The Wines of Austria

The Wines of Austria

by Philipp Blom

MITCHELL BEAZLEY

First published in Great Britain in 2000
by Faber and Faber

This edition published in Great Britain in 2006
by Mitchell Beazley, an imprint of
Octopus Publishing Group Limited,
2–4 Heron Quays, London E14 4JP.

Copyright © Octopus Publishing Group Ltd 2006

Text copyright © Philipp Blom, 2000, 2006

Maps copyright © Octopus Publishing Group Ltd, 2006

Cartography: Encompass Graphics Ltd

A CIP catalogue record for this book is available from the British Library.

ISBN 13: 978 184533 132 0

ISBN 10: 184533 132 X

The author and publishers will be grateful for any information which will assist them in keeping future editions up-to-date. Although all reasonable care has been taken in the preparation of this book, neither the publishers nor the author can accept any liability for any consequences arising from the use thereof, or the information contained therein.

Printed and bound in England by Mackays, Chatham.

For
Thomas
wine companion of the first hour
and my friend

Contents

Acknowledgments

It is a well-used phrase to say that a book could not have been written without the help of so many people, but this project really did depend on the collaboration and kindness of people many of whom were, or have become, good friends, and many wine producers have very kindly given me hospitality above and beyond the call of duty or the fear of journalists – Austrian hospitality is always a great experience.

Toni Bodenstein kindly let me partake of his encyclopaedic knowledge of the scientific aspects of wine – geology, climate, and plant biology – and Willi Bründlmayer found time to read the chapter on winemaking and to suggest improvements despite the fact that the harvest was in full swing. In Paris, the eagle-eyed Joanie Wolkoff made sure that I had my numbers right.

For general advice and for many discussions I am also very grateful to Thomas Klinger, Jasper Morris, Jan-Erik Paulson, David Schildknecht, Dr. Josef Schuller, Dr. Viktor Siegl, as well as to many colleagues and friends whose good company made my tastings and wine trips a more pleasurable and informative experience.

Last but by no means least, the Austrian Wine Marketing Service financed my trips to Austria, organized tastings and wine transports, helped me with factual information, and was professional, flexible, and welcoming. My special thanks go here to Michael Thurner, Susanne Staggl, Caroline Linz, Andrea Krautstoffl, and Iris Kovacs.

Map of Austria

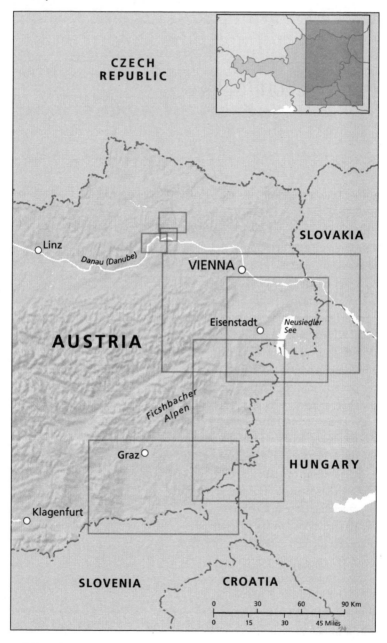

Introduction

When I lived in Vienna in the early 1990s, studying philosophy at the university, I fell in love with the opera. Before long I was hell-bent on becoming a tenor, and so took singing lessons with an eccentric Scot. While I was straining for that elusive C, my eyes drilled into a grotesque caricature of Rossini behind my teacher's piano.

Suffering induces comradeship, and I started talking to another hopeful who was financing part of his studies by working as a chef. "You realize, of course," said my fellow student as we trotted down the stairs after a lesson, "that Austria produces some of the finest wines in the world." At this I 0emitted a loud guffaw of derision. I might not be a food expert, but I knew a little about wines, I thought. I had tasted the local offerings at the *Heurige*, the country inns scattered all around Vienna, and had even bought the two-litre bottles available at every greengrocer. Nothing to write home about.

The effect of my hilarity was surprising. My otherwise gentle friend took me by the scruff of the neck and dragged me into his cellar. He did not lock me up, as I had feared, but chose instead four bottles from his collection and marched me up to his flat. Several hours and said bottles later I had to admit defeat. These wines were quite astonishing, and my visit was the beginning of something close to an obsession.

Austrian wines are the best-kept secret of the wine world. Their palette of aromas and their indigenous vine varieties make them unique, and the country's geographic position in central Europe, right at the meeting point of two climatic systems, creates ideal conditions for growing very different wine styles; which a substantial number of growers exploit for making thrilling, even world-class wines. Indeed, probably no other country in the world produces such a wide range of wine styles from so many different vine varieties on so relatively little space. For all those who love the individuality of well-crafted wines (the very opposite of speculative hype and factory winemaking), Austria offers immense pleasures.

Austria is a small country in wine terms. The annual average yield of 2.4 million hectolitres (between 1993 and 2003) from 48,500 hectares of vineyards in the east of the country accounts for one per cent of world production. The Californian wine giant Ernest & Julio Gallo sells twice as much wine as that; France makes on average just under 70 million hectolitres, and exports five times as much wine as Austria makes; Austria's production is roughly equivalent to that of the Loire Valley.

The structures of wine production in this country, too, are still very small and date from a time (until only about thirty years ago) when grapes were often just one of many crops on a farm. Although there are about 27,800 viticulturists, only about 3,000 of these are full-time growers and wine-makers. The majority of wine-growers work small plots of less than a hectare and sell their grapes to larger producers. Moreover, of the total produced during any year, a quarter is sold either as grapes or as cheap wine by the barrel. Another ten per cent is produced and sold in the local *Heurige* and *Buschenschanken*. Of the remaining sixty-five per cent, roughly four-fifths are simple wines sold in two-litre or litre bottles. Only the remaining twenty per cent, i.e. about nine per cent of the entire vintage, is vinified as wine of high quality: about 200,000 hectolitres, though the proportion of these wines is now on the rise. For comparison, the fine-wine sector in neighbouring Germany comprises only about two per cent of the total.

This guide does not pretend to be comprehensive. A guide should choose and distil, not drown the reader in a flood of data. This one presents a personal selection of leading estates, with one criterion in mind: to reflect what is best in Austria, from world-class producers to consistently interesting ones, and to show the fascinating and complex interaction of individuals and nature.

Many things have happened in Austrian wine since the first edition of this book appeared, in 2000. The most notable is that these wines no longer need an introduction. Nowadays it is taken for granted that leading wine critics admire and rank Austrian wines as world class. The noted American critic, Robert Parker's 2005 report on Austria, for instance (written by David Schildknecht), rated no fewer than eighty wines with ninety points or more, and today there is hardly a great restaurant or dealer in the world without some outstanding Austrian growths on their list. Austria has established itself as a select but important voice, and since 2000 exports have not only doubled in volume but also risen in quality.

This new edition has been an opportunity for me to review my own impressions of Austrian wine. Apart from rocketing exports and international accolades, there has been a considerable consolidation and a refinement of styles and techniques. While a few estates did not make it into this second edition, a considerable number of young and up-and-coming producers have been included, or have had their entries considerably enlarged. The most significant developments, however, are the renewed focus on terroir wines that are less dominated by alcohol and oak, and a growing interest in ecological viticulture and biological sustainability, which can create not only vines with deeper roots but also, I believe, wines with more and more individual local character.

I have not rated producers with points, stars, grapes, or happy faces. Every estate that appears in this guide has been included because its wines are worth tasting, and good wine is a living, evolving thing, not suited to fixed scores and hierarchies. To give scores to wines seems to me to miss the point, and to ignore the fact that every tasting (even if based on knowledge and experience) is a unique encounter between the momentary constitution of a wine and that of the taster.

There are, of course, producers who have a proven track record of excellence, and estates producing consistently high or even great quality are profiled in more depth. Other growers listed are those who are reliably solid and interesting, or up-and-coming, with a lot to prove.

In retrospect, I am glad that I once laughed at the idea of Austrian wines being good, for otherwise I might never have discovered them. My friend, by the way, did become a singer, though he still enjoys cooking. I have long since given up my battle with the high C. Perhaps Rossini's grin above the piano was a little discouraging. I blame him, anyway.

Philipp Blom
Paris, November 2005

Part 1

The Background

1

History

There is a paradox at the heart of Austrian wine culture: it is arguably both one of the oldest in Europe and one of the youngest in the world. Today's Austria is one of the most ancient settled regions in Europe, particularly the wine-growing areas of the Kremstal, the Kamptal, and the Wachau: the Willendorf Venus (a small stone statue of a well-rounded fertility goddess, dated 25,000 to 20,000 BC and now in the Naturhistorisches Museum in Vienna) was found, unsurprisingly, in Willendorf, a village only a few kilometres from what is now the wine village of Spitz. The oldest finds of cultivated grape seeds in Austria date back to the ninth or tenth century BC, and were made in the region of Lake Neusiedl, which was then called Pannonia. An excavation of a Hallstatt period grave (c. 700 BC) found a clay bowl with grape seeds, which were identified as vines genetically similar to the modern Chardonnay and Sylvaner, a result of breeding and improving the native Pannonian wild grapes. The region was part of the Amber Road, a trade route linking the Baltic coast with the Mediterranean. Finds from Celtic times also included tools such as vine knives, and vessels with resin residues, suggesting the use of resinated wines in Celtic cults, and possibly the importation of such wines from Greece or Rome. Other sources describe the wine culture of the Celts and say that they even drank their wine undiluted with water, an act of great culinary daring.

While it is possible that Celtic wine production and consumption have been underestimated until recently, it seems that the Romans brought large-scale wine-growing here after conquering the region in 15 BC. The Danube marked part of the northeastern border of the Roman Empire, and the new lands therefore had considerable strategic significance both in military terms and as a part of the Amber Road. There were substantial Roman settlements throughout Austria, most notably the city of Carnuntum, capital of the province of Pannonia Superior, which had 70,000 inhabitants.

The Romans supplanted the wine culture of the indigenous Celts: they brought with them their own expertise, administration, and culture, and tilled the soil in order to guarantee the flow of provisions for their army outposts. Wine was grown in areas already cultivated by the Celts, along the Danube in today's Wachau, in Pannonia, and in Styria, the last of which produced wines so good that they were even exported to Rome at the price of one young slave per amphora.

For reasons remarkably reminiscent of today's European Union, the Roman emperor Domitian upset the wine world of his provinces in AD 92 by ordering vines to be torn out of the ground. The cause of this was, curiously enough, the eruption of Mount Vesuvius in AD 79 ; the eruption that buried Pompeii. The volcano also buried some of Italy's most important vineyards, and to compensate for this loss, large amounts of new vineyard had been planted, and the market was quickly swamped. Imported wine from the colonies did not improve things.

As the Roman historian Suetonius relates, a poor grain harvest compounded the problem, convincing the emperor that the balance of wine and grain production was askew and needed to be rectified. Some vineyards had to go, and the colonies were the first to suffer. Today, historians question how efficiently this edict was implemented in the farflung outposts of the empire, and it is probable that a significant number of vineyards in Austria remained unscathed, but Domitian still gets a bad press.

Two hundred years later, Emperor Aurelius Probus (276-282) lifted the edict of his predecessor and even sent soldiers to help with the planting of new vineyards, mainly in Pannonia, today the border region of Hungary and Austria. He seems to have thought highly of Pannonian wine, as he specifically mentioned the Pannonian plains along with Gaul as areas to be replanted: "*Probus…Vineas Gallos et Pannonios habere permissit.*" ("Probus permits the Gauls and Pannoneans to have wine", as the Roman historian Eutropius summarizes in Book IX of his *Breviarium Historiae Romanae.*)

This laid the foundation for Austria's wine culture for almost two millennia. According to a time-honoured Roman custom, Probus also gave parcels of land in Pannonia to his veterans for cultivation, thus both supporting wine-growing and consolidating his hold on one of the border areas of his empire.

MIGRATIONS AND MONKS

With the demise of the Roman Empire and the great migrations of the early Middle Ages, wine cultivation in the former Roman province came under severe pressure. Pannonia especially was to be overrun by almost every horde or army crossing from east to west, and it changed hands several times in the process. Wine-growing, however, requires continuity. The vineyards (and the wine stocks) were vulnerable to the invaders' thirst for destruction, as well as their thirst for alcohol, and continuity was conspicuously absent from the region. During the fifth century it was the base of Attila's Huns, and was later taken by the Gepides, the East Goths, the Langobardes, and the Awares, until Charlemagne conquered it in 803. From the tenth century onwards it belonged to Hungary.

Styria, historically one of the biggest wine-growing areas, suffered an equally turbulent history. It changed hands between the Quades, the Vandals, the East Goths, Huns, Slovenes, Bavarians, the Franconians under Charlemagne, the Hungarians, and the Germans, before passing, in 1282, to the House of Habsburg.

In the Wachau, wine culture could develop with less severe interruptions. After being ruled by the Langobardes and Awares, the region fell to France in 803 and became the Ostmark of Charlemagne's empire, with Salzburg as its administrative and cultural centre.

Charlemagne's conquest of the region that is now Austria, at the end of the eighth century, was to be a great influence. Grapes were classified, and those which were deemed superior were called "Fränkisch" ("Franconian", as in Blaufränkisch), while lesser varieties were apostrophized as "Heunisch" (i.e. "of the Hun", the greatest insult after Attila's hordes had ravaged Europe). Ironically, Heunisch grapes (the word was more a description of appearance than of a particular variety) became very prevalent throughout the vineyards of Germany and Austria during the following centuries, and Riesling is their genetic descendant.

Under the title *Capitulare de villis* (*"Landholding Regulations"*) the emperor (or more probably his son, Louis the Pious) formalized rules for the husbandry of vineyards and for vinification methods for the first time. Hygiene was an important issue: the practice of treading grapes with bare feet was prohibited, and tree-presses were to be used instead. It is doubtful whether this decree had much practical effect (grapes were trodden with bare feet in Austria, as indeed in France, until well into the twentieth century), but it illustrates the importance accorded to viticulture under Charlemagne.

After military campaigns at the beginning of the tenth century, the eastern parts of modern Austria were again in the hands of the Magyars. When they were defeated in the Battle of Lechfeld in 955, the House of Babenberg became Margraves of the Ostmark. The battle also proved the last great military adventure for the Magyars, who would now become increasingly settled and Christianized and would themselves eventually turn to wine-growing. In this new atmosphere of stability, Styria and other Austrian regions were be planted with vineyards on a much larger scale than had earlier been possible.

The high-medieval wine history of Austria is a tale of saints and bishops. After the demise of the Carolingian empire and the establishment of the Duchy of Austria in 1156, most vineyards in the Wachau and in Burgenland were in the possession of monasteries, and monastic foundations set the pattern for agricultural practice and landownership more generally in Austria. The Nikolaihof in Mauthern, founded as a feoff of the diocese of Passau in Bavaria and today a top estate, can look back on more than a thousand years of continuous winemaking. Margrave Leopold (1073-1136), the national saint of Austria, founded the monasteries of Heiligenkreuz, Mariazell, and Klosterneuburg, the last of which still owns a great deal of vineyard throughout Austria, notably in the hills around (and suburbs of) Vienna: Nussdorf, Weidling, and Grinzing. The bishopric of Salzburg had owned extensive vineyards in the Wachau since the days of Charlemagne. These possessions had been managed as one large estate, and today the successor of the Bishop of Salzburg is a modern cooperative, the Freie Weingärtner Wachau.

The Und monastery in nearby Krems is another survivor from medieval structures. Krems, the largest town in the Wachau region, was an important point for wine-growing and trade, and was recorded as a wine-producing area in 995; two hundred years later, no fewer than sixteen different monasteries had estates and vineyards in and around the city. It was not until well after World War II that the Wachau overtook Krems in reputation and quality, even if the first "*crus*" of the Wachau, individual vineyards and plots of recognized quality, were recorded during the thirteenth century.

In the region to the west of Vienna, Bavarian monasteries and especially Göttweig Abbey (still standing in all its baroque splendour), dominated wine-growing and most other aspects of life in the province.

The history of viticulture in the Burgenland, the eastern part of modern Austria and then still part of Hungary, was dominated by the Cistercians, members of a Burgundian monastic order who were given land between the river Leitha and the north bank of Lake Neusiedl in 1203 by the Hungarian King Imre. His successor, King Andrew II, added to this gift. The Cistercians studied climate and soils, built drainage installations, and imported Burgundian grape varieties such as Pinot Gris and, probably, Pinot Noir from their home in France.

While the north of the Burgenland was essentially a colony, administered by monasteries, the south of the area was under feudal rule, especially the rule of the families of Lutzmannsburg, Seifried, and the Counts of Güssing. Even today, the landscapes of the southern Burgenland and neighbouring southeastern Styria are dominated by large medieval fortifications such as Burg Lockenhaus and the Riegersburg, attesting to the violent territorial disputes between neighbouring feudal overlords and people that were such a strong feature of life in these parts. Despite the importance of feudal families the proper cultivation of wine here, too, owes more to the Cistercians than to the robber barons.

Medieval wine consumption was robust, partly due to the scarcity of clean drinking water, and one should spare a thought for the fact that our ancestors were very probably almost constantly inebriated. Even damsels residing in the very basic fortifications of Burgenland and Styria were entitled to about seven litres of good red wine a day, easily enough to make them forget their grim surroundings.

Wine, however, was not made for domestic consumption alone. By the eleventh and twelfth centuries, Austrian wine was being exported all over Europe, especially from Vienna and Krems. Wine from these regions was drunk in Bohemia and Moravia, in north Germany, the Baltic states, and even in England, making it a distinct possibility that England imported more Austrian wine during the Middle Ages than it does now.

While expanding their exports, Austrian rulers also protected their internal markets. Foreign wines were not allowed into Lower Austria for two centuries after 1364, and, much like their French counterparts, the burghers of Vienna were entitled to sell wine within the city limits, just as farmers producing wine could sell their products at local markets. The Viennese have always loved their wine, and during the Middle Ages they protected it with truly medieval measures: people caught stealing grapes were liable to have a hand cut off. In 1430, a particularly bad vintage, the sale of beer was prohibited in Vienna to boost the sales of wine.

Despite the efforts of the Cistercians and other monastic orders, wine-making techniques and technology were still in their infancy, and the weather was all-important. In 1456, following a bad season, the wine was so sour that the growers decided to pour it all away. The wine was known as "*Reifenbeisser*", or "hoop-biter", as it was said to be so acid that it corroded the hoops of the casks it was kept in. The Emperor Frederick III, however, decreed that no divine gift was to be wasted, and so the wine was used for mixing mortar. Some of it stands petrified today between the stones of St Stephen's Cathedral.

SWEET WINES AND BITTER WARS
During the sixteenth century the area under vine in what is now Austria was up to five times larger than it is today. New laws, new taxes, and the rising popularity of beer were to stall and then reverse the expansion of Austrian wines for the next three centuries.

There were exceptions, of course, most notably in the region of the Hungarian, though German-speaking, town of Rust. The town is situated on the western banks of Lake Neusiedl, and the mists rolling across the vineyards make this an ideal area for the production of sweet wines from grapes affected by botrytis, or noble rot – the magic fungus that both causes grapes to shrivel and changes their biochemical make-up, and produces many of the great sweet wines of the world.

Even in the Middle Ages the Cistercian monks had experimented with sweet wines of this kind, and by the beginning of the seventeenth century the first Ausbruch wines were being produced by the addition of a small amount of healthy grapes (usually Furmint) to grapes affected by botrytis. The Ausbruch wines were similar to that other famous sweet wine, Tokaji, which was produced further inside Hungary. (In the production of Tokaji, the must of botrytized grapes is added to unbotrytized Tokaji wine.) The first Trockenbeerenauslese, a sweet wine made exclusively from nobly-rotten grapes, and a great rarity until the twentieth century, had been made even earlier, in 1526, in

Donnerskirchen by Lake Neusiedl. This wine was then regarded as a delicacy, and whenever an amount of it had been taken from a cask, washed pebbles would be added to make up the volume and keep out air, thus preventing oxidation. This technique worked so well that the last of this 1526 wine was not in fact drunk until 1852, 326 years after it had been made. Donnerskirchen being a Protestant enclave in an otherwise Catholic region, the wine came to be known as Lutherwein. To this day it remains a local legend. It is worth noting that it was produced centuries before nobly-rotten grapes seem to have been vinified in Sauternes.

The originally small proportion of healthy grapes in Ausbruch wines later grew and became relatively high, largely because of a court case of 1655, when the peasants rose against their masters over what they regarded as the unreasonable amount of work involved in picking the shrivelled botrytized grapes. The judges ruled that Ausbruch wines would thenceforth be required to contain a significant quantity of healthy grapes, to lessen the pickers' workload.

The burghers of Rust soon found out how to produce these wines, and before long they were doing a roaring trade. Ruster Ausbruch was enjoyed by princes and emperors, and was exported as far as the Baltic states. The wine-growers and merchants of the town grew wealthy, and displayed their new riches in their beautiful baroque town houses, still standing in Rust today.

With the rising popularity of the wine came the need to protect it against competitors, and in 1524 the Hungarian Queen Maria granted the town the privilege of branding its casks with the letter "R", an early form of trademarking, with the nearby cities of Jois and Neusiedl being given similar privileges at about the same time.

Rust escaped lightly from that scourge of so many seventeenth-century populations: the Thirty Years' War. Winemaking in the area was not strongly affected, but by the end of the war, in 1648, control over the region was in dispute. The Turkish invasion was a severe threat both to the people of Rust and to their wines. In 1683, the town was laid waste by the Turkish army, en route to lay siege to Vienna. During the siege, Prince Esterházy, who held lands in Hungary and Pannonia, appointed the wine of his homelands to a patriotic role: every day, between eleven in the morning and five in the afternoon, casks of wine were distributed gratis to the defenders of the city.

The winemakers of Rust were to exact their own peculiar revenge on one Turkish soldier at least: the now legendary Purbach Turk, enthusiastically ignoring his religion's ban on intoxicating substances, missed the retreat of his own troops. He came to, surrounded by his victorious Austrian enemies. The fleeing Turks, meanwhile, had left behind intoxicating substances of their own, as Jan Sobieski, a Polish spy who had aided the Austrian cause, was to find. The curious beans in the Turkish army sacks were to create a legend of their own: the Viennese coffee-house.

The vineyards of the Burgenland recovered. Tokaji was unavailable, as Hungary was still under Turkish influence. Moreover, many wine-growers had fled from Hungary and were now cultivating wine in the Burgenland, bringing Hungarian expertise to the area. By 1681, Ruster Ausbruch had become so successful and so widely known that the town of Rust was made an Imperial Free City. The price for this distinction, however, was considerable: 500 buckets of the prestigious Ausbruch itself, and 60,000 guilders in addition.

CONNOISSEURS AND SCHOLARS

The Turks, pushed back first into Hungary, were driven even further by Prince Eugen of Savoy, in a protracted campaign lasting twenty-five years. After centuries of invasion and upheaval, the eastern regions of Austria were finally secure. In this time of peace and stability, wine cultivation flourished alongside many other industries. A new confidence spread through Viennese culture and social life, and the city regained its characteristic *joie de vivre*. Wine production – and consumption – rose markedly. The land under vine increased accordingly with countless men and women hard at work each year, not to mention some 1,200 horses. The Viennese were proud of their wine, and a veritable gourmet culture had developed around it. The traveller Lady Mary Wortley Montagu, who visited Vienna in 1716, remarked in a letter that dinners for the "first people of quality" were served in silver or the finest china, "but the variety and richness of their wines, is what appears the most surprising. The constant way is, to lay a list of their names upon the plates of the guests, along with the napkins; and I have counted several times to the number of eighteen different sorts, all exquisite in their way."

As the eighteenth century progressed, Vienna developed its own hierarchy of *Rieden*, or *crus*, with some wines being aged in casks for up to twenty years before being drunk. Considerable rivalry was apparent between the *Rieden* of Grinzing, Weidling, and Nussdorf, and even comparative tastings were arranged, so that an official decision might be made as to the best wine-producing area of all.

For Pannonia, too, a new era had begun. In many cases, the ruling families had taken over as the Church's influence had waned, with significant effects on winemaking. The monasteries lost their role as centres of innovation to the cellars of princes in Eisenstadt and Forchtenstein, and to the imperial possessions of Rust, Lutzmannsburg, and Purbach.

By now, Hungarian Tokaji had again eclipsed the Ausbruch wines of Rust, which were now also burdened by a special tax. The popularity of Pannonian sweet wines, however, persisted so much so, in fact, that heavy penalties were introduced to combat the increasing numbers of fraudulent winemakers who aped the sweet Ausbruch wines by mixing other wine with honey, sugar, and raisins. The export business, too, was flourishing again, and barrels were shipped not only to the traditional markets of the Baltic region, but even as far as St Petersburg.

The export trade was often carried out by Viennese merchants taking advantage of favourable tax regulations, or by Pannonian wine merchants, many of whom were Jewish. Jews had been forbidden to live in Austria proper from the Middle Ages, and this prohibition remained in force until the passing of the Edict of Tolerance by Emperor Joseph II at the end of the eighteenth century. In the intervening period, the borderland Pannonian cities of Deutschkreutz, Eisenstadt, Frauenkirchen, and Mattersburg had developed sizeable Jewish communities.

The eighteenth century saw a decline in Austrian wine production. Having covered a surface of more than 150,000 hectares during the three previous centuries, vineyard surfaces shrunk, affected by the after-effects of the Thirty Years' War, by price collapses due to over-production, and by the rising popularity of beer. Empress Maria Theresa saw to it that surplus wines were made into vinegar, mustard, and brandy in special, newly founded manufactures. Her unjustly unloved son, the reforming Joseph II, set limits for wine production and dissolved a third of all monasteries in his empire, thereby changing the patterns of land ownership. Finally, in 1784, the emperor placed the popular *Buschenschanken* and *Heurigen* (country inns and taverns in the Viennese suburbs) on a secure legal footing, by allowing his subjects to sell food and wines freely on their own land, provided everything offered had been produced by the vendors themselves.

In the early years of the nineteenth century, Napoleon conquered the Austrians and his armies overran Imperial Austria. Both their progress along the Danube through the Wachau in 1805 and the battle of Wagram in 1809 were fought in the very heart of Lower Austria's wine country, as cannon-balls incorporated in the walls of some Wachau houses still testify. The *ossuarium* at the medieval church of St Michael there still contains the skulls of soldiers fallen during the battle – one of them belonging to a child who had not yet grown his second teeth, probably a drummer boy. As is the custom of armies, Napoleon's soldiers wreaked havoc along the way – not least by blowing up the wine cellars of the Klosterneuburg Abbey, and in so doing destroying a "wine library" going back several centuries. The monks of the abbey had used the old wines for medicinal purposes, as old wines were then regarded as an effective treatment for fatigue. Napoleon's soldiers also drank whatever wine they could find, earning themselves the honorific title of "thirstiest army in Europe". Over the ensuing decades, the abbey cellars were restocked, only to be emptied again by Russian soldiers at the end of World War II. What they could not guzzle down, they simply machine-gunned.

There were, however, more encouraging developments during the nineteenth century. Vine nurseries sprang up, and in 1819 a certain Hofrat von Görög founded a nursery containing a seemingly infinite variety of grapes: no fewer than 565 French varieties, 453 from the Austrian Empire, 257 from Venice, forty-eight from Milan, forty-eight from Dalmatia, forty-five from Sicily, thirty-two from Ragusa, thirty from Florence, twenty from Tripoli, thirteen from Naples, and six from Smyrna. The collection seems to have vanished with the good Hofrat's demise in 1833. It is perhaps a significant footnote that he did not seem to have found it necessary to collect German vines, unless, of course, they were subsumed in the "imperial" varieties.

During the 1830s, the Austro-Hungarian oenologist and writer Franz Schams made a study of the wines grown in the Habsburg Empire, which he published in two volumes in 1832 and 1835 under the exhaustive title *Vollständige Beschreibung sämmtlicher berühmter Weingebirge in Österreich, Mähren und Böhmen in statistisch, topographisch-naturhistorischer und ökonomischer Hinsicht* (*"Complete Description of all Famous Wine Mountains in Austria, Moravia, and Bohemia in Terms of Statistics, Natural History, and the Economy"*). Schams compared some Habsburg wines favourably to the wines of Burgundy and also writes that some wines were aged as long as fifteen or twenty years. Not everyone, though, was so enthusiastic about Austrian, and especially Viennese wines.

As in the eighteenth century, the most highly regarded wines of the Austro-Hungarian empire, with the possible exception of Tokaji and Ruster Ausbruch (which had by now recuperated from its many woes), were those growing around Vienna, particularly in Nussdorf, Weidling, Grinzing, and Klosterneuburg. Another wine with a good name was the "Vöslauer", or that from around Vöslau in the Thermenregion. Until World War II, Austrian wines were generally referred to not by their grape but by their geographical origin. Wine was largely limited to these areas, and to Styria: the Burgenland was still Hungarian, and wine production in the Wachau had declined in favour of orchard plantations.

Schams paid a good deal of attention to red wines, too. In today's Thermenregion near Vienna, he wrote, "the Blauer Burgunder [Pinot Noir] and the Portuguese grape [Blauer Portugieser] are thought of most highly for red wines, though now and then the Schwarzfränkische, which is also called Mährische appears. It is a product of the most recent times, and has been known for some thirty years." Blaufränkisch had made its debut in Austria.

A keen observer of innovation, Schams also applauded the idea of planting vines in orderly rows, so facilitating work in the vineyard, which he found in the Cistercian monastery of Heiligenkreuz. Elsewhere, as in the Middle Ages, vines were planted at random. Schams also commented on another practice that only reappeared in Austrian winemaking a century or so later: he found that the growers in Mauer (now part of Vienna) were pricing their wines higher when they had been fermented in new oak barrels. He confessed himself puzzled: "I am quite unable to clarify," he wrote in the above title, "what beneficial influence the wines might derive from the process of having their alcoholic fermentation take place in new oak barrels," but he decided nonetheless to try the method in his own winemaking.

During the mid-nineteenth century, the entire structure of grape production was changed through the efforts of one man, Robert Schlumberger, an enterprising German wine merchant who who was the first to plant Cabernet Sauvignon, Cabernet Franc, and Merlot in Austria (in the Thermenregion, still a good spot for fine reds) and, in 1846 introduced his "white sparkling wine from Vöslau". Schlumberger's sekt was such a success that only a few years later it was exported as far as Turkey,

India, and North America, listed in Europe's best hotels, and needed a large number of farmers to produce the grapes for the base wine. The Schlumberger house still exists, as does the production of Austrian sparkling wines. (Today these are also made by other large producers such as Kattus, whose Hochriegl Sekt is ubiquitous in Austria.) A significant proportion of grapes from the Weinviertel are still produced for sekt.

In 1880, new steps were taken to regulate the wine industry. The first comprehensive Austrian law governing wine was introduced in 1907, and was reviewed four times before being radically recast in 1985. A whole flood of wine literature and oenological tracts from the nineteenth century provides more than enough material to build up a picture of Austrian viticulture during this period. We know about dominant varieties, about the methods of treating vines, grapes, and wine in the vineyards and in the cellars, and about the experiments that were conducted.

Many of the wines produced then would be difficult to recognize as Austrian wines today. Furmint and Zierfandler are still cultivated in the Thermenregion today, but the Griechische ("Greek") grape, once used widely for wines of lesser quality, has now vanished, along with the Augustrebe and Silberweisse varieties.

Of the vines most common today, only a few were grown during the nineteenth century. One exception is Pinot Gris, which has been cultivated in Austria since the Middle Ages; Pinot Noir and St Laurent were probably known as well. There was a little Grüner Veltliner, but it was then known as Grüner Muskateller and was not widespread. This vine, today almost the embodiment of Austrian wine, accounting for roughly a third of production, gained primacy only with Lenz Moser and his method of high-training vines in the 1950s. Muskateller, Riesling, and Welschriesling were already grown in Austria, though not on a large scale. There would also have been some Blaufränkisch, then known as Blauer Zierfandler and/or Schwarzer Muskateller in southern Burgenland, and as Schwarzfränkisch or Mährisch in Vöslau, and Blauer Portugieser. Neuburger is an interesting special case, because according to legend a bunch of vine branches was fished out of the Danube in the Wachau and planted in that region – a Moses, as it were, among Austrian vines. There is another version of this legend, according to which it was another vine that came floating down the Danube, and was planted in, and named after, the Rizling vineyard. This, however, is doubtful.

International varieties that are very successful now, such as Sauvignon

Blanc and Merlot, had to wait until the late twentieth century, but Chardonnay and Cabernet Sauvignon had come in already in the nineteenth. The structure of the wine landscape, too, was different, as the German system of classifying wines into Prädikat, Spätlese, Auslese, Beerenauslese, and so on was introduced in two separate waves of wine-related laws in 1972 and 1985.

In the Wachau, which today produces some of the very finest Austrian wines, the wine landscape was not quite so exciting. The grape favoured here, and incidentally around Vienna, was the Grobe (the "rough one") about which writer Franz Schams said in his *Full Description* that it produced good wines in good years and good vinegar in bad ones. Only after World War II did Riesling show how perfectly suited it was to the Wachau. During the nineteenth century the locals stuck to their unshakeable faith in the Grobe, dismissing most other vines as foreign nonsense.

Langenlois, to the east of the Wachau, was even then one of the best wine-producing cities in the empire, with a huge area under cultivation. The two main vines here were Roter Muskateller and Grüner Muskateller, or Grüner Veltliner. Langenlois was therefore one of the very few places that would have looked much the same to a wine enthusiast one hundred years ago as it does now, with extensive vineyards and an emphasis on Grüner Veltliner.

By 1860, a school of viticulture had been established in Klosterneuburg in an attempt to breathe new life into the local culture and to spread new knowledge and winemaking technology. The school is still one of the most important centres of learning and research in Austria. Wine was on its way back. Many important new developments have emanated from this school, among them the Klosterneuburger Mostwaage (KMW) – a method, still used, of measuring the sugar content of must – and important new grapes such as Zweigelt and Goldburger.

The Universal Exhibition of Vienna in 1873 was an opportunity for the Habsburg Empire to show off its wines to the world. Wines from everywhere were invited to present themselves for a competition, to be judged by experts. The British representative at this occasion was one Henry Vizetelly (later to be Emile Zola's English publisher), charged by Her Majesty's Commissioners to draw up a report. In 1875 he published a popular version of his report, drawing on his experiences in Vienna. He was an honest man, a good taster, and not given to flattery. In his 1875 book *The Wines of the World Characterized & Classed: with some particulars respecting the beers of Europe* he wrote: "The wines of Austria are as diverse as its population. At the extreme south they are so dark and full-bodied that when mixed with an equal quantity of water they are quite as deep in colour and as spirituous as the ordinary wines of Bordeaux.... While in less favourable districts they are excessively poor and so sour as to rasp the tongue like the roughest cider. Many have the luscious character of Constantia and the Muscat growths of Frontignan and Lunal. Several, on the other hand, are disagreeably bitter, others again so astringent as to contract the windpipe while swallowing them, whereas a few of the lighter varieties possess the delicacy, if not the fragrance, of certain growths of the Rheingau. It must be confessed, however, that althought the specimens were remarkably varied and numerous, the better qualities were extremely rare."

The nineteenth century also brought the terrible blights of oidium and phylloxera. The latter almost completely destroyed wine production throughout Europe. Oidium, or powdery mildew, was first observed in France in 1847, and in central Europe soon afterwards. Phylloxera, a louse that feeds on the roots of vines and destroys them in the process, came hard on its heels and proved far worse. It first surfaced in France during the 1860s, and production of French wine collapsed from 85 million hectolitres in 1875 to 23 million hectolitres in 1889. In Austria, phylloxera first came to the attention of wine-growers in 1872, in Klosterneuburg.

During the 1880s, phylloxera ravaged the Thermenregion, and then went on into other areas. Within twenty years it destroyed 9,029 hectares of vines throughout Lower Austria, a quarter of the total. There are no figures for the Burgenland and Styria, but the extent of the destruction was considerable here as well. Recovery was brought about only with the grafting of European vines onto resistant American rootstocks, a solution that produced a rather curious viticultural footnote.

Some of the poorer growers, especially in Styria, proceeded to make wine from the American *Vitis lambrusca* vines, instead of just grafting European grapes onto labrusca rootstocks. Wine from some of the imported vines were reputed to cause imbecility, and any sale of these wines was forbidden by law. The descendants of these labrusca wines still survive in South Styria, where they are known by the collective name of Uhudler, apparently because the growers who had downed it came home drunk as owls, the word for "owl" being "*Uhu*". Limited production of

Uhudler was legalized only in 1992, and only in certain districts of South Styria and South Burgenland.

Before phylloxera destroyed the vineyards of the Burgenland, the red wines of this region flourished as well-regarded substitutes for French wines, which had been afflicted by phylloxera. After the disaster red grapes were planted again.

The early twentieth century brought the catastrophe of World War I and the collapse of the Austro-Hungarian Empire. In 1921 the Burgenland held a referendum to establish which state, Austria or Hungary, its inhabitants wanted to join. The result was, as expected, that German Hungary, as it was still called, finally became the Burgenland, and the wine country of Austria attained the shape familiar to us today.

Before the country settled into its new pattern, however, the wine of Austria had been that of the Section Donauland of the Third Reich. Austria was part of the Ostmark, and so after 1938 the German wine law of 1930 became the basis of Austrian winemaking. After World War II, one Austrian cellar even became a theatre of European history when, or so the legend goes, the Austrian Foreign Minister Leopold Figl invited the victorious Soviet delegation into the cellars of the Freie Weingärtner Wachau to discuss whether his young country was to belong to the Eastern Bloc or to the West. It is fondly claimed that Figl had a larger capacity for Wachau wines than his Russian counterparts, and that Austria's postwar freedom is a result of these negociations.

THE GLORIOUS REVOLUTION OF 1985

Despite the efforts of Austria's wine professors, and of a few growers who strove for the highest quality throughout much of the twentieth century, the majority of winemakers had other ideas. After World War II, commercial opportunities for selling cheap, sweet plonk in domestic and German supermarkets meant that the majority of growers went down this road, selling their wines to dealers by the barrel to be marketed under the dealers' names. New technologies and over-optimistic consumption forecasts led to domestic over-production. An almost universal triumph was enjoyed by Grüner Veltliner as a reliable, mass-yielding grape, and by staples such as Müller-Thurgau and Blauer Portugieser. Dry, characterful wines were a rarity, though some were produced for domestic consumption by committed growers who were widely seen as loveable but unrealistic dreamers.

Fritz Hallgarten's 1979 book *The Wines and Wine Gardens of Austria* provides an intriguing picture of the country's postwar wine landscape just before the, enormously beneficial, catastrophe that was to befall it. Hallgarten's Austria is a country in which there are some extraordinary wines, but few international grape varieties or styles. "Austria does not produce heavy wines full of alcohol", he declares, a statement very much at odds with the style of modern Austrian winemaking. The "most loveable, finest and most elegant" Austrian wines, according to him, were grown in the Burgenland.

The wines Hallgarten lists as remarkable (often with tasting notes such as "we like it") are commonly chaptalized, so much so that he devotes an entire chapter to this practice, which is still legal for some wines in Austria, but now very much frowned upon. International grape varieties feature hardly at all, and grapes such as Müller-Thurgau and Blauer Portugieser are used widely.

Hallgarten describes wines that are often semi-sweet, have German-sounding names such as Loibner Katzensprung ("Loiben Cat's Leap"), and are made by wine-growers most of whose names have vanished from the modern map, while the majority of the growers famous today hardly feature in his lists.

The wines of postwar Austria were overwhelmingly competing at the bottom end of the market, notably with the worst Italian products. It was in the spirit of undercutting the competition at the lowest end that in some merchants in the Burgenland and in Lower Austria began adding diethylene glycol, a poisonous, viscous substance widely used as an antifreeze agent, to cheap export wines to make them appear sweeter and richer in body and aromas. When analyses in Austria and Germany found evidence of this fraud in 1985, the scandal erupted like a volcano. Four fraudsters were sentenced to prison, and during the ensuing investigations it appeared that diethylene glycol had been added by some wine merchants since about 1976.

The effects were instant and devastating. Collapsing exports (Belgium outlawed all imports of Austrian wines) led to a breakdown of the entire commercial structure established in the postwar years, whereby growers, who were mostly small-scale and part-time, delivered grapes to merchants. A string of bankruptcies followed.

Germany was caught up in the same scandal, but with far less catas-trophic results than Austria. In Germany, some wine merchants had used dyethylene glycol or already adulterated Austrian wines in their trade-mark plonk. In Italy, the far more toxic methylene alcohol was added to wines. More than twenty people died in Italy, though nobody was hurt as a consequence of drinking the adulterated Austrian wines. Italian grow-ers, however, had already begun to promote their wines internationally.

In retrospect, nothing better could have happened to Austrian wine-making. New wine laws, the strictest in Europe, were introduced to ensure quality, and with the demise of the old networks for the distribution of poor, sickly-sweet wines, and a wave of retirements among the older growers, a new generation, with new ideas and international travel behind them, was soon taking over the business. There were some examples they could follow. In the Wachau, a group of friends around Josef Jamek, Franz Hirtzberger senior, and Franz Prager, had slowly and patiently built their reputation on dry, terroir-oriented wines. Their colleagues had thought them crazy, and there had been little political support, either, since the group also spearheaded protests against a dam project that would have produced electricity at the price of destroying the uniquely beautiful landscape of the Wachau and ending wine production there.

The generation that became dominant during the late 1980s and early 1990s had horizons and goals very different from those of its fathers. New vinification methods and international travel had changed perspectives and raised ambitions. The old generation looked on in disbelief as workable mixed farms were converted to wine only, and large sums were invested in new cellars; as high yields were abandoned, and as growers increasingly bottled and sold their own wines. New grape varieties were planted, some of which, such as Chardonnay (which had, as Morillon and as Pinot Blanc, already been grown to some extent) and Sauvignon Blanc proved very successful, though they still represent only a small fraction of the vineyard. Within a very few years, one of the most backward wine-producing countries in Europe had become one of the most bubblingly exciting.

THE FACE OF AUSTRIAN WINE CULTURE TODAY

Austria sports one of Europe's most vivacious and dedicated wine cultures. In a country with considerably fewer inhabitants than London, three journals, *Falstaff*, *Vinaria*, and *A la Carte*, are devoted to discussing and reviewing local (and international) wines, and at the annual Salon

Tasting wine journalists and other recognized connoisseurs nominate growers whose wines are then entered for a series of blind tastings and ranked in a "hall of fame" of the 200 best wines and growers in Austria.

The Austrian Wine Academy runs not only diploma courses in wine appreciation but is also a European outpost of the Institute of Masters of Wine in London. In addition to this, there is a plethora of wine seminars, regional tastings, cellar tours, open days in wineries, blind tastings, wine concerts, and other events, while wine culture in Austrian restaurants is world-class. Every good restaurant has suitable glasses (can we say, the variety of which can occasionally be carried to excess), a varied and well-chosen wine list, and a knowledgeable sommelier.

Formal wine education in Austria is, as might be expected, very thorough. Its centre is the Weinbauschule Klosterneuburg, a vocational secondary school and a port of call for most aspiring growers. There is also a well regarded school of viticulture in Krems, and another one in the Styrian town of Silberberg. In addition, the Viennese Universität für Bodenkultur (BOKU) carries on work with a stronger emphasis on academic research into soil types, clones and climate, vine training methods, and so on.

Appreciation, teaching and research are also supported by an active and professional marketing organization, the Austrian Wine Marketing Board, which promotes Austrian wines abroad, invites journalists and makes trading connections. At a biannual wine fair in Vienna's Imperial Hofburg, the VieVinum, visitors can taste the best the country produces.

One widely publicized recent development has been the introduction in 2003 of the Weinviertel DAC (*Districtus Austriae Controllatus*, or Controlled District of Austria), a system intended to be similar to French *appellation contrôlée*. Under the rules of the Austrian DAC initiative, committees of growers in each region are invited to determine which wine types or varieties should represent the region; submitted wines are then tasted annually for quality and characteristics such as colour, varietal fruit, and vinification method. The Weinviertel DAC (which has been defined as a fresh, peppery Grüner Veltliner without wood aromas and with no more than six grams of residual sugar and at least twelve degrees of alcohol), has generated a good deal of publicity, and currently some three per cent of Weinviertel wines are sold as DAC wines. The region has greatly profited from this initiative, both in terms of public exposure and in terms of wine quality. It has been the intention to expand the system to other regions, but no other DAC declaration is imminent at the time of writing, since political interests between and within regions diverge. The Wachau points out that its own organization, Vinea Wachau, effectively already operates a DAC system. Other regions have created their own structures (for instance the associations Pannobile in Neusiedlersee, or Steirische Klassik in Styria), which also serve the purpose of promoting regional identity.

Stylistically, among the top flight of growers, the last few years have shown a rise in confidence as well as a movement away from international styles and grape varieties, especially for red wines. Blaufränkisch and Zweigelt (and, to a certain extent, St Laurent) are now widely seen as the best candidates for great Austrian reds, even if they are often blended with Merlot and Cabernet Sauvignon. Pinot Noir, a vine that has been cultivated in Austria for some two centuries, is also on the way up. There is now a small but growing band of producers around Lake Neusiedl, in the Kamptal, in Styria, and in some other regions, who make outstanding Pinot Noir. This is a very encouraging development, and if temperatures in Europe continue to rise, Austria could even become one of Europe's most important sites for Pinot.

So, what lies ahead? Many good producers have set their sights on exports, which have increased almost twentyfold since 1985, and are continuing to rise. Responsible for one per cent of world production, Austrian wine will always remain a niche in the world market, but one of the very highest quality. The smaller to middle-sized names have been enthusiastically welcomed abroad, but so far Austria has no very large producer of a quality sufficient to compete with the great commercial names of other countries. This would be a logical next step, helping to consolidate Austrian wines abroad, and realizing the considerable and as yet untapped potential of many high-quality vineyards.

2

Vines and vineyards

The climate is changing. Mean temperatures in winter in Austria are now about one degree Celsius higher than sixty years ago, and summer temperatures have increased by two degrees. Along with this, rainfall patterns have shifted and there is more likelihood of late hail or early frosts.

Two degrees Celsius may not sound much, but it makes a crucial difference to the vegetative cycle of plants, whose development is triggered, among other things, by key temperatures that now occur much earlier in the year. The vegetation period of vines is some two weeks longer today than it was fifty years ago, resulting in higher ripeness or indeed overripeness; Austrian vineyards also increasingly suffer from sunburn, as well as heat and drought stress. UV radiation increased by twenty per cent between 1990 and 1999, and levels of ozone close to the soil, too, have rocketed up, causing increased strain on the plants. In very hot summers like 2000 and 2003, the berries of varieties susceptible to sunburn responded by producing thicker skins with more tannins.

Among Austrian wine-growers, responses to this phenomenon are varied. Many dismiss these changes as ordinary variations that don't have much significance, but some growers, notably Prager's Toni Bodenstein, and Willi Bründlmayer, accept it as a long-term trend and react with particular measures both in canopy management and in the planting of new vineyards. Leaving part of the leaf canopy to shade the fruit zone can counter the risk of sunburn and heat stress, and a move toward "greener", more ecologically diverse vineyards with less chemical intervention can allow the plants to defend themselves, for instance by growing deeper roots to access water reserves. Recent research suggests that the increased biodiversity of biologically healthy soils makes plants more resistant to stress and infection. Green cover between the rows can absorb excess moisture and help regulate competition between the vines. In case of drought it can be cut, providing natural fertilizer. There are, of course, as many different regimes as there are wine-growers.

Another effect is that, in Lower Austria at least, vineyards have begun to climb up the hillsides as temperature differences make new sites viable. If a vineyard was ideal for a delicate Gelber Muskateller after World War II, it may soon look like a good place for Pinot Noir or even Merlot. If temperatures continue to rise traditionally "hotter" varieties will spread northward and push out vines that prefer cooler conditions. This will be one of the great issues in European viticulture in the next few decades.

THE TERROIR QUESTION

Terroir is the greatest gift and challenge to any winemaker, and the DAC initiative was partly a recognition that not all Austrian wine-growing regions have a strongly terroir-based identity as yet. Historically, only the Krems region (the Wachau alone has some 900 historically recognized vineyard names) and the Thermenregion have a strong and unbroken terroir tradition reaching back several centuries. Other regions have individual vineyards that have long been recognized, but they may have only a few producers making wines with a strong terroir character.

Defining terroir has become perhaps the greatest challenge for the more ambitious winemakers, especially in the Burgenland, in Styria, and in the striving Lower Austrian regions. An increasing number of growers is meeting it by concentrating on Austrian varieties like Grüner Veltliner and Riesling in Lower Austria, Blaufränkisch and Zweigelt in the Burgenland, and, less unmistakably Austrian though fully justified, Sauvignon Blanc and Chardonnay in Styria, and with a winemaking style less influenced by wood, extraction and concentration.

Most of these Austrian varieties have so far received little attention from international wine research institutes, so there are few attractive commercial clones around. Existing Austrian commercial clones of Grüner Veltliner, Blaufränkisch, and Riesling were usually developed during the 1950s, 1960s, and 1970s, when they were selected for high yields and resistance to pests and frost. This renders them less interesting for modern, quality-oriented production, as they usually have larger berries, thinner skins, and a more vigorous vegetation, which means more canopy work during summer if yields are to be restricted.

Under new EU legislation, particularly directive 2005/43/EC, only certified clones that have been tested for viruses may be planted in the EU. This may seem a good idea, but it necessarily restricts the gene pool of European vines, leading to genetic erosion, less variety, and possibly to increased pest and virus problems in the future, as vineyards with little genetic diversity are more vulnerable to threats targeting their specific genetic profile. It was, at the time of writing, uncertain whether this legislation was likely to present a problem or whether the directive, itself amending a previous one, would be changed.

The Austrian tradition of massal selection (planting cuttings from one's own best vines) is in direct opposition to such a policy, if the cuttings are not tested for viruses. But massal selections may be more adapted to local conditions and individual preferences, and they can preserve genetic diversity. Increasingly, growers are turning to old, pre-World War II vineyards for material. Toni Bodenstein of Prager in the Wachau has planted two "Noah's Ark" vineyards, one dedicated to 118 different Grüner Veltliners, another to a rather more modest sixteen different Rieslings.

Planting densities and training methods during the second part of the twentieth century are connected to the economics of the day. During the harsh postwar years, mechanization and yields were paramount. Almost all wine-growers produced vegetables as well as wine, and one tractor had to be used for both, forcing growers to leave more space between the traditionally narrow rows of vines. The average density of vineyards created during this period dropped from between 5,000 and 6,000 vines per hectare or more, to 2,500 per hectare. The loss in yields had to be made up by greater productivity per vine. Enter the Lenz Moser training system, developed by grower and merchant Lenz Moser in the 1950s. Vines trained on this system are characterized by their tall trunks, with the grapes at about 1.3 metres (four feet) off the ground, and the rows spaced about 3.5 metres (11.5 feet) apart. Its obvious advantage is that it makes mechanized vineyard work easier, simplifies the tending of the vines and is also less hard on the backs of workers, who can remain upright when pruning and harvesting. And, of course, yields are high.

Unfortunately, the grapes tend to lose warmth reflected from the soil and are more exposed to wind; they also have less leaf surface as the height of the canopy is limited by the reach of workers or mechanical cutters. Less warmth and less leaf surface means less ripeness, though producers who limit yields and are careful to manage their leaf canopy can achieve very good results with this training method. On the shores of Lake Neusiedl, Lenz Moser training is used for high-quality dry wines: in this warm, foggy area, the greater ventilation of the airy Moser system can help keep botrytis at bay. Apart from this regional particularity, though, almost all good producers have abandoned the system.

Individual growers also experiment with other methods. Willi Bründlmayer, for example, has trained the vines in some of his best vineyards according to the lyre system invented by Henri Latour in Auxey-Duresses and developed by Dr. Alain Carbonnneau. The lyre system increases the leaf canopy (and thus the ability of the wine to photosynthesize) while leaving the grapes with just the right amount of exposure to the sun and protection from the elements. Unlike Lenz Moser, this system is very labour-intensive. Around Vienna, other, individual high-canopied, traditional training methods persist. One interesting experiment is undertaken by Sepp Muster in South Styria, who uses high trunks and leads part of the canopy downwards, sloping toward the soil.

The most prevalent training methods for interesting wines are now the classic double guyot, the arched cane method, and the *cordon de Royat*, though the Austrian adaptation of these tends to be a little higher than the usual thirty to forty centimetres (twelve to sixteen inches), in recognition of the lower temperatures in the vineyards. In the terraced vineyards of the Wachau, where mechanized work is ruled out by the steep stone terraces, normal planting densities can reach up to 7,000 vines per hectare, 5,500 being the average.

The higher the planting density of a terraced vineyard the more skilled manual work is necessary. This puts high-density vineyards out of the reach of less affluent producers who have to rely on their small tractors. Top producers, however, actively seek out old, steep, high-density vineyards, though there are still good producers who believe that the increased pruning is not reflected in increased quality. They prefer lower densities of around 4,000 vines per hectare, with correspondingly more yield per vine, ranging from one kilogram for high-density vineyards to 1.5 kilograms for lower-density ones. In the Wachau and in the neighbouring Kremstal and Kamptal, hillside vineyards are usually irrigated during summer, adding a further sixty litres per square metre to the Wachau's 300 litres of rainfall during summer, an amount on the low margin of tolerance for vines. Only through irrigation can the Wachau hold its present high quality levels.

Most Lower Austrian vineyards show a picture similar to that of the Wachau, with planting densities dropping dramatically for vineyards planted around 1950, and more than doubling in recent years. The Weinviertel, still the source of the vast majority of Austria's simple whites, has a great proportion of unreconstructed, Lenz Moser-trained vineyards with low density and high yields per vine. An exception here is Hans Setzer's 8,000 vineyard, planted with Grüner Veltliner and named after its extremely high planting density. In the Kamtal and Kremstal, many vineyards operate with less than 4,000 vines per hectare on the flat land and up to 6,000 for terraced vineyards, an average density also reflecting a relatively higher degree of mechanization than in the Wachau.

Around Lake Neusiedl, densities of 5,000 to 6,000 vines dominate. Some growers such as Heinz Velich prefer 4,000 for their dry wines in recognition of the high botrytis risk in the area. These lower densities are compensated for by a slightly higher yield per vine, up to 1.5 kilograms for high-quality wines. Irrigation is necessary here, too, particularly as viticulture is directly competing with the intensive irrigation of vegetable fields and the attendant lowering of groundwater levels during the vegetation period. In Middle and South Burgenland, planting densities are also on the rise, as is wine quality.

Styria shows a similar, relatively low density per hectare, with the initial 3,000 vines planted after the war gradually increased to 4,500 or thereabouts to allow for the use of specialized tractors in the often extremely steep and widely scattered vineyards. The significantly higher rainfall in the region makes irrigation unnecessary. As elsewhere, yields for high-quality wines are usually restricted to under 1.5 kilograms per vine.

BETTER WITH BIO?

Austria claims to be Europe's greenest wine producer. The federal ÖPUL programme (its initials hide the hideousness of its full name: Österreichisches Programm zur Förderung einer umweltgerechten, extensiven und den natürlichen Lebensraum schützenden Landwirtschaft, or "Austrian Programme for the Support of an Environmentally Friendly Extensive Agriculture Conserving the Natural Environment") subsidizes environmentally friendly practices in agricultural production and covers seventy per cent of all farmers and ninety per cent of all agricultural surface area in Austria. Under the (strictly controlled) guidelines of the programme, producers may not use certain chemical fertilizers, must limit their use of chemical pest controls, and must secure their fields against erosion and/or actively maintain a varied and sustainable ecosystem on their land.

While ÖPUL has effectively managed to steer Austrian agriculture towards ecological sustainability, and practically all Austrian wine-producers are part of it, some go much further. Organic or even Biodynamic production is slowly spreading, particularly in Lower Austria and the Lake Neusiedl area. As everywhere, the picture is more complex than it may seem. Many top Austrian producers today practise what the French call "*lutte raisonnée*", which means using chemical products only when necessary. Some of these producers claim to be organic, but only those who are certified by institutions like Bio Ernte Austria, Bioveritas, AGÖL, Ecocert, or Demeter (for Biodynamic produce) are entitled to do so. Nor is organic viticulture in itself free of problems: a high dosage of copper sulphate, for instance, is entirely permissible as well as legal as a fungicide, but the build-up of copper in the soil can be considerable.

Austria also has Europe's highest proportion of Biodynamic vineyards in relation to its total vineyard surface. Biodynamic viticulture adviser Andrew Lorand is soon to help a group of winemakers, among them the majority of the Pannobile growers (*see* Appendix III) and several in the Kamptal, to make the transition to Biodynamic wine-growing. The Nikolaihof in the Wachau was a trailblazer for Biodynamic viticulture when this was still thought to be mad, bad, and dangerous. Now even the most conservative must acknowledge that neither the state of the Nikolaihof vineyards even in wet years, nor the quality of the wines, leave anything to be desired.

The suitability of Biodynamic or organic methods is also partly a result of the climate. In dryer regions (particularly in Lower Austria and Burgenland) it is easier to avoid fungicides as the main threat comes from *oidium* or powdery mildew, which is relatively simple to deal with organ-ically, as opposed to *peronospera* or downy mildew, which is not. Here, significant losses of crop are a constant risk. In Styria, high rainfall renders organic viticulture very difficult. Even so, the remarkable Sepp Muster in South Styria is demonstrating that it is possible to produce outstanding wine even here according to a strictly Biodynamic regime.

HARVEST

The most important single decision of the year is the date of picking. Within the last ten years the criteria have changed: after the war, and with an eye to reliable, production-oriented winemaking, it was Klosterneuburg viticultural school orthodoxy that sugar content determines ripeness, and that high sugar translates into ideal ripeness. For a long time most growers simply whipped out their refractometer to determine when they should harvest. They tended to produce unsophisticated wines with plenty of rustic tannins and high alcohol.

Outstanding growers have always trusted their palates more than technology. Now the majority of growers tend to emphasize tasting the grapes as the main factor in deciding when to harvest. As a result there has been a noticeable increase in ripeness (but not overripeness) and finesse.

Average harvest dates vary according to area. The hot Burgenland plains are usually first, with some growers beginning to pick their reds around September 15, a week earlier than most of their colleagues. Growers in Styria and Lower Austria typically begin harvesting in early October, while their more ambitious, and more courageous, colleagues will wait some three weeks longer for perfect ripeness, a gamble against rain and rot that is only possible for producers who are financially relatively secure. Nobly-sweet wines and then Icewines bring up the rear, with some grapes occasionally hanging as long as late December or even early January.

With climate change and a longer vegetation period and a general trend to harvest as late as possible, the hang-time of the berries has increased by almost a month compared to the 1950s. During the late 1990s, when fashion dictated a search for extremes, hang times were sometimes carried to excess. Now most growers have found a more balanced approach, and many accept that the latest possible harvest date may not always be the best, as acidity is reduced and aromas become less fresh and clear.

For top wines it is normal to select rigorously and to go through the same vineyard several times, cutting out diseased or less than perfect material and harvesting berries with perfect ripeness. Alois Gross in Styria repeats this procedure up to five times for his top wines. Almost all top growers in Austria harvest by hand.

GRAPE VARIETIES

Percentages in brackets indicate the share of the entire Austrian vineyard.

White grapes

BOUVIER
Less than one per cent.

A soft, fat variety named after Clothar Bouvier, who cultivated it on his estate in Bad Radkersburg in Styria at the end of the nineteenth century. It was probably brought into Austria from Slovenia, and to there from Switzerland. Today it is used mainly for botrytis wines, where it can achieve good quality, and for the popular *Sturm*, wine drunk while still fermenting, and produced almost exclusively in the Burgenland, with some additional vineyards in Vienna and Styria. Bouvier needs fertile soils and ripens early. On its own it tends to lack acidity and character and is therefore often blended with Welschriesling, which has higher acidity. Bouvier is golden in colour and has an aroma reminiscent of Muscat. There is also some Bouvier grown in Hungary.

CHARDONNAY
Also called Morillon in Styria and Feinburgunder in the Wachau;
six per cent, 2,936 hectares.

Officially, Austria did not have any Chardonnay until 1986, when suddenly 300 hectares appeared on the map. The reason for this miraculous transformation was that a great deal of Chardonnay had previously appeared in the statistics as Pinot Blanc. Chardonnay can therefore be regarded as a traditional Austrian variety, certainly at least as much as other, more recent arrivals that are thought of as typically Austrian, such as Zweigelt and Blauburger.

The origin of the name Morillon is somewhat mysterious. According to Austrian sources, Chardonnay shoots were imported into Styria from the village of Morion in Champagne after phylloxera. There is, however, no such village in Champagne, though there is one by that name close to Lyon. No wine is made there. Several villages throughout France are called Morillon, but it seems more likely that the grape has its name from an old name for Chardonnay (and occasionally Pinot Noir) used in Burgundy and in northeastern France.

Chardonnay is produced in most Austrian wine-growing regions. Powerful and often aged in oak, it can reach great heights in Styria and around Lake Neusiedl, while in Lower Austria it is often dense and lean, and usually fermented in steel or in large barrels.

In general there are both international, oaked Chardonnays, and tighter, more traditional, "classical" wines. The latter are vinified reductively in steel tanks (and occasionally in large barrels) and without malolactic fermentation to emphasize the finesse of the fruit and the acidity. Most growers will vinify some of each.

FURMINT
Also known as Gelber Furmint, Mosler, or Zapfner;
less than one per cent.

In Hungary, Furmint is the main ingredient of Tokaji. Just across the border, in the Burgenland, it is now making a slow comeback for Ausbruch and other sweet wines, and recently some outstanding dry Furmints have heralded a mini-renaissance of this grape. Furmint is thought to have been brought to Hungary by Italian immigrants during the thirteenth century. It is high in acidity and has a reputation for being difficult to grow, requiring warm, dry soils, and producing variable yields. Some growers, especially in Rust, have good successes with it, and are often rewarded with finely-tuned aromas and high alcohol and acidity. It ripens late. As it has relatively thin skins, it is particularly sensitive to noble rot, which makes it an ideal candidate for Ausbruch.

FRÜHROTER VELTLINER
Also known as Malvasier;
one per cent.

No direct relative of the Grüner Veltliner (though they may share a common ancestor, Roter Veltliner), or indeed of Malvasia, despite its names, the reddish-skinned Frühroter Veltliner is related to the Malvoisie family of grapes and thought to have originated in Greece, and been imported to Austria via northern Italy. Originally often used in *Gemischter Satz*, traditional mixed plantings, it is now also planted on its own, especially in Lower Austria, and traditionally in the Thermenregion. It is not easy to master, being very sensitive to frost and yielding often neutral wines with little acidity and high alcohol. It is tolerant of lime and thrives on dry soils, where it is early ripening. Frühroter Veltliner is cultivated almost exclusively in Austria. Its wines are hardly ever of very high quality. At their best, they have a pleasant, earthy aroma reminiscent of bitter almonds, but their low acidity and high alcohol often make them unbalanced.

GOLDBURGER

Less than one per cent.

A variety bred in 1922, this is a crossing of Welschriesling with Orangentraube made by the Austrian wine pioneer F. Zweigelt. It has gold-coloured skins and ripens well on poor soils, mainly around the Neusiedlersee, in the Weinviertel, and Southeast Styria. As dry wine it tends to lack character, but as it tends to reach high must weights it can be be used for sweet wines up to TBA.

GRÜNER VELTLINER

Also known as Weissgipfler, Bielospicak, Dreimänner, Falkensteiner, Fehérhegyue, Grüner Muskateller, Grünmuskateller, Nemes Veltelini, Manhardsrebe, Manhardtraube, Manhartsrebe, Mouhardsrebe, Ryvola Bila, Tarant Bily, Valteliner, Veltlini, Veltlinske Zelené, Weissgipfler, Weissreifler, Weissmuskateller, Yesil Veltliner, Zeleny Muskatel, Zleni Veltinac, Zöld Muskotaly, and Zöld Veltelini.

Thirty-six per cent, 17,479 hectares.

The most common grape in Austria by far, this is also found in eastern Europe. Its origins are obscure, though it is certain that it does not, in fact, derive from the Italian vine Valtellina, or from the Swiss Veltlin Valley. Like the popularity of the grape in Austria, the name Grüner Veltliner is quite recent. First documented in 1766 as Grüner Muskateller, the vine began to supplant the Heunisch grape throughout the then Habsburg empire. According to the wine historian Norbert Tischelmayer the name Grüner Veltliner was first mentioned in 1855 but was not common until the 1930s. Genetic research has now identified Traminer as one of its parents, the other one being still unknown, though it is likely that Roter Veltliner belongs to its more distant ancestry.

The great success story of Grüner Veltliner in Austria begins with the oenologist Lenz Moser and his high vine-training system, to which the grape was well suited. The first great Grüner Veltliner with the complexity, ripeness, and depth now associated with the grape was, however, a product of the oenological revolution of the 1980s and 1990s.

While Austria's *Heurige* culture would be inconceivable without Grüner Veltliner, growers in the Wachau, the Kamptal, Kremstal, and also in the Weinviertel, the Donauland, and the Traisental vinify it as a high-quality wine. In its most simple incarnation it is pleasantly fruity, with notes of pepper and grapefruit, but it can evolve into extraordinarily complex wines with aromas reminding one of tropical fruit, pineapple, and even walnuts, backed up by high acidity and alcohol.

Although eminently drinkable in their youth, the best wines have an extraordinary ageing potential and will have lost nothing of their power and structure after thirty years. The grape is often compared to Riesling and, growing in the same areas, especially the Wachau, great Grüner Veltliners often age better than Riesling. Those grown on primary rock miraculously take on the buttery depth and complexity of *grand cru* white burgundy – with which they are sometimes confused in blind tastings – while Grüner Veltliners from the loess and loam soils in the Kamptal and Kremstal can acquire a note reminiscent of Riesling. As the revolution in Austrian winemaking took place relatively recently, it is not yet possible to gauge the full ageing potential of Grüner Veltliners produced with all the benefits of modern vinification, but some Veltliners from the sixties and even the fifties still retain their youthfulness and structure and are wonderfully enjoyable.

As already mentioned, Grüner Veltliners often display tones of honey, citrus, and grapefruit with a distinctive peppery note in youth. Wines from riper grapes tend to have pronounced tropical fruit aromas, while the Veltliners of the Wachau also display a remarkable mineral backbone. Depending on vinification, the wines can be light and fragrant, or powerful battleships, often weighing in at fourteen to fifteen degrees of alcohol, a strength only the best winemakers are able to control. The grape is also, however, high in acidity, which helps to balance the power.

A supremely adaptable variety, Grüner Veltliner takes well to poor and to rich soils, and to both loess and to lime, and can yield up to a hundred hectolitres per hectare. For high-quality wines, however, the yields have to be severely limited, at times down to around twenty hectolitres per hectare on the steep terraces of the Wachau. The best and most characteristic results are achieved on primary rock soils, such as those in the Wachau and the Kamptal, where it can produce wines that are a beautiful expression of their terroir. On loam and loess the wines can become too fat and lose much of their character and potential.

Grüner Veltliner is planted throughout Austria, but overwhelmingly in the Weinviertel, where it produces spicy and quaffable wines.

It can be found throughout eastern Europe, and is cultivated in the

Sopron district of Hungary, where it is known as Zöldveltelini; in the Czech Republic and in Slovakia as Veltlin Zelene or Veltlinske Zelené; in Yugoslavia, and in Germany. Experiments with the variety in New York State did not prove successful, but Grüner Veltliner seems an ideal candidate for export to New World countries; indeed, there is already an experimental planting in New Zealand.

MÜLLER-THURGAU
Also known as Riesling/Sylvaner and Rivaner;
seven per cent, 3,390 hectares.

This vine was developed in Geisenheim, Germany, in 1882, and was long believed to be a crossing of Riesling and Sylvaner, though it is now thought to be a crossing of two Riesling grapes, or possibly Riesling and Chasselas. Whatever it is, it has not been a success in qualitative terms, and there is little or no Müller-Thurgau of true interest around.

The grape can be grown in most conditions and on most soils, ripens early and produces bountifully, especially on fertile soils and in cool climates: 150 hectolitres per hectare, and more in some years, almost twice of what can be expected from Riesling. In Germany, it is virtually synonymous with the dreaded Liebfraumilch. In Austria, it is also responsible for mass-produced wines, especially in the Burgenland. If treated with great care Müller-Thurgau can produce wines similar to Riesling in fruit, though not in depth or structure. It can also have a pronounced Muscat aroma. Low alcohol and acidity do not help. It is still very common, especially at the lower end of the market, but is now progressively being abandoned by more ambitious growers, and is no great loss.

MUSKATELLER
Also known as Gelber Muskateller or Muscat-Lunel;
less than one per cent.

Cultivated since the fifteenth century, Muskateller (a gold-skinned variation on the French Muscat Blanc à Petits Grains) is still one of the most consistent grape varieties in Austria. A late-ripening variety with a preference for sandy or gravelly soils, Austrian Muskatellers are produced mainly in the Wachau, in Southeast Styria, and in the Burgenland, especially around Rust, where they are used for Ausbruch wines, turning the grape's sensitivity to rot into an advantage. There is beautiful dry Muskateller made in the Wachau, where it is light and aromatic, with a characteristic aroma of roses and nutmeg. In Styria, a more muscular version has evolved during the last ten years.

MUSKAT-OTTONEL
One per cent.

A popular variety despite its often low yields, Muskat-Ottonel produces mild wines with low alcohol and acidity. Its name probably derives from confusion with the French Muscat-Lunel, which is in fact another name for Muskateller. Like the latter, Muskat-Ottonel ripens late and is sensitive to diseases, noble rot among them. Popular in Austria in the sixties and seventies, there is little Muskat-Ottonel cultivated now, and it is found mainly in the Burgenland. With its intensive Muscat aroma and light fruit it can be vinified dry as an aperitif. Nowadays, however, it is more commonly used in nobly-sweet wines, especially in the Neusiedlersee, where it can often be found in blends.

NEUBURGER
Also known as Grüner Burgunder, Brubler, Neuburger Alb, Neuburger Blanc, Neuburgske, Neuburske, Novogradski, und Ujvari;
two per cent, 1,094 hectares.

This is the Moses of Austrian wine: according to legend it was fished out of the Danube in the 1860s and planted in the Wachau, though another story has it going back to the Thirty Years' War; either way it seems to have originated in Austria. Genetically speaking it is a natural crossing of Roter Veltliner and Sylvaner. In vinification it is usually treated like the Burgundian grapes and is often vinified in cask, where it can produce wines with good ageing potential, a nutty, fleshy character, and very pleasant acidity. Neuburger is a relatively early ripener and prefers crystalline, dry to heavy soils. It is grown throughout Austria, with the exception of Styria. After the war it was used for unremarkable, sweetish, mass-produced wines, and this reputation is still dogging it. Today, however, it has been recognized that Neuburger can make wines of considerable complexity and interest, particularly in the Burgenland and Lower Austria.

PINOT BLANC
Also known as Weisser Burgunder, Weissburgunder, and Klevner;
four per cent, 2,935 hectares.

A relatively late arrival, Pinot Blanc is a mutation of Pinot Gris, which was first observed in Burgundy at the end of the nineteenth century. Pinot Blanc was long confused with Chardonnay, which it resembles very closely. It is a demanding variety and needs very good conditions in order to ripen well. It prefers deep, chalky soils with plenty of nutrients and good sun exposure, and will not yield high quantities. If and when these requirements are met, especially in the Burgenland, in Styria, and the Wachau, the Kamptal, and other parts of Lower Austria, Pinot Blanc can achieve good must weights and can be made into beautifully full-bodied wines, which are characteristically round and almond-scented, high in alcohol and often very powerful, with plenty of ageing potential.

PINOT GRIS
Also known as Grauer Burgunder, Grauburgunder, and Ruländer; less than one per cent.

A red-skinned mutation of Pinot Noir, this grape was probably brought to Austria in the thirteenth century by Cistercian monks. In the appropriate conditions and on the right soil it can produce soft and gracious wines with lovely fruit and full body. Styria seems to be ideal. Here it develops the acidity necessary to give it bite and can be made into remarkable wines, though it tends to be underestimated even there; obviously a case of the prophet not being recognized in his own land.

RIESLING
Also known as Rheinriesling; three per cent, 1,643 hectares.

Sometimes called the queen of white grapes, Riesling in Austria is not important in terms of quantity, but is hugely important in terms of quality. Long regarded as the German grape, Riesling is one of the few white varieties to age well for many decades and can produce great wines that may be very dry, high in residual sugar, or affected by noble rot. Famous for its combination of acidity and fruit extract, the typical taste of Riesling is often described as flowery yet tart, with petrol overtones in maturity, and always strongly affected by its terroir.

Riesling is thought to have originated in the Rhine Valley in Germany, though some authors believe that a vineyard by the name of Rizling in the Wachau (first mentioned in the thirteenth century) may in fact be the oldest recorded place of Riesling cultivation.

The grape is famously wedded to its terroir and is often thought to provide the most perfect expression of the conditions it finds in soil and microclimate. While Riesling will grow on most soil types it is sensitive to high chalk content, and will not develop great character on loess or loam. The wood of Riesling vines is harder than that of many others, and the grape is consequently not very sensitive to frost, although it does need sheltered, south-facing vineyards with good sun exposure to ripen fully.

In view of its sensitivity to terroir, it is not surprising that in Austria Riesling is associated not only with particular areas, mainly in the Wachau and the Kamptal, but with particular vineyards that have long been known to offer ideal conditions for its cultivation: dry, deep soils of primary rock able to retain the warmth of the sun and to release it gradually for the benefit of the vines. In the Kamptal, Zöbinger Heiligenstein, Lamm, and Gaisberg are famous sites for Rieslings, while in the Wachau there are various renowned Riesling *Reiden*, among them Singerriedel, Steinborz, Achspoint and Tausendeimerberg in Spitz; Hochrain and Kollmitz in Wösendorf; Pichlpoint in Joching; Achleiten in Weissenkirchen; Kellerberg in Dürnstein; and Loibenberg in Loiben – all of which, incidentally, are also great for Grüner Veltliner.

While the Rieslings of the Wachau are justly famous for their vigour, complexity and their strong mineral note, those of the Kamptal and the nearby Kremstal tend to be a little fuller, while the Rieslings around Vienna are somewhat broader. The Austrian Riesling idiom is closer to that of Alsace than to that of Germany: often high in alcohol and extract with clear mineral character and usually vinified dry, though there are some nobly-rotten Rieslings in years that lend themselves to this.

ROTER VELTLINER
Also known as Roter Muskateller;
less than one per cent.

This very old variety is an ancestor of many other grapes of the Veltliner family, such as Frühroter Veltliner and Neuburger (with Sylvaner), and Rotgipfler (with Traminer), though it is probably only a distant relative of the most famous family member, Grüner Veltliner.

If the yields are kept down – and Roter Veltliner yields unreliably – it can show very good fruit and finesse. It is, however, sensitive to frost, rain, and rot. It also ripens unevenly and needs rich loam and loess soils to mature fully. Most is made in the Weinviertel, in Wagram (Donauland), in the Kamptal, and around Krems and Gedersorf. Both the dry and sweet styles can be successful. Nowadays a rarity, it is by no means negligible and can produce beautiful wines, especially in Kremstal and Donauland. Weisser, Brauner, and Silberweisser Veltliner are all mutations.

ROTGIPFLER
Less than one per cent.

Probably originating in Styria, Rotgipfler has now firmly established itself in the Thermenregion, where it is often blended with Zierfandler. Rotgipfler is certainly the lesser of the two: late-ripening, very demanding in terms of soil and location, and sensitive to wind chill and botrytis, it can produce some full-bodied wines with marked acidity, golden colour, and characteristic aromas of clementine and almonds. Often, though, it produces light and fresh wines that are not remarkable in terms of sophistication and complexity. Blends with Zierfandler may be called Spätrot-Rotgipfler.

SAUVIGNON BLANC
Also known as Muskat-Sylvaner;
less than one per cent.

The global Sauvignon Blanc boom has produced its fair share of techno wines in Austria as everywhere else. There are producers in Austria who have made it their passion and, especially in South Styria, it is capable of great things. Sauvignon Blanc ripens late and needs fertile, not-too-dry soils to flourish, all of which it gets in Styria as well as in parts of the northern Burgenland. Some of these wines have wonderful fruit and complexity. There is also some Sauvignon Blanc in Lower Austria. In other parts of the country, Sauvignon Blanc can be a valuable added string to the wine-grower's bow, without reaching the dizzying heights it can achieve in Styria or Burgenland.

SCHEUREBE
Also known as Sämling 88;
less than one per cent.

Originating in Alzey, Germany, in 1916 from a crossing of Riesling and Sylvaner (unlike Müller-Thurgau, which is often said to be Riesling x Sylvaner but is not), the Scheurebe, named after its inventor Dr Georg Scheu (and sometimes after its "greenhouse name" Sämling, or "Seedling" 88), produces good yields, regularly reaches a high must weight, and is popular in Germany, where it can produce some interesting wines. It places few demands on the soil, but needs good vineyards in order to mature fully. It is also sensitive to frost. In Austria, Scheurebe wines are often quite bland when vinified dry. Prone to botrytis it is, however, a good variety for the production of nobly-rotten wines, both on its own and in blends. In this incarnation it is quite common around the Neusiedlersee, especially in Illmitz.

SYLVANER
Less than one per cent.

Probably originating in Austria (in Germany it used to be called Österreicher) and still common in Alsace and in Franken in Germany, this variety used to be more common before the introduction of the high training of vines in Austria. Copious in yield and high in acidity, this early ripener is a typical workhorse vine that rarely produces exciting wines. It used to be widely planted in the Burgenland, and after its almost total demise it is now occasionally planted again as for light aperitif wines. Nevertheless, its earthy and often bland aromas have not made it many friends in Austria.

TRAMINER
Also known as Gewürztraminer, Gelber Traminer, Roter Traminer, and Weisser Traminer;
less than one per cent.

A pink-skinned grape, Gewürztraminer, as its most common clone is called in Germany and in Alsace, is one of the oldest known grapes in the world. It is documented as having been grown in Austria, in the Tyrol, around the year 1000 AD, though the Greeks are supposed to have already known it by then, and the Roman historian Pliny the Elder (23-79 AD) mentions Aminea (today, to add to the confusion, a synonym for Welschriesling), a grape that might well be Traminer. Many modern varieties are descended from it, among them Pinot Noir, Pinot Gris, and Pinot Blanc, Sauvignon Blanc, Grüner Veltliner, and even, more distantly, Cabernet Sauvignon.

Traminer mutates easily and there is a certain amount of confusion about the differences between Gewürztraminer, Roter Traminer, and Weisser Traminer. According to ampelographer Pierre Galet, Gewürztraminer is a variation on Traminer, which is also called Roter Traminer in Austria, Savagnin Rosé in France, and Klevner d'Heiligenstein in Alsace. (Not to be confused, of course, with what is sometimes called Klevner in Austria: Pinot Noir.) Gewürztraminer, the most popular mutation of Roter Traminer, is also called Gelber Traminer in Austria, and Savagnin Rosé Aromatique in some areas of France. Weisser Traminer is called Savagnin Blanc in France, and, just to compound the chaos, Gelber Traminer in some parts of Styria. Traminer grapes are also grown under different names in eastern Europe.

In Austria, different cousins of the Traminer family are often planted together in one vineyard and can be distinguished in autumn by the different colours of their berries, especially in the case of the Roter Traminer and Gewürztraminer. Ripening late, Traminer prefers warm and deep soils. Occasionally there are quite exceptional Traminers in Austria, Muscat-like and full-bodied with rose and lychee notes on the nose. They typically have a deep golden colour and can have a high alcohol content. Traminer is scattered all over Austria, with the notable exception of the Wachau. There are fine exponents of this variety in the Burgenland and in Styria, but there are also very good Traminers in the Weinviertel.

WELSCHRIESLING
Nine per cent, 4,323 hectares.
Welschriesling is the second most commonly grown grape variety in Austria after Grüner Veltliner. As indicated by its name, which translates as "foreign Riesling", it is not related to the Riesling. Its origins are lost in the infamous mists of time, though the name points to an origin outside of Austria, possibly Romania.

High in acidity, Welschriesling is most commonly used for simple, light wines for summer drinking, as a base wine for Sekt – and, in the Burgenland, for nobly-sweet wines. It needs deep, warm, and nutrient-rich soils and ripens late, best in sheltered, south-facing vineyards. Most Welschriesling is grown in the Burgenland, in Lower Austria, and in Styria. It is vinified mostly as a classical *Heurige* wine. It is usually distinguished by good acidity and an appealing green-apple fruit. In the hands of good growers it can be made into wines with fine, lemony acidity, and an ideal blending partner for sweet wines up to TBA level, especially around Lake Neusiedl, where it reaches its apogee.

ZIERFANDLER
Also known as Spätrot;
less than one per cent.
Planted mostly in the Thermenregion and much less in the Donauland, Zierfandler makes lean, spicy wines up to the higher reaches of the

Prädikat range, distinguished by an aroma reminiscent of quinces. It is a relation of Roter Veltliner, without having either its potential for depth or its adaptability. It is certainly superior to Rotgipfler, and can be full-bodied, high in alcohol (up to fifteen degrees), and have good ageing potential. A blend of Zierfandler and Rotgipfler may be called Spätrot-Rotgipfler.

Despite its name, Zierfandler is no relation to California's Zinfandel. Zierfandler remains very much a local speciality, though some is also produced in Hungary, where it is called Cirfandli.

Red grapes

BLAUBURGER
Two per cent, 884 hectares.
Created in 1922 by the legendary Prof. Zweigelt from Blauer Portugieser x Blaufränkisch, Blauburger's main claim to fame seems to be that it can lend colour to pallid reds, without, however, being capable of greatness. It is undemanding, but nevertheless sensitive to frost, mildew, and rot. It can still be found throughout Austria, in the Weinviertel, Kamptal, Carnuntum, Thermenregion, around Lake Neusiedl, and, in small quantities, in Styria and in Vienna.

BLAUFRÄNKISCH
Five per cent, 2,641 hectares.
Documented first in Austria in the second half of the eighteenth century, Blaufränkisch is, after Zweigelt, the most important red variety in the country. Its name suggests that its origins are probably medieval, when by Charlemagne's decree the superior grape varieties were called "fränkisch", or Franconian. This would mean that Blaufränkisch was already well established in the eighth century. In the nineteenth century it was called Blauer Frankentaler, and a great many legends exist, both about its name and its origin.

Its best wines are made in the Burgenland, where it can create powerful, tannic wines with characteristic pepper and bramble fruit. The wine-growers in the Middle Burgenland, where it has swept to victory over the last thirty years and is now the majority vine, even call their part of the world "Blaufränkischland". Here it finds the deep, nutrient-rich soils it needs to flourish. It is tolerant to chalky soils, but needs good sun exposure and shelter from strong winds, all of which are provided by the gentle hills of the middle and south Burgenland. There is a small-berried and a large-berried variety, the latter of which produces more rustic wines. A late ripener, Blaufränkisch needs sunny years to ripen fully.

Blaufränkisch wines have a characteristic midnight-blue colouring, the darkest of all red wines made in Austria. If the vines are cut back and the yields limited, Blaufränkisch can have an overwhelming, deep bouquet of cassis, bramble, eucalyptus, and black pepper, and characteristic notes of liquorice, with notably high acidity balancing its tannins. In less ripe years green aromas can dominate, but recently, notably in 1997, the grape has realized its potential. The most ambitious growers treat it very much like Syrah and vinify Blaufränkisch in small, new oak barrels. The results can be very impressive wines with good ageing potential, sometimes reminiscent of Rhône wines. It is also often used in blends, either with Zweigelt, or with Cabernet Sauvignon, or even (less convincingly) with Pinot Noir.

Blaufränkisch is also grown in Germany, where it is called Limberger or Lemberger, and throughout central Europe. As it was long thought to be identical with the Beaujolais grape Gamay it is still called Gamé in Bulgaria, while in Hungary it is known by its translated Austrian name of Kékfrankos, or as Nagyburgundi. In Slovakia it is called Frankovka, while in the northeast of Italy, in Friuli, it is called Franconia. Winegrowers in Washington State in the USA know it as Lemberger.

BLAUER PORTUGIESER
Five per cent, 2,358 hectares.

This grape was imported to Austria from Portugal in 1770 by the Austrian Count Fries. From there a Johann Philipp Bronner brought it to Germany in 1840. A high yielder (it can produce up to 160 hectolitres per hectare) that ripens early, grows practically everywhere, and is resistant to disease and frost, Blauer Portugieser is popular for mass-produced wines that are almost invariably cheap and relatively cheerless: thin, low in acidity, colour, and character, although some producers do their best to elevate it into a wine with more individuality. I have not yet been convinced that it does indeed have this potential – it seems to take up a great amount of perfectly good vineyard that could be planted with more promising varieties.

Blauer Portugieser is also grown in Hungary and Romania as Kékoporto, and in Croatia as Portugizac Crni, or Portugaljka. It was also known widely as Portugais Bleu in Southwest France, but many growers there are sensibly ripping it out.

BLAUER WILDBACHER

Also known as Schilcher, Kracher, or Krätzer; less than one per cent.

Blauer Wildbacher was already planted in Styria in the fourth century. A local speciality, this grape is traditionally vinified as a light rosé, a process that seems to involve doing everything one would otherwise try to avoid: planting it where it will not have much too sun and harvesting it early in order to make a wine high in acidity and low in sugar. Its name is derived from "schilchern" or "schillern", the interplay of colours between white and red, indicating that this wine is hardly ever vinified red. Another name, however, displays a different dimension of the wine: Heckenklescher, or "hedge-crasher". After a few glasses of this innocuous thirst-quencher on a hot summer's day, you fall into the hedge.

Sensitive to spring frosts and rot, Blauer Wildbacher needs airy sites to ripen well. The yields are typically no higher than sixty hectolitres per hectare, and the hallmark acidity is very high. In West Styria, it has been used for this rosé wine for at least two hundred years. Some Schilcher is also used for the production of sparkling wine, and there's even occasionally a nobly-rotten, amber-coloured TBA.

CABERNET FRANC

Less than one per cent.

This French grape exists in Austria mainly because it was mistaken for Merlot. It has had little impact in Austria, and is planted on less than half a per cent of the total area under vine, mainly in the Burgenland. It was sanctioned in Austrian wine law as a Qualitätswein grape in 1986.

CABERNET SAUVIGNON

Less than one per cent.

One of the most popular red grapes worldwide, Cabernet Sauvignon originates in France, where it is the backbone of much Bordeaux. A classical variety for blends, it lends power, tannic backbone, and structure to varieties with a more mellow, softer profile. Cabernet Sauvignon was introduced to Austria experimentally in 1860, in Vöslau, where it was made into a Bordeaux-style blend with Merlot. In spite of having become fashionable in Austria recently, it has turned out disappointingly in most regions apart from the Burgenland, where some very interesting wines are made from it, both on its own and in Bordeaux-style blends. Part of the problem is that it is late-ripening and rarely ever achieves full physiological ripeness in Austria, though it has benefited from the recent run of warm and very warm vintages. It grows on most soils and has good frost resistance. Like some other international varieties, it was recognized by the wine law only in 1986. It can be good blended with Blaufränkisch.

MERLOT
Less than one per cent.

As already mentioned, much of what was thought to be Merlot in Austria is actually Cabernet Franc. The soft, velvety blending partner in many Bordeaux wines, Merlot has not had the success in Austria that it has had in the New World. It was one of the first of the international varieties to be planted in Austria, and has established itself firmly in the repertoire, especially in the Neusiedlersee-Hügelland, Kamptal, and in Mailberg in the Weinviertel, where it is commonly blended with Cabernet Sauvignon, but hardly ever achieves much complexity.

SANKT LAURENT
Also known as Pinot St Laurent;
less than one per cent

St Laurent hails from France and is probably a descendent of Pinot and an unknown grape. Its name is derived from the fact that it usually begins to ripen on St Laurence's day, August 10, if the yields are limited. It was probably imported to Austria via Germany in 1870, although Joseph Umathum, one of the best St Laurent growers in Austria, believes that it might have come to the country with the Cistercian monks who colonized the Lake Neusiedl region during the thirteenth century and who introduced Pinot Gris to the region.

St Laurent is a capricious and difficult grape variety and most growers think it is not worth their while, particularly because of its dangerously early flowering, which makes it sensitive to late frosts and causes it to yield unreliably. It is also sensitive to rot. It does, though, tend to ripen much earlier than Pinot Noir and can therefore reach full physiological ripeness in less warm years.

St Laurent has an interesting recent history in Austria, which has led to its partial rehabilitation. Until a few years ago it was usually treated like Pinot Noir (which it was supposed to resemble in aromatic profile in the same way that the vines resemble each other) and made into wines with relatively low tannin and little extraction. In this incarnation it has long failed to be entirely convincing, because the wines tended to lack the depth and sophistication that make Pinot so magical. During the last five years, some producers have started making it into much more dense, tarry, and brambly, almost inky wines, more like Syrah. This new style has proved wonderfully successful. The wines can be fascinating; somewhat rustic perhaps, but deeply satisfying. St Laurent is also used in blends with Blaufränkisch, Cabernet Sauvignon, Pinot Noir, and Zweigelt.

St Laurent is also grown, as Vavrinecké or Svatovavrinecke, in Slovakia and in the Czech Republic, as Sentlovrenka in Kroatia and Slovenia, and to a lesser extent in the German Pfalz.

PINOT NOIR
Also known as Blauer Burgunder, Blauburgunder, Blauer Spätburgunder, or Klevner;
less than one per cent.

The most successful red import from France, Pinot Noir, the main red grape of Burgundy, has been grown in Austria for almost two hundred years. Pinot Noir is difficult both in the vineyard and in the cellar: it demands good, light and fertile soils that are not too dry, and good sun exposure. In addition to this, it is sensitive to late frosts, rot, and viral diseases. Pinot Noir usually ripens early but does not achieve high yields, a fact that effectively rules it out for mass production. Austria's climate favours it, especially with climate change; there are also few other red grape varieties that so successfully express their terroir, a fact that makes it highly interesting for ambitious growers.

In the hands of a less able winemaker, however, the wine will turn out overoaked, jammy, or simply dull. In Austria, the hunt for great Pinot is on, and in 2002 and 2003 Austria produced its first really serious Pinots, particularly around the northern shores of Lake Neusiedl and in the Kamptal. It has taken most growers a while to get away from the overwrought, jammy style, but now there are wines of considerable finesse and depth, and the fine notes of summer hay, cherries, and autumn leaves that so distinguish this grape are now being captured here, too.

UHUDLER
Less than one per cent.

A Styrian speciality, Uhudler is hardly grown anymore. It originated from American varieties intended as rootstock after phylloxera in the late nineteenth century, but used by some Styrian growers as direct producers. Uhudler is therefore not a single variety but the collective name for such wines. It was not allowed to be sold in Austria until 1992. There are about twenty-three hectares of Uhudler remaining in Southern Styria and in Heiligenbrunn in South Burgenland. It has a curious, foxy taste, reminiscent of strawberry wine.

ZWEIGELT
Also known as Blauer Zweigelt or Rotburger;
nine per cent, 4,350 hectares.

Zweigelt is the cocker spaniel of Austrian grapes: always friendly, always happy to oblige, and never aggressive. A cross between St Laurent and Blaufränkisch, Fritz Zweigelt's 1922 creation can probably be regarded as the Austrian red grape par excellence. It is the most common red, can be found in every region, grows well on all but the most chalky soils, and is not sensitive to frost or disease. It yields reliably and plentifully, in good years up to one hundred hectolitres per hectare. It ripens quite early, typically in the second half of September or in early October.

Zweigelt wines are dense and dark, with characteristic mellow, cherry fruit. They are usually aged in large wooden barrels, but can also be vinified in small barriques to add backbone to their otherwise round structure. If restricted to low yields the grape can make beautifully concentrated wines that have a distinctive liquorice note in good years. The ageing potential of high-class Zweigelt is not yet clear, as such wines have been produced only relatively recently. Another factor in the continuing ascent of this grape is that many vineyards are only now coming of age, yielding more concentrated and more interesting wines.

Zweigelt is sometimes blended with Blaufränkisch, the Zweigelt being the softer and more mellow of the two. This can work superbly well and produce some wines that marry fruit and tannic backbone. These wines, though, are still in their infancy, and we may expect more yet.

Some Zweigelt is grown in Saxony, in eastern Germany, and, experimentally, in England.

Other varieties

There are experiments with Nebbiolo, Syrah, Sangiovese, Gamay, Tannat, and Zinfandel, but these are, as yet, of little consequence. There is the occasional Austrian red rarity like Rösler. Other native grapes such as Grüner Hainer, Kardarka, and Trollinger are being pushed out of the game altogether, which is not necessarily a bad thing, as their names tend to be their most interesting aspect.

3

Vinification

One of the abidingly fascinating aspects of great wine is that it can be made in a shack by the light of a single light-bulb or in an avant-garde architectural temple; by instinct and a few barrels or by the combined forces of science and technology. Only the outcome counts. Every grower has his or her own procedures and style of vinification, but it is at least possible to make some general statements about individual areas. The last five years or so have brought with them a significant re-orientation, especially in the case of reds and wood-aged whites. During the 1990s, the realization that Austria can produce powerful wines, plus many innovations in cellar technology, often resulted in cellar-heavy wines, dominated by extraction, concentration, and oak. International grapes such as Cabernet Sauvignon and Chardonnay were all the rage and the wines often tasted so international that in blind tastings it was difficult to tell which country or even which continent they came from.

This has now changed. A combination of competition and experience means that a good proportion of top producers are now pursuing regional character by being less interventionist in the cellar and relying more strongly on the best Austrian grapes.

The most homogenous and traditional winemaking in Austria is found in the Wachau. Most of the whites are rigorously selected, harvested by hand, destemmed, and then pressed by pneumatic presses (these are almost universally used by high-quality producers), with the notable exception of the Biodynamic Nikolaihof, which has taken its old tree press back into use and generally vinifies much more oxidatively than most of its colleagues. Fermentation is usually in steel tanks (some concrete or plastic tanks are still in use, notably by the

Freie Weingärtner) with roughly equal proportions of the best growers relying on ambient and industrial yeasts.

No aromatic yeasts are allowed by the Vinea Wachau, and while the ideal here is to produce dry wines, several growers, Emmerich Knoll and Rudi Pichler among them, prefer to use ambient yeasts and allow their wines to dictate both the pace and temperature of the fermentation and the amount of residual sugar. In general, temperature control, lees contact, and wood ageing vary from producer to producer, and there is no malolactic fermentation. Botrytis is usually avoided, though in extreme years such as 1995 a small percentage can create fascinating wines.

Some estates, such as Nikolaihof and Knoll, put their faith in little or no temperature control during fermentation, relatively long lees contact (Nikolaihof has one wine, Vinothek, that is aged on the lees for fifteen years, but that is a wonderful freak), and ageing in large, used barrels. Others, such as Franz Hirtzberger and Toni Bodenstein of Prager, believe in more intervention, cooled fermentation, and more reductive vinification to maintain the clear varietal aromas associated with the Wachau. Even they, however, do not use fully computer-controlled cooling systems. Concentration is not allowed by the Vinea, and not practised. Ageing is mainly in steel tanks, while some large wood is also used.

In neighbouring Kremstal, largely the same grapes are used and vinification is very similar to that in the Wachau, though the style is not controlled by any powerful growers' association. The most ambitious growers here have shown a great openness to innovation combined with a sound sense of priorities. Willi Bründlmayer has transferred his scientific training to the cellar and experimented widely, using different woods and degrees of toasting – he now uses both acacia and a lot of local oak – selected and natural yeast, lees contact, and every other conceivable technique. Throughout the Kamptal, both steel and wood ageing are common, and some wood character and malolactic fermentation are favoured for the more powerful whites. Schloss Gobelsburg's excellent Riesling and Grüner Veltliner Tradition are indeed vinified much as they would have been a century ago.

Some of the best Kamptal wines, by contrast, have been made possible only by modern cellar technology, specifically pneumatic presses (though, ironically, tree presses may be just as gentle). Late-harvest Grüner Veltliners, which have done so well at several prestigious blind tastings and are among the country's very finest, rely on gentle pressing to free their bewitching aromas without grinding out the bitter tannins in their thick skins.

The country's largest wine-growing area, the Weinviertel, is not as international, though there is a handful of exceptional producers. Most winemaking harks back to the ideas of the 1950s, with Grüner Veltliner fermented with mainly industrial yeasts, vinified in steel, and made for clear primary fruit and quick consumption. The enterprising Roman Pfaffl (one of the fathers of the region's DAC project) and the Schlossweingut Graf Hardegg have demonstrated that it is possible to create outstanding and innovative wines using temperature-controlled fermentation and vinification in steel or in wood. Other producers are following, but not many compared to the size of the area.

The Donauland is one of Austria's most dynamic regions. Its reputation rests mainly on a group of young growers who often age their top Veltliners in new wood and allow malolactic fermentation to give them an extra dimension, an extreme and excellent example being Josef Ehmoser's Grüner Veltliner Aurum, a wine fermented with ambient yeasts, aged in small barrels, and bottled as early as possible. Similar in style is the Traisental's Ludwig Neumayer, the only producer in this area to show consistently very high qualities.

The wines of the Thermenregion are very different. Zierfandler and Rotgipfler are often handled much like Chardonnay with some pre-fermentation oxidation, and fermented and aged in steel or wood. Top wines may get some small oak, and the use of this is less heavy-handed than it used to be. Some wines undergo malolactic fermentation.

Carnuntum is increasing its proportion of reds, which are produced using the entire range of modern, international techniques, including fermentation with industrial yeasts and in temperature-controlled tanks, and ageing in small, new wood, most of all in Gerhard Markowitsch's Californian-style winery.

Vienna produces almost only white wines that are usually vinified, without much ambition, for local use. The producers swimming against the tide are Fritz Wieninger, the Zahel brothers, and Michael Edlmoser, all three quite assertive in their use of internationally inspired techniques.

In Burgenland, winemaking has almost been reinvented in the last twenty or thirty years. During the 1990s, EU subsidies and necessity resulted in a wave of new cellars filled with gleaming technology. Initially this resulted in some very technology-heavy wines packed with alcohol, tannins, and oak. Now, however, there is a significant trend away from power.

Most producers in the Burgenland, as well as in Styria, make a "classical" line of wines, so called because it corresponds to the traditional tastes of Austrian drinkers. This is typcially fermented and aged in steel, and emphasizes varietal and primary fruit. They also make an "international" one, which is vinified in oak. Vinification methods for red wines in the four Burgenland regions are not significantly different among top growers; the differences are in individual styles, blends, and, most importantly, terroir.

Red wines are macerated for between three days and four weeks, depending on the grower, though for most wines around three weeks is normal. In recent years there have been frequent problems with over-extraction, but this is now less common. Fermentation temperatures vary, but an average of 28°C (82°F) appears to be the norm. Some producers (such as John Nittnaus) use only ambient yeasts and spontaneous fermentation, while other high-quality producers are more comfortable with the more predictable industrial yeasts.

In recent years, must concentration by reverse osmosis or vacuum extraction has unfortunately been practised by a considerable number of producers, often resulting in jammy, stewed, mulled-wine aromas. I am certain that I have tasted concentrated wines without noticing, but concentrators seem to be rather like toupées: a bad idea generally and catastrophic when noticeable. Today many winemakers have sold their concentrators (or so they say) while others have become much more discreet in their use, so that the problem has become much less significant.

Along with extraction, controlled fermentation, and concentration, the use of wood has been greatly modified in recent years. Some producers used to announce proudly that they had aged their top reds twice in new wood; unfortunately the wines tasted exactly as you'd expect. Today most producers will use a mixture of new and used French oak, mostly medium toast, and the results are wines of great sophistication that begin to show true terroir character. Red wines and some white wines are allowed to undergo malolactic fermentation and are aged in casks normally for about a year, and in some cases up to two years.

Dry white wine production is situated mainly around Lake Neusiedl, and usually concentrated on Chardonnay vinified in a very Burgundian manner, with some oxidation during a maceration of between two and twelve hours, followed by ageing in small, usually French oak. How long these wines remain on the lees depends on the individual producer.

In Styria both ambient and industrial yeasts are used. Together with the Neusiedlersee area and the Middle Burgenland, Styria is the region that has most enthusiastically taken up modern winemaking techniques. Most top growers here favour reductive vinification and use steel tanks and temperature-controlled fermentation for their "classic" single-varietal wines. "International" wines are aged in small oak. The Polz winery, the largest producer in the area, has recently invested in wooden fermentation vats, however, and has adopted a more oxidative style for its top wines. Top whites in the region sometimes undergo malolactic fermentation, though the region's emphasis on varietal fruit mitigates against it.

CORK

This has been, and still is, even more controversial in Austria than in other countries. Despite paying high prices (up to one Euro) for corks, and despite taking every possible precaution, Austrian wine producers have had more than their fair share of cork problems. This may, as some producers feel, be a result of the cork industry fobbing them off with inferior corks, but it is equally possible that the fine and aromatic white wines that are mainly hit by this problem are simply more vulnerable to cork taint, just as they are more able to express their terroir. When one opens four bottles of an excellent wine and finds all of them tainted (as recently happened to me in the Wachau, where another famous producer had just under half of his wines affected by cork taint during a tasting) the extent of the problem becomes apparent. Some producers have stopped using cork for good, while others believe that even to consider other closures is the end of civilization. The young Kamptal producer Hannes Hirsch caused a good deal of controversy when he decided to fill his best wines under screwcap, but many others have followed suit. Screwcaps appear to have convinced most quality-conscious producers, while glass stoppers, which are aesthetically more interesting but newer and less tried and tested, are still regarded with some scepticism despite possibly offering the most satisfying and attractive solution. Plastic corks have not proved a good alternative and are on their way out for high-quality wines.

The argument against alternative closures is that there is little or no knowledge of their long-term behaviour, though in the case of screwcaps there are Australian wines dating back to the 1980s that appear to have aged very well. Opponents argue that wine may need the tiny amount of oxygen that migrates through the cork, and that an air-tight closure may hinder ageing. However, the ageing process of wine and its oxidative versus anaerobic processes are still very little understood. Very probably the oxygen in suspension in the wine and that contained in the air space present in every bottle is ample for ageing, and there is no reason to suppose that wines closed hermetically do not age well over long periods of time, as centuries-old wines found in historic wrecks on the bottom of the sea have proved. Whatever the closure used, every Austrian producer is alive to the problem and has an opinion on it.

Part 2

The Regions

4

Burgenland

During the Habsburg era, Burgenland was, administratively speaking, a part of the Kingdom of Hungary, and a wistful, central European atmosphere still prevails. Old women in headscarves and old men with cloth caps still on benches in front of their houses, watching the world go by.

Much has changed here during the lifetimes of the oldest among them. After the collapse of the Austro-Hungarian Empire in 1918, the people of the Burgenland decided in a referendum to stay with Austria. The name "Burgenland" has its roots in the thirteenth and fourteenth centuries, when the region reached its greatest size and included the districts of Eisenburg, Ödenburg, Weiselburg, and Pressburg (now Bratislava). It was called the Vier-Burgen-Land ("Four Fortress Country") after these cities, and then simply the Burgenland, though this name was not adopted officially until a new designation had to be found for the area of German West Hungary in 1921, when that became part of Austria. After an interlude during the Third Reich, when the region was split up, it regained its autonomy in the Second Austrian Republic.

It was only after World War II that a small area on the eastern side of Lake Neusiedl began to make wine in earnest: the region around Illmitz and Apetlon. Vineyards had been recorded here since the late sixteenth century, but even at the end of the nineteenth century, there were little more than sixty hectares under vines. Today the 1,500 hectares planted here produce some of the finest nobly-sweet wines in the world. The whole region has 14,500 hectares under vine.

The Burgenland is still a very rural landscape, and is recognized as an area worthy of special funding by the EU, funding which has enabled great investments to be made in cellars and technology. It is a small and traditional community reminiscent of many towns in neighbouring Hungary. This observation, however, is not likely to endear one to the locals, who pride themselves on their Austrian identity. Hungarians are used mainly as cheap labour, and it is perhaps not only because of the difficulty of the neighbouring country's language that hardly any wine-growers in the Burgenland speak Hungarian, even if they may deal with Hungarian workers most days of the year.

On the eastern side of the lake especially, the architecture bears out the Burgenland's restless history, its lack of natural stone for building, and its recent wealth. The traditional farmhouses, whitewashed cottages with reed roofs, were built from soft mud bricks and had to be rebuilt regularly, if indeed they did not burn down first. Today, most have disappeared and been replaced by squat, practical, new bungalows in cheery colours. Driving through these villages it is not easy to remember that they were once very beautiful in a romantic, impractical sort of way.

In terms of scenic and architectural beauty, the eastern shores of Lake Neusiedl with their villages of Gols and Illmitz have little to offer (though this is more than made up for by the wines). Aesthetic requirements are satisfied on the other bank, in the beautiful Baroque town of Rust.

The Burgenland lies on the cusp of two climatic zones, broadly speaking the Pannonian, with its hot summers and cold winters, and the western European – an important factor for its wines. Moreover, it divides into four distinct wine-growing areas: Seewinkel or Neusiedlersee, Neusiedlersee-Hügelland, Middle Burgenland, and South Burgenland.

The two northernmost areas take their names and their unique climatic conditions from Lake Neusiedl, a lake thirty-six kilometres (22.4 miles) in length, divided between Austria and Hungary. Geologically, the Neusiedlersee is, like Lake Sopron in Hungary, a steppe lake typical of the Hungarian plains. It is fed from ground-water and by springs. Only two metres (6.6 feet) deep at its lowest point, its shallowness is one of its most important features for wine production on its banks.

As does every large body of water, Lake Neusiedl has a moderating effect on temperature change. In late summer especially, the shallow waters act like a huge heat reservoir as the water is heated up by the sun to as much as 30°C (86°F). Because of its shallowness, however, it is more susceptible to temperature change itself than deeper water would be: in the exceptionally cold January of 1929 it froze into one huge block of ice, killing all the fish. In the early mornings, evaporating water is cooled by the cold air from the Hungarian plains and moves across the surrounding vineyards as fog, creating ideal conditions for the development of botrytis, the noble rot that is the basis of the area's world-famous sweet wine production.

Because of intensive irrigation of both vineyards and vegetable fields, there are now concerns that falling ground-water levels may lead to the lake drying out once again, endangering not only sweet-wine production but the entire mesoclimate of the area. As the different agricultural interests (broadly speaking intensive, yield-oriented agriculture versus the opposite) are in conflict, this issue is likely to become more pressing in the future.

NEUSIEDLERSEE
Vineyards: 8,326 hectares.
Soils: mainly loess, black earth, gravel, and sand.
White grapes (seventy-five per cent): Grüner Veltliner, Welschriesling, Pinot Blanc/Chardonnay, Müller-Thurgau, Neuburger, Bouvier, Scheurebe, Muskat-Ottonel, Pinot Gris, Traminer, Gemischter Satz, Riesling, Frühroter Veltliner, Sauvignon Blanc, Jubiläumsrebe, Gelber Muskateller, Sylvaner, Roter Veltliner, Rotgipfler, Zierfandler, Furmint, Chardonnay, Neuburger.
Red grapes (twenty-five per cent): Zweigelt, Blaufränkisch, St Laurent, Cabernet Sauvignon, Blauburger, Pinot Noir, Merlot, Gemischter Satz, Cabernet Franc, Blauer Portugieser, Blauer Wildbacher.

Situated on the northeastern and eastern shores of Lake Neusiedl, this region has made the largest qualitative jump of all, transforming itself within two decades from a local backwater and source of cheap bulk grapes into one of Austria's, and Europe's, most exciting and versatile regions, with outstanding dry reds and whites as well as sweet wines.

It was the sweet-wine guru Alois Kracher who first brought world recognition to the area during the early 1990s with his fabled Trockenbeerenauslesen, and soon other growers took up the challenge of producing top-class wines here. According to the vintage, most producers make sweet as well as dry wines, though naturally specialities do develop.

This is one of the few wine-growing areas in the world where it is possible to harvest good quantities of nobly-rotten grapes almost every year. Made

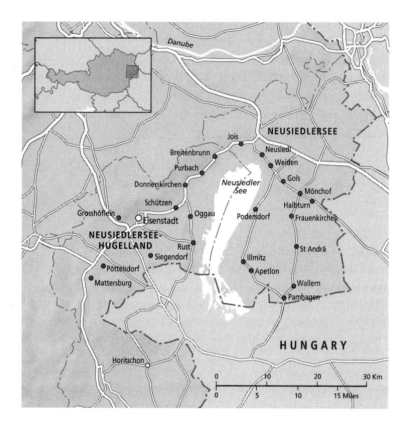

ii Neusiedlersee & Neusiedlersee-Hügelland

mainly from aromatic and thin-skinned varieties, the secret of these wines lies in the fact that despite very high sugar levels in the must, they are never just sweet, but bolstered by fresh acidity that can give them a dazzlingly complex, dancing, and never cloying character, particularly in great sweet-wine years such as 1995 and 2002. Such years are often not ideal for dry wines, as they tend to have wet, at times very rainy autumns.

The rapid spread of botrytis also allows growers to harvest before other rot can set in, thus preserving a great purity of fruit together with the botrytis tone in the wine. Growers are usually content to allow these exceptional musts to stop fermentation well below twelve degrees of alcohol, though only rarely do they have the problem faced by Alois Kracher (and, on the opposite bank, Feiler-Artinger): a "wine" of less than five degrees of alcohol, which the law refuses to define as wine. Beerenauslesen and Trockenbeerenauslesen have an almost unlimited ageing potential (as proven by the famous 1526 Luther wine made in Rust, the last sip of which was enjoyed in 1852) and only appear to increase their aromatic complexity and length with age. Barrel ageing in French oak frequently adds a dimension of aromatic complexity.

In years when botrytis is less prevalent, the growers have other options if they want to make sweet wines: grapes can be dried on straw and reed mats for Strohwein and Schilfwein and, in cold winters, the grapes can be left to freeze on the vines for Eiswein.

Botrytis can be a threat to dry wines, and is usually countered by relatively low planting densities and higher trellising to allow air circulation to dry off the grapes. The whites, particularly Chardonnay, are often remarkably fine and usually aged in oak. At their best, they can develop a Burgundian complexity. Most growers, however, put their pride in their red wines, which have undergone a huge stylistic evolution that is still continuing. After a brief period of Parkerized bombs exploding all over the place, the best growers are now seriously interested in defining and expressing their terroir, and attention is shifting away from the likes of Cabernet (which is still used in blends) to creating great Blaufränkisch and Zweigelt wines. Important *Rieden* are Altenberg and Gabarinza in Gols; Kreuzjoch, Kurzberg, Pohnbühel, and Waldacker in Mönchhof; and Hallebühl in Frauenkirchen.

In recent vintages it has come as a surprise to me to find these wines are not only full of character and depth, but are also quite feminine and elegant, very unlike the broad-shouldered macho wines that used to be made here in some cellars. This is a compliment, even if it may not be current consumer orthodoxy. The Neusiedlersee, I think, could well establish itself as a light but very subtle terroir suitable for finely tuned Blaufränkisch, dark and velvety Zweigelt, and seriously decadent Pinot Noir. Already the best reds show great class and should have very good ageing potential, even if the pace of change in winemaking here has made it impossible to taste back for comparable offerings. It is all in the future.

The northeastern shores of Lake Neusiedl, right around the northern tip of the lake and down to the villages of Weiden, Gols, Mönchhof, and Halbturn, has mainly loess, loam, and black soils suitable for red wine production, as well as for white grapes. Going south along the lake, we come to the Seewinkel, the eastern shore with its numerous small, shallow, saline ponds (saline because this region was at one stage under the sea), which are mainly filled by rainwater and are not connected to the lake. The surrounding soil is sufficiently loamy to insulate the alkaline soil surrounding the saline ponds and allow wines to be grown only a few metres away. On the edges of the vineyards the warm ponds effectively act as fog machines for botrytis wines. Here loam and sand are layered on a gravelly subsoil.

The wine villages of Podersdorf, Illmitz, and Apetlon are directly by the lake, while Frauenkirchen, Andau, St Andrä, Wallern, and Pamhagen lie some kilometres inland. It is here, in the vineyards up to two kilometres (1.2 miles) from the water (and on the western shore around Rust) that the influence of the lake has its greatest effect on wine.

In terms of climate, the region is part of the Puzta, the great central European steppe stetching across Hungary and further east. The climate here is Pannonian. There is less annual rainfall (500 millimetres/twenty inches) and more sun here than on the other, western shore of the lake. Partly due to the lake's regulating influence on temperature, the vegetation period here is 250 days, up to two weeks longer than in the rest of the Burgenland. The influence of the lake is very beneficial, too, as the summer highs can reach up to 40°C (104°F), with minimum winter temperatures of -25°C (-13°F).

Some 3,300 growers around Lake Neusiedl cultivate 8,326 hectares of vines, which is less than a decade ago. The proportion of red wines is rising steadily with more and more producers switching from cheapish white wines to the more upmarket red varieties; they are also switching to better white varieties, though the move to reds is more pronounced. In terms of area planted Grüner Veltliner still has the lion's share of the vineyards, though visits to the top producers would never make one think so.

Top growers

PAUL ACHS

Neubaugasse 13, A-7122 Gols. Tel: 02173 2367. Fax: 02173 3478. Website: www.paul-achs.at. Vineyards: 26 ha. White grapes: Welschriesling, Chardonnay, Pinot Blanc, Traminer, Muskat Ottonel. Red grapes: Blaufränkisch, Zweigelt, Cabernet Sauvignon, St Laurent, Pinot Noir.

"Before I had worked in California for some months and had gathered experience in 1990," says Paul Achs, "we did not make red wines worthy of the name." Things have certainly changed, for today Achs is one of Austria's most individual and most thoughtful red-wine producers. His flagship is a Pannobile blend built around that most capricious of Austrian red grapes, St Laurent, together with varying parts of Cabernet Sauvignon and Pinot Noir, a very stylish wine made to age. Achs is also among the pioneers of Pinot Noir in Austria, and his wines from this grape are consistently fascinating in their search for precision and the perfect expression of Neusiedlersee terroir. A fine series of three single-vineyard Blaufränkisch wines, Goldberg, Altenberg and Spiegel, explores the great stylistic range of this grape, and is one of the best illustrations of red wine terroir in Austria.

Never going for huge blockbusters, Achs has become recognized as one of the outstanding growers of the area, and of the Pannobile association. Yields per hectare are limited to thirty-five hectolitres and the wines are harvested with the utmost care. The wines age in small and large oak, and in large acacia barrels, and Achs is also constantly experimenting with producing unfiltered and unclarified wines.

WERNER ACHS
Goldberg 5, 7122 Gols. Tel: 02173 23900. Fax: 02173 23996. Website: www.wernerachs.at. Vineyards: 17 ha. Red grapes: Zweigelt, Blaufränkisch, St Laurent.

Werner Achs is an ambitious new face on the local wine scene. Having started in 1999 with a little over a hectare, he is now making wines from seventeen hectares. Achs was trained by Alois Kracher as well as on internships in France and Italy, and he has set his sights very high. His blend Xur (Zweigelt/Blaufränkisch/St Laurent) combines power with delicate floral and berry aromas – a most interesting debut from a talented young winemaker.

BECK
Untere Hauptstrasse 108, 7122 Gols. Tel: 02173 2755. Fax: 02173 27554. Website: www.weingut-beck.at. Vineyards: 12 ha. White grapes: Pinot Blanc, Pinot Blanc, Chardonnay. Red grapes: Zweigelt, Blaufränkisch, Cabernet Sauvignon, Merlot.

Known for its solid wines, the Beck estate has begun to flourish since daughter Judith became increasingly involved in the winemaking after gathering experience in Bordeaux, Italy, and Chile. Recent vintages are showing better balance and structure. Appropriately, the blend Judith stands out with its notes of cassis and liquorice, followed by a dense and sappy St Laurent and a nicely styled new-generation Pinot Noir.

GOLDENITS

Untere Haupstrasse 8, 7162 Tadten. Tel: 02176 2294. Fax: 02176 229411. Website: www.goldenits.at. Vineyards: 14 ha. White grapes: Sauvignon Blanc, Chardonnay, Welschriesling. Red grapes: Cabernet Sauvignon, Zweigelt, Blaufränkisch, Syrah.

The energetic Robert Goldenits is a relatively new face in the wine landscape. With his consciously contemporary approach – labels, wine names, architect-designed winery, vinification *et al* – he leaves no doubt as to his ambition. His stylish Tetuna is a blend of Blaufränkisch, Cabernet Sauvignon, and Zweigelt, expensively vinified in French oak; Mephisto (Cabernet Sauvignon and Syrah) is equally dense. Both are perhaps a little eager to please, but they have plenty of structure and good potential.

GSELLMANN & GSELLMANN

Obere Hauptstrasse 28 & 38, 7122 Gols. Tel: 02173 2214. Fax: 02173-3431. Website: www.gsellmann.at. Vineyards: 22 ha. White grapes: Pinot Gris, Pinot Blanc, Chardonnay. Red grapes: Zweigelt, Blaufränkisch, Cabernet Sauvignon, Pinot Noir.

The Gsellmann brothers are among the most reliable red-wine producers in the area. Eighty per cent of the vineyards are planted with red grapes and the style of the wines is solid and ample, especially for their Pannobile and Ungerberg blends.

HAIDER

Seegasse 16, 7142 Illmitz. Tel: 02175 2358. Fax: 02175 23584. Website: www.weinguthaider.at. Vineyards: 13 ha. White grapes: Welschriesling, Traminer, Chardonnay, Riesling, Neuburger, Scheurebe, Bouvier, Sauvignon Blanc. Red: Cabernet Sauvignon, Zweigelt, Merlot.

Martin Haider is a quiet and unassuming man, very much in contrast to his expressive sweet wines, which keep winning national and international prizes. His small estate, which looks little different from the private houses around it, is only a few hundred metres from Lake Neusiedl. He makes a surprising variety of wines, including an increasing number of dry reds. Among the sweet wines, Welschriesling especially has him in its spell and he vinifies TBAs of great finesse and complexity.

SCHLOSS HALBTURN

Im Schloss, 7131 Halbturn. Tel: 02172 20162. Fax: 02172 20114. www.schlosshalbturn.com. Vineyards: 64 ha. White grapes: Chardonnay, Sauvignon Blanc, Grüner Veltliner, Riesling. Red: Cabernet Sauvignon, Merlot, Cabernet Franc, Blaufränkisch, St Laurent, Pinot Noir, Zweigelt.

This is an amazing story. Until some years ago, Schloss Halbturn was distinguished only by its history, its fine baroque architecture, and its park. Wine has been made here since 1214, but it was never remarkable. Enter Karl-Heinz "Carlo" Wolf, a German wine specialist, who convinced the owner (a descendant of a branch of the Habsburg dynasty) to make major investments, including the tearing out and replanting of forty hectares of vineyard and the construction of an entirely new cellar with top technology, a French cellarmaster, and a young Burgundian oenologist especially for the estate's Pinot Noir.

This well-directed largesse has made an also-run estate into a major player in the area; indeed, its Pinot Noir 2003 is, I believe, quite simply the best of the vintage, a bewitchingly complex wine proving that the elegance and depth of *premier cru* burgundies can be achieved in this region if priorities are right and the finance is there. Also remarkable are the Impérial (Cabernet Sauvignon/Merlot/Cabernet Franc/Blaufränkisch), beautifully structured and in view of the young vines one to watch, and a fine St Laurent. More is certainly to come.

HEINRICH

Baumgarten 60, 7122 Gols. Tel: 02173 31760. Fax: 01273 317604. Website: www.heinrich.at. Vineyards: 32 ha, plus 35 ha contract growers. White grapes: Chardonnay, Pinot Blanc, Pinot Gris, Neuburger. Red grapes: Zweigelt, St Laurent, Cabernet Sauvignon, Blaufränkisch, Merlot, Syrah.

Gernot Heinrich's winery, a post-modernist palazzo with large, stylish rooms decorated with contemporary art, was one of the first bold statements in Austrian wine. He has not stopped at architecture: he and his wife Heike invested "every cent we had" into new vineyards (he originally had just eight hectares) and new equipment.

The new wines created in this cellar were marked for a few vintages by a striving for power and concentration; but in recent years Heinrich, like other top growers in the area, has abandoned this style in favour of a more complex, more elegant, and balanced line, which is wonderfully successful. One of the greatest Austrian reds vintage after vintage, Salzberg (Merlot/Zweigelt) shows an inimicable floral elegance and depth combined with great concentration. The equally famous Gabarinza (Zweigelt/St Laurent/Merlot/Blaufränkisch) reveals density and subtlety in equal measure, combined with an astonishing play of berry, smoke, and game aromas. While these two wines are always priced at the upper end of the market, the Pannobile (Zweigelt/Blaufränkisch) also shows fine tannins and good complexity with characteristic salty notes, an ocean breeze caught in a glass. Among the varietal wines from this estate, Pinot Noir shows interesting notes of nutmeg and spice, while St Laurent has firm tannins and fine varietal fruit.

HILLINGER

Hill 1, 7093 Jois. Tel: 02160 8317. Fax: 02160 8129. Website: www.leo-hillinger.com. Vineyards: 15 ha, plus 12 ha under contract. White grapes: Welschriesling, Sauvignon Blanc, Chardonnay. Red grapes: Zweigelt, Blaufränkisch, St Laurent, Cabernet Sauvignon, Merlot.

Leo Hillinger had spent several stints in California before he took over the family estate, and he has brought a decidedly modern outlook to the banks of Lake Neusiedl. His rather New-World approach (witness the address) to winemaking caused a bit of a stir, but he has proved that he knows his craft thoroughly. His Hill 1 (Cabernet Sauvignon/Merlot/Syrah/Zweigelt) is big, well structured, and shows interesting, elegant aromas, while the ambitious Cabernet Sauvignon is convincing only in warmer vintages. Other varietal wines, such as Blaufränkisch, Sauvignon Blanc, and a pleasantly leathery Zweigelt, all maintain a high standard.

JURIS-G. STIEGELMAR

Untere Marktgasse 12-18, 7122 Gols. Tel: 02173 2203. Fax: 02173 3323. Website: www.juris.at. Vineyards: 18 ha. White grapes: Welschriesling, Sauvignon Blanc, Chardonnay, Muskat Ottonel. Red grapes: Pinot Noir, Blaufränkisch, Zweigelt, St Laurent, Cabernet Sauvignon.

Axel Stiegelmar spent time working and learning in Germany, California, and Bordeaux before taking over the family estate. His approach to wine-making is marked by an insistence on elegance and balance before all, a stylistic choice that has made him particularly well regarded abroad.

Stiegelmar refuses to pare down his range, and offers more than a dozen different wines. His flagship blend, the red Ina'Mera (Merlot/

Blaufränkisch/Cabernet Sauvignon) is a beautifully floral and finely wrought wine with delicate tannins and good ageing potential. St Georg (Pinot Noir/St Laurent) surprises with an agreeably earthy tone from its St Laurent component, while the Pinot Noir is a little too thickset to let the grape really shine. The Muscat Ottonel Selection is a beautiful surprise, a lovely, floral wine with clear, deep aromas.

KRACHER-WEINLAUBENHOF

Apetloner Strasse 37, 7142 Illmitz. Tel: 02175 3337. Fax: 02175 33774. Website: www.kracher.at. Vineyards: 20 ha. White grapes: Welschriesling, Chardonnay, Scheurebe, Traminer, Muskateller, Bouvier. Red grapes: Zweigelt, Blaufränkisch.

Alois Kracher has done it again. Having earned a place among the world's top wine producers with a series of sweet wines in the late 1990s, in more recent years he made wines that were still outstanding, but no longer sparked in wine lovers the kind of religious awakening that his 1995 had done. Then came 2002, and with it a range that confirmed his status as a master of sweet wine.

Describing himself as "just a simple farmer", Kracher is, in fact, one of the main movers and shakers in Austrian wine, whose mastery, canniness, charm, energy and *gourmandise* have played a significant part in creating the Austrian wine miracle over the last two decades. Despite his phenomenal international success, however, Kracher has never lost touch with his origins, or with the customs of a rural world: three generations are now working on the estate. Kracher's father is mainly in the vineyards, and son Gerhard works more and more independently in the cellars.

As always, the wines are vinified in two styles: Zwischen den Seen, aged in large barrels for up to fifteen months, and the internationally-oriented Nouvelle Vague (the name is an homage to French cinema), which is vinified in new oak. Among the former, his Schreurebe TBA No 6, with its finely chiselled aromas of yellow fruit and delicate spice, and his Welschriesling TBA No 8, all blossoms and apricot notes and a dazzling progression of secondary aromas, are masterful. To choose only two from an embarrassment of riches among the Nouvelle Vague wines: Chardonnay TBA No 2 with hints of beeswax and oriental spice, outstanding even in this series; Chardonnay TBA No 9 with summer flowers and hay, supported by clear wood, and long on the palate. Grande Cuvée TBA No 7 is also great, and Kracher No 12 is not actually a wine, as it did not reach the legally required five degrees of alcohol. It is therefore called "partially fermented grape juice".

One of the hallmarks of these wines is their harmonious structure, based on an interplay between sweetness and acidity: they are never cloyingly sweet. These wines are produced only if conditions are right, and in years such as 2003, which are less suitable for botrytis, only a handful are produced. Kracher also makes a dry red of which he is very proud. Next to a dozen sweet miracles, however, it seems less than miraculous.

LANG

Quergasse 5, 7142 Illmitz. Tel & Fax: 02175 2923. www.helmutlang.at. Vineyards: 15 ha. White grapes: Chardonnay, Welschriesling, Pinot Blanc, Scheurebe, Sauvignon Blanc, Gewürztraminer, Gelber Muskateller. Red: Zweigelt, Merlot, Blaufränkisch, Pinot Noir, Cabernet Sauvignon.

Helmut Lang is one of Lake Neusiedl's finest and largest sweet-wine producers. His Scheurebe and Welschriesling TBAs are perhaps the most consistently convincing, though his 2002 Sämling 88 TBA is excellent. Recently, Lang has also developed a renewed interest in dry reds and especially in Pinot Noir. The first efforts are solid rather than overwhelming, but he has both the ambition and the skill to do better.

LEITNER

Quellengasse 33, 7122 Gols. Tel: 02173 2593. Fax: 02173 21547. Website: www.leitner-gols.at. Vineyards: 8 ha. White grapes: Welschriesling, Pinot Blanc, Muskat Ottonel. Red grapes: Zweigelt, Blaufränkisch, Cabernet Sauvignon, Syrah.

Syrah is not a vine one associates with Austria, but the Leitner winery has made a speciality of it and makes it very well, not perhaps with the generosity of warmer climes, but it is nevertheless dense, with fine tones of nutmeg and red fruit. Among the others, Blaufränkisch and Pinot Blanc are particularly successful. The best from this producer, however, is the Eiswein that he makes regularly, most recently the excellent Welschriesling 2003.

WEINGUT FRANZ LENTSCH

Neusiedlerstrasse 40, 7141 Podersdorf/See. Tel: 02177 2398. Fax: 02177 20056. Vineyards: 12 ha. White grapes: Pinot Gris, Pinot Blanc, Chardonnay. Red grapes: Zweigelt, St Laurent, Blaufränkisch.

Honest, solidly made wines at fair prices are the strong suit of this small producer, whose Zweigelts and Remanenz (Zweigelt/ Blaufränkisch/St Laurent) are good examples of Neusiedlersee reds.

LENTSCH (ZUR DANKBARKEIT)

Hauptstrasse 39, 7141 Podersdorf/See. Tel: 02177 2223. Fax: 02177 2224.
Website: www.dankbarkeit.at Vineyards: 1.5 ha plus 4 ha under contract. White grapes: Welschriesling, Pinot Gris, Pinot Blanc, Muskat Ottonel. Red grapes: Pinot Noir, St Laurent, Zweigelt.

Lentsch runs a restaurant, but his heart is in the cellars, where he is always experimenting, and becoming better with every passing year. With its porty aromas, his Pinot Noir may still be on the rustic side, but it is a very satisfying wine, while his other dry reds and whites all show good winemaking. His sweet wines are at times very fine, particularly his Pinot Noir TBA with its wonderfully layered aromas of hazelnut, quince, and honey.

NEKOWITSCH

Schrändlgasse 2, 7142 Illmitz. Tel: 02175 2039. Fax: 02175 2034.
www.nekowitsch.at. Vineyards: 4 ha. White: Welschriesling, Scheurebe, Traminer, Grüner Veltliner, Müller-Thurgau. Red: Zweigelt, Blaufränkisch.

Gerhard Nekowitsch is not only a fine sweet-wine maker but also a civil servant who commutes to Vienna every day. It is all the more astonishing that he finds the time to produce a dazzling variety of very complex wines, including botrytis, Eiswein, and an excellent Schilfwein, which is his particular favourite, usually a blend of Welschriesling, Grüner Veltliner, and Scheurebe. He also makes rare red Schilfwein from Zweigelt and Blaufränkisch. It seems that every possible combination of grape varieties is employed, understandably in very small quantities. Nekowitsch also makes some dry wines.

HANS & ANITA NITTNAUS

Untere Hauptstrasse 49, 7122 Gols. Tel: 02173 2248. Fax: 02173 2220.
Website: www.nittnaus.at. Vineyards: 25 ha. White grapes: Welschriesling, Sauvignon Blanc, Chardonnay, Grüner Veltliner. Red grapes: Cabernet Sauvignon, Blaufränkisch, St Laurent, Merlot, Zweigelt.

Not to be confused with another Hans Nittnaus down the road (or with six others in the same village, for that matter), Hans "John" Nittnaus had initially intended to become a professional musician, but he now puts his hands to good use in the vineyard. There is something curiously modest and traditional about this winemaker, who is one of the very few top growers not to have constructed an architectural extravaganza for himself, but instead still lives in a traditional farming estate behind a simple gate in the middle of the small town of Gols.

The wines mirror Nittnaus' considered approach to life and are the result of continual experimentation and improvement, as well as his commitment to organic viticulture. Oak is used sparingly, none of the wines are artificially concentrated, only natural yeasts are used, and the wine is left on the lees for long periods. All this indicates a stress on elegance and depth over power. The flagship wine is the excellent Commondor (Merlot/Zweigelt/Cabernet Sauvignon), whose fine tannins and elegant, dark fruit clearly show Bordeaux influences, while the Pannobile (Blaufränkisch/Zweigelt) shows salty, berry tones and depth. With its aromas of fresh hazelnut and butter, the Chardonnay is constructed with the same ideal in mind, and the Grüner Veltliner, a rarity in this area, shows surprising spice, creaminess, and elegance. All are made with balance in mind, and older vintages show how harmoniously they can age.

HANS & CHRISTINE NITTNAUS
Untere Hauptstrasse 105, 7122 Gols. Tel & Fax: 02173 2186. www.nittnaus.net.
Vineyards: 18 ha. White: Sauvignon Blanc, Pinot Blanc, Chardonnay, Riesling.
Red: Zweigelt, Blaufränkisch, Cabernet Sauvignon.

The jovial Hans Nittnaus is newly installed in an architect-designed winery and has his sights set high. His wines show his commitment to quality, and to modern winemaking. Nit'ana (Zweigelt/Blaufränkisch/Syrah/St Laurent), a red blend, shows smoky sweetness but little complexity, while second wine Vigor Rubeus (Zweigelt/Merlot/St Laurent) has more structure. The best of the reds is the fine Zweigelt, called Luckenwald, with its dense tannins and notes of cherry and smoked ham. Vigor Albus, made of Chardonnay and Pinot Blanc, has a pleasant, appley nose, but is often dominated by its high alcohol. The TBA Pinorama, made of all three Pinots, shows beautiful complexity.

OPITZ
St Bartholomäus-Gasse 18, 7142 Illmitz. Tel: 02175 2084. Fax: 02175 20846.
www.willi-opitz.at. Vineyards: 14 ha. White grapes: Welschriesling,
Weissburgunder, Scheurebe, Grüner Veltliner, Gewürztraminer, Muskat Ottonel.
Red grapes: Blauburger, St Laurent, Zweigelt.

Willi Opitz is a phenomenon, not only because he came to wine from another industry and is self-taught, but also because he imported from his previous job a robust attitude to marketing and product placement.

His wines are very solidly made. The dry Muskat Ottonel is a delicious rarity in the region, while the Zweigelt makes up with fruit what it may lack in complexity. Growing directly on the shore of Lake Neusiedl, the sweet wines are always important for this estate. The finest among them is another speciality, a reed wine (for which healthy grapes are dried on reed mats), Schilfmandl, of astonishing richness and complexity. His botrytis wines are also fine examples of their kind, too, *primus inter pares* perhaps being the Goldackerl, a blend of Welschriesling and Scheurebe.

PITTNAUER

Neubaugasse 81, 7122 Gols. Tel & Fax: 02173 3407. www.pittnauer.com.
Vineyards: 12 ha. White grapes: Pinot Blanc, Chardonnay. Red grapes: Zweigelt, Blaufränkisch, St Laurent, Cabernet Sauvignon, Pinot Noir.

Gerhard Pittnauer is a relative newcomer who started out with just a few barrels only ten years ago and is now ensconced in an architect-designed cube in the middle of twelve hectares of vineyards. Always image-conscious, Pittnauer's most recent wine is called Red Pitt. Despite the inane name its dense, elegant tannins and fruit show a wine of considerable potential. Equally good is the smoky, lingering Pannobile red (Zweigelt/St Laurent/Blaufränkisch); the white blend Weisse Reben (Chardonnay/ Pinot Blanc/Sauvignon Blanc), which nicely integrates woody, caramel tones into pear and quince fruit; and the Pinot Noir, a soft example with notes of mulberry and dry leaves, though a little overwhelmed by high alcohol. The best wine, however, is the outstanding new-generation St Laurent, a slender but powerful wine with notes of blueberry, liquorice, and finely integrated wood.

PÖCKL

Baumschulgasse 12, 7123 Mönchhof. Tel: 02173 80258. Fax: 02173 80244.
Website: www.poeckl.com. Vineyards: 23 ha. White grapes: Chardonnay, Scheurebe. Red grapes: Zweigelt, Blaufränkisch, Pinot Noir, Merlot, Cabernet Sauvignon, St Laurent, Syrah, Cabernet Franc.

Josef Pöckl is one of the pioneers of red wine in the area. His Admiral and Rosso e Nero blends were right at the forefront of the Austrian wine revolution and showed its most important characteristic, an opening up to international styles and expertise. Pöckl is both a professional and a visionary, and his wines, now made with the aid of son René, who has taken over work in the cellars, show that his ideals lie beyond Austria's borders. The Rosso e Nero (Blaufränkisch/Cabernet Sauvignon/Merlot/St Laurent/Zweigelt) combines soft, roasted notes with chocolate and red fruit; not a deeply complex wine, but always reliable. Similar in style, the powerful Pinot Noir offers nutmeg and roasted notes and good length. The Pöckl style of intensity, power, and a good dollop of oak, does not come into its own until the top wines are reached, and here it works beautifully: the Admiral (Cabernet Sauvignon/Merlot/Syrah/Zweigelt) is always one of the region's most interesting reds, wonderfully dense and ripe with elegant tannins and impressive persistence. It is outshone only by the Rêve de Jeunesse (Cabernet Sauvignon/Zweigelt/Syrah/Merlot), a wine with lovely, complex aromas of forest fruits, and fine wood tones supported by firm, fine, and ripe tannins. There are also some good sweet wines produced here.

PREISINGER
Obere Hauptstrasse 33, 7122 Gols. Tel: 02173 2592. Fax: 02173 20000.
Website: www.clauspreisinger.at. Vineyards: 8ha. White: Chardonnay,
Weissburgunder. Red: Pinot Noir, Zweigelt, Cabernet Sauvignon.

Claus Preisinger started making his own wines in 2000, after having served an apprenticeship in the Tyrol and with Hans "John" Nittnaus in Gols. Like his mentor, Preisinger strongly believes in a vinification that is guided, but not strongly controlled, including fermentation in open vats, the use of ambient yeasts, and long lees contact; wines that are "totally pure and made by instinct", as he says. The results have quickly established Preisinger among the country's most hopeful young winemakers. His fine blend Paradigma (Zweigelt/Cabernet Sauvignon) presents a dense aroma of berry fruit and vanilla, elegant and finely wrought. The Pinot Noir is soft and elegant with notes of red fruit and autumn foliage, one of the most accomplished Pinots in the country.

HELMUT & GABRIELE PREISINGER
Neubaugasse 19, 7122 Gols. Tel: 02173 236200. Fax: 02173 236240.
www.weingut-preisinger.at. Vineyards: 12 ha. White: Pinot Gris. Red: Zweigelt,
Blaufränkisch, St Laurent, Cabernet Sauvignon, Syrah, Pinot Noir.

Helmut Preisinger is young and full of initiative, and his ambition shows in his wines. He made a great deal of noise in Austria with his S.EX., an unsubtle, punning abbreviation for Sehr Extrem ("Very Extreme"), a Pinot Gris with fifteen degrees of alcohol. Some Austrian critics loved it, but I found this wine quite painful to taste. Much better is his Merlot, which is still well above fourteen degrees, but has enough fruit not to collapse under it.

RENNER

Obere Hauptstrasse 97, 7122 Gols. Tel: 02173 2259. Fax: 02173 2254.
Website: www.rennerhelmuth.at. Vineyards: 13 ha. White grapes: Pinot Blanc,
Chardonnay. Red grapes: Zweigelt, Blaufränkisch, St Laurent, Syrah.

Helmuth Renner's persistence has earned him a place among the region's most dependable producers. His two top wines are Altenberg (Blaufränkisch/Merlot/Zweigelt), powerful and generous with assertive, firm tannins and fine aromas of red fruit, and Pannobile Weiss (Chardonnay/Pinot Blanc), a sophisticated wine with fine aromas of yellow fruit, discreetly supported by French oak.

SCHWARZ

Hauptgasse 21, 7163 Andau. Tel: 02175 240240. Fax: 02175 240241.
Website: www.thebutcher.at. Vineyards: 12 ha. White grapes: Chardonnay, Grüner
Veltliner, Semillon. Red grapes: Zweigelt.

Johann Schwarz appeared on the wine scene quite suddenly, with two excellent wines. The reason for this apparent miracle is that Schwarz, who had until then produced grapes for Alois Kracher, decided to team up with him instead. He is now advised by Kracher and Manfred Krankl, an Austrian who made it big in California, though mercifully in the wine world, not politics or bodybuilding. Schwarz's red wine, Schwarz Rot, is a pure Zweigelt, and surely one of the most serious Zweigelts around. His white wine, Schwarz Weiss, is also successful, though not quite as remarkable.

TSCHIDA-ANGERHOF

Angergasse 5, 7142 Illmitz. Tel & Fax: 02175 3150. Website: www.angerhof-
tschida.at. Vineyards: 15 ha. White grapes: Pinot Blanc, Scheurebe,
Welschriesling, Grüner Veltliner, Muskat-Ottonel. Red: Zweigelt.

Johann Tschida concentrates almost exclusively on sweet wines, and although he is not widely known internationally his sweet wines are among the very finest of the region. The botrytis wines (the great majority of his production) are complex and finely judged, their sweetness unlocking the aromas without overwhelming them. His Welschriesling, Muskat-Ottonel, and Scheurebe are particularly outstanding examples, and recently his Chardonnay BA was a triumph of depth and complexity. Tschida also produces very good Eiswein and Schilfwein.

UMATHUM

St Andräer Strasse 7, 7132 Frauenkirchen. Tel: 02172 24400. Fax: 02172 21734. Website: www.umathum.at. Vineyards: 25 ha. White grapes: Welschriesling, Pinot Gris, Chardonnay, Sauvignon Blanc. Red grapes: Zweigelt, St Laurent, Pinot Noir, Blaufränkisch, Cabernet Sauvignon.

It is always a great pleasure to visit Josef "Pepi" Umathum on his estate just outside the little town of Frauenkirchen. An apprenticeship in France gave him the confidence to turn around a farm with a sideline in mainly white wines to become one of Austria's foremost and largest red wine estates. Umathum is quietly passionate not only about the quality of his wines but also about the surrounding countryside and goes to great lengths at the slightest provocation to explain its geology, architecture, and history. His wines reflect this single-minded devotion to the land. Although he, unsurprisingly, takes his stylistic leads mainly from France, he wants to create, or help to create, a red wine style that is distinctly Austrian, and he is happy to talk and speculate about this in his beautiful, newly built cellar, taking and discussing barrel samples with friends and interested visitors.

An inveterate experimenter, Umathum has recently begun to think seriously about Biodynamic viticulture, and respect for the environment is his great preoccupation. He is currently involved in a project of selecting the best vines from his vineyards and propagating this selection for later planting, a strategy that his father followed successfully. Generally, Umathum's wines are less chunky than other reds made here, and with more emphasis on length and secondary aromas. His top wine Ried Hallebühl (Zweigelt/Blaufränkisch/Cabernet Sauvignon) typically shows beautifully defined fruit and good balance, a dense wine made to age. The second-most famous wine here is the St Laurent vom Stein, one of the first wines to show the potential of this variety. I have at times found this wine too strongly groomed for elegance, with too few of the more rustic, earthy characteristics so typical of the grape. In good years, such as 2002, however, this is a gem of a wine, with balance, extract, and focus. Among Umathum's other wines, the Blaufränkisch Kirschgarten and several sweet wines are very beautiful.

VELICH

Seeufergasse 12, 7143 Apetlon. Tel: 02175 3187. Fax: 02175 31874. Website: www.velich.at. Vineyards: 9 ha. White grapes: Welschriesling, Chardonnay, Pinot Gris, Pinot Blanc, Bouvier.

The brothers Heinz and Roland Velich are a formidable team, and their approach to winemaking is marked both by their attachment to the region, and by an intellectual streak: Heinz studied philosophy and psychology, Roland was a researcher in agricultural science. The estate's great wine is Chardonnay Tiglat, with which the name Velich has become almost synonymous, a Burgundian wine of immense finesse and mineral depth with fruit and wood suspended in equilibrium. (The wood is never 100 per cent new – the brothers' cautious use of small oak barrels was always years ahead of some of their more trigger-happy colleagues.) This is what Chardonnay can do if handled well. The Chardonnay Darscho must pale in comparison, but is also a fine achievement, while the blend O.T. (Chardonnay/Welschriesling/Sauvignon Blanc) offers a dazzling multiplicity of aromas. Last but by no means least, an array of excellent and often meditative sweet wines completes the range.

While Heinz is mainly concerned with the production of these white wines, brother Roland is in charge of another project, which is of equal importance to the brothers: Moric, a range of Blaufränkisch wines made in the Middle Burgenland and discussed in more detail in that chapter.

NEUSIEDLERSEE-HÜGELLAND

Vineyards: 3,912 hectares.

Soils: loess, black earth, sand, loam.

White grapes (sixty-three per cent): Chardonnay, Welschriesling, Muskat-Ottonel, Pinot Blanc, Neuburger, Pinot Gris, Bouvier.

Red grapes (thirty-seven per cent): Zweigelt, Blaufränkisch, Cabernet Sauvignon, St Laurent.

The western shore of Lake Neusiedl, less than fifteen kilometres (9.3 miles) away, comes under the influence of the Leitha-Gebirge, a small mountain range, technically the last ripple of the Alps, which lies toward the southwest of the area. There are three bands of soil types here, with intensely varied soils throughout. By the lake shore, sand, loam, and black earth predominate. Further up the slopes, there is chalky loam and marl with loess layers, while the vineyards on the higher parts of the softly rounded hills have soils of crystalline slate with chalk deposits.

The vineyards on the hills of the western shore of Lake Neusiedl are open to the Pannonian climate while being protected from cold northerly and westerly winds. The proximity of the hills, however, increases the annual rainfall to 800 millimetres (31.5 inches) per year, while the increase in height also lowers the average temperature and the degree to which grapes are affected by botrytis. Needless to say, the closeness of the lake is a tempering influence here, too. While the vineyards near to the lake, around Rust, Oggau, Mörbisch, Donnerskirchen, and Purbach, are used overwhelmingly for white wines, many of them sweet, those in the hills, especially around Grosshöflein and to the west of Rust, are increasingly used for powerful dry white and red wines.

The largest town is Eisenstadt, seat of the Esterházy family and the unloved domicile of Joseph Haydn. Eisenstadt has a long tradition as a wine trading centre on the route between Hungary and Germany, but the wine produced in the town is on the whole not exceptional. Growers in nearby Grosshöflein, however, produce great reds, and Rust offers a whole complement of excellent sweet and dry wines, both white and red. It is also a town of considerable beauty. Its most famous wine is Ruster Ausbruch, a botrytis wine not quite high enough in sugar to be TBA, and different in style, with more alcohol than sugar, and more acidity.

During the last few decades, the terroir principle has been rediscovered here for dry wines. The *Rieden* of Grosshöflein and Rust have produced outstanding wines. Some of the best *Rieden* are Bartsatz, Point, Steinzeiler, and especially Tatschler in Grosshöflein; and, Hoher Baumgarten, Marienthal, Pandkräftn, Rieglband, and Turner in Rust. These are excellent vineyards, suitable especially for red grapes – Blaufränkisch, Cabernet Sauvignon, Zweigelt – and Chardonnays of Burgundian proportions. Other good *Rieden* in the area are the Goldberg near St Margarethen, Eisner and Rosenberg in Purbach, and Lehmgrube in Kleinhöflein.

Top growers

BRAUNSTEIN
Hauptgasse 18, 7083 Purbach. Tel: 02683 5913. Fax: 02683 591322. Website: www.braunstein.at. Vineyards: 20 ha. White grapes: Chardonnay. Red grapes:

Blaufränkisch, Zweigelt, St Laurent, Cabernet Sauvignon.

Birgit Braunstein's wines are in the solid upper middle of the quality pyramid in this region. Both her Oxhoft (Cabernet Sauvignon/ Blaufränkisch/ Zweigelt) and her top wine, Gemini (St Laurent/ Blaufränkisch/Zweigelt) are generously expressive.

FEILER-ARTINGER

Hauptstrasse 3, A-7071 Rust. Tel: 02685 237. Fax: 02685 23722. Website: www.feiler-artinger.at. Vineyards: 23 ha (19 ha in use). White grapes: Welschriesling, Pinot Blanc, Sauvignon Blanc, Chardonnay, Traminer. Red grapes: Blaufränkisch, Zweigelt, Cabernet Sauvignon, Merlot.

One of the most famous names in the Burgenland, the Feiler estate is renowned both for its wines and for its wonderful Baroque house in the heart of the equally beautiful town of Rust. While great Ausbruch wines laid the foundation of Hans Feiler's international success, his son Kurt, who served his apprenticeship in Bordeaux, has given the reds much more attention than before, with excellent results. The Blaufränkisch Umriss shows sophisticated winemaking, a beautifully peppery wine with fine tannins and hints of dark chocolate. Solitaire (Blaufränkisch/ Cabernet Sauvignon/Merlot/Zweigelt), the top red, is more velvety, very much in the French tradition, and needs time to develop.

Despite the success of the red wines, the sweet wines are still the jewel in the crown. With its aromas of summer blossoms, wax, and honey, the Ruster Ausbruch (various varieties, depending on the year) continues the century-old tradition this wine has here, and the Ruster Ausbruch Essenz is marvellous, balanced between luscious intensity and precision.

GIEFING

Hauptstrasse 13, 7071 Rust. Tel: 02685 379. Fax: 02685 60748. www.wein-rust.at. Vineyards: 6 ha. White: Chardonnay, Welschriesling. Red: Zweigelt, Blaufränkisch, Cabernet Sauvignon, Pinot Noir.

When Erich Giefing, who has already had one career as a chef, produced his first wine in the mid-1990s, the artist-designed labels, fantasy names, and almost aggressively powerful style seemed the perfect embodiment of an Austrian winemaking fad, cloyingly unattractive. An extremist in everything he does, but a man who will always seek out good advice, Giefing quickly put this phase behind him and is now producing wines that are still powerful and still in many ways extreme, but at the same time elegant and layered. A particular passion is Furmint, which here shows density and pleasant bitter-almond notes. Chardonnay Contessa is perhaps a little too international, but Pinot Noir Cavallo shows profile and elegance. Giefing's flagship wine is the Cardinal (Blaufränkisch/Zweigelt/Cabernet Sauvignon), aged in new oak for twenty-six months – something that would usually make me find an excuse to leave. This dark and intense wine, however, shows such an array of roasted notes, eucalyptus, and bitter chocolate, and such beautiful length that I declare myself convinced.

HARTL

Florianigasse 7, 2440 Reisenberg. Tel: 02234 806360. Fax: 02234 80634. Website: www.toni-hartl.at. Vineyards: 20 ha. White grapes: Welschriesling, Grüner Veltliner, Chardonnay, Sauvignon Blanc. Red grapes: Zweigelt, Blaufränkisch, Syrah, Pinot Noir.

The energetic Toni Hartl used to be a civil servant before he began to make wine. As may be expected, his first wines were somewhat on the rustic side, but hard work and an intelligent approach have quickly earned Hartl the respect of fellow winemakers in the area. His list reaches from the intriguing, wood-aged Grüner Veltliner L'Importance to the fine Blaufränkisch Tout Feu Tout Flamme, uncompromisingly powerful and over the top. Like his colleague Erich Giefing, Hartl leaves no extreme unexplored. To my taste, always more interested in elegance than power, this is not necessarily a recommendation, but Hartl's many national and international awards prove that he has many admirers.

KLOSTER AM SPITZ

Waldsiedlung 2, 7083 Purbach. Tel: 02683 5519. Fax: 551920. Vineyards: 13.5 ha. White grapes: Grüner Veltliner, Merlot, Chardonnay, Riesling, Sauvignon Blanc. Red grapes: Blaufränkisch, Syrah, Pinot Noir, Cabernet Sauvignon, Zweigelt.

Thomas Schwarz is an ambitious winemaker who has only recently achieved his breakthrough with some outstanding reds, particularly with his dense and classy Antonius (Blaufränkisch/Zweigelt/Cabernet Sauvignon), one of the new wave of Austrian reds, and the brambly and profound Nepumuk (Cabernet Sauvignon/Blaufränkisch/Zweigelt). The Chardonnay Muschelkalk shows Schwarz to be interested in structure rather than just weight.

KOLLWENTZ-RÖMERHOF

Hauptstrasse 120, 7051 Grosshöflein. Tel: 02682 65158. Fax: 02682 6515813.

Website: www.kollwentz.at. Vineyards: 20 ha. White grapes: Welschriesling, Chardonnay, Sauvignon Blanc, Pinot Blanc. Red grapes: Blaufränkisch, Cabernet Sauvignon, Zweigelt.

The Römerhof is one of the great Neusiedlersee estates, not only in terms of its size – it has more than twice the area under vine than many other growers around here – but also in terms of the consistently outstanding quality produced here. For about forty years now, Anton Kollwentz has been an innovator. He was among the first to plant international grape varieties like Cabernet Sauvignon and Chardonnay, and to produce international, oak-fermented wines with standards in a different league to those of many of his colleagues. Son Andreas was sent to Bordeaux (Château Palmer, Château La Tour Blanche, Château Bonnet) and to study trips to various destinations in the New World.

Anton Kollwentz was one of the first in his area to pay close attention to the terroir and to vinify his wines by vineyard. Steinzeiler (Blaufränkisch/Cabernet Sauvignon/Zweigelt), aged in fifty per cent new oak for one year, is the flagship wine, and what a flag it flies. Complex and deep with firm, mature tannins over a core of intense black fruit, it is a wine of great finesse and stature. Wines from as far back as 1969 (which, for Austria, is ancient) still show good structure and lively fruit, even if they have lost much of their weight and punch; but, as Kollwentz says, "we didn't know a tenth back then of what we know now." Also very fine among the reds are the dense Blaufränkisch Point, Eichkogel (Blaufränkisch/Zweigelt) and a very classical, powerful yet elegant Cabernet Sauvignon.

The white wines have always been important here, too, especially the excellent Chardonnay Tatschler, all opulent fruit and mineral complexity. Sweet wines are produced only if the conditions are right. They, too, can be very fine.

LEBERL

Hauptstrasse 91, 7051 Grosshöflein. Tel: 02682 67800. Fax: 02682 67814. www.leberl.at. Vineyards: 14 ha. White grapes: Sauvignon Blanc, Chardonnay. Red grapes: Zweigelt, Blaufränkisch, Cabernet Sauvignon.

Josef Leberl's ambition is to produce great Austrian wine. Best known is his red blend Peccatum (Blaufränkisch/Cabernet Sauvignon/Zweigelt) which shows a beautiful core of dark berries and liquorice. Interesting, too, are the leathery Cabernet Sauvignon and the Sauvignon Blanc with its intense notes of grass and elderflower.

MARIELL

Hauptstrasse 74, 7051 Grosshöflein. Tel & Fax: 02682 61522. Vineyards: 6.5 ha. White grapes: Chardonnay, Gewürztraminer, Welschriesling. Red grapes: Blaufränkisch, Pinot Noir, Zweigelt.

Gabi Mariell is best known for her fruit brandies, but she also makes increasingly good wine. Her Wetzlesberg (Blaufränkisch/Zweigelt) is a fine example of the succulent depth Blaufränkisch-based wines can have in this region. Also good is the Blaufränkisch Haussatz, and the Pinot Noir Point, too, is a step in the right direction, while the Chardonnay Neusatz lacks a little complexity.

MOSER

St Georgener Hauptstrasse 13, 7000 Eisenstadt. Tel: 02682 66607. Fax: 02682 6660714. www.hans-moser.at. Vineyards: 11 ha plus 11 ha under contract. White grapes: Sauvignon Blanc, Chardonnay. Red: Zweigelt, Blaufränkisch, Cabernet Sauvignon, Cabernet Franc, Merlot, Pinot Noir.

Possibly one of Austria's most complicated blends, Hans Moser's VTS (Vintage Top Select) is assembled out of Cabernet Sauvignon, Cabernet Franc, Merlot, Blaufränkisch, and Zweigelt, and somehow the French grapes lend the wine a cedary spice that makes it very attractive. Moser also makes a good Cabernet Sauvignon/Merlot, dense and tannic, with notes of blackcurrant. The white wines are quite dominated by wood and often high alcohol levels.

PRIELER

Hauptstrasse 181, 7081 Schützen am Gebirge. Tel: 02684 2229. Fax: 02684 22294. Website: www.prieler.at. Vineyards: 20 ha. White grapes: Welschriesling, Chardonnay, Pinot Blanc. Red grapes: Blaufränkisch, Cabernet Sauvignon, St Laurent, Pinot Noir.

Engelbert Prieler's estate is marked by a meeting of tradition and openness to innovation. Prieler has run the estate since 1972 and now works with his daughters Michaela and Silvia – the latter is the oenologist and a microbiologist by training – and their brother Georg, who contributes international experience.

Always very good, during the last decade or so the Prielers have joined the top producers in the area, especially with their excellent (though not cheap) Blaufränkisch Goldberg, a wine of great (natural) concentration, elegance, and length, all eucalyptus, liquorice, and Christmas spice. Also outstanding are the aristocratic Cabernet Sauvignon Ungerbergen; the Schützener Stein (Blaufränkisch/Merlot), whose beautiful cassis nose and complexity are often locked in hard tannins in their youth but open up later; and a project by Silvia Prieler, a lovely Pinot Noir with roasted aromas, fine tannins, extract, and sweetness, and great length. Among the whites, the mighty Chardonnay Seeberg carries its weight well, while the Pinot Blanc Seeberg shows beautifully exotic notes.

SCHANDL

Haydngasse 3, 7071 Rust. Tel: 02685 265. Fax: 02685 2654. Website: www.schandlwein.com. Vineyards: 16 ha. White grapes: Pinot Blanc, Pinot Gris, Chardonnay. Red grapes: Pinot Noir, Cabernet Sauvignon.

One of Rust's most dependable producers, cellarmaster Paul Schandl has a knack for creating outstanding Ausbruch wines. His dry wines, among them a good Sauvignon Blanc, Pinot Blanc, and a very decent Pinot Noir, never show much complexity but are always satisfyingly full and round.

SCHRÖCK

Rathausplatz 8, 7071 Rust. Tel: 02685 229. Fax: 02685 2294. Website: www.heidi-schroeck.com. Vineyards: 9 ha. White grapes: Furmint, Muskat Ottonel, Sauvignon Blanc, Pinot Blanc, Welschriesling, Muscat Lunel. Red grapes: Zweigelt, St Laurent, Blaufränkisch.

The labels of this estate proudly proclaim "Heidi Schröck, Weinbäuerin in Rust" ("woman wine-grower in Rust"). After serving an apprenticeship in Germany, Bordeaux, and South Africa, she went on to make a name for herself with her Muskateller/Welschriesling Ausbruch, as well as with dry Muskateller and Pinot Blanc; she is also a champion of Furmint. Hers are wines of radiant originality and purity, from the mandarin- and pear-scented dry Furmint and the riper Furmint Pepa to a fine, almost filigree Pinot Gris and a St Laurent Kraxner of great earthy stylishness and length. Schröck's Ausbruch wines are always among the best in Rust. Their purity, intensity, and length are testimony to an approach combining a healthy respect for tradition and landscape with constant, thoughtful innovation.

SCHUSTER

Prangergasse 2, 7062 St Margarethen. Tel & Fax: 02680 2624. Website:

www.rosischuster.at. Vineyards: 8 ha. White grapes: Sauvignon Blanc, Chardonnay.
Red grapes: Zweigelt, Blaufränkisch, St Laurent, Cabernet Sauvignon, Merlot,
Pinot Noir.

The entry of son Hannes in Rosi Schuster's estate has galvanized an otherwise dependable range of wines and made this one of the names to watch
in the area. CMB, previously the top wine and a blend of Cabernet
Sauvignon, Merlot, and Blaufränkisch, shows mature tannins and fruit
sweetness, a wine of character and good potential. Also good are
Sauvignon Blanc and Chardonnay. The show-stopper, however, is Hannes
Schuster's excellent St Laurent, an immensely exciting, tarry wine with
notes of currant and chocolate, reminiscent of the northern Rhône Valley.

TINHOF
Gartengasse 3, 7000 Eisenstadt. Tel: 02682 62648. Fax: 02682 68232.
Website: www.tinhof.at. Vineyards: 11 ha. White grapes: Pinot Blanc, Neuburger.
Red grapes: Zweigelt, Blaufränkisch, St Laurent.

After studying at Vienna's Agricultural University and at Mas de Daumas
Gassac in the Languedoc, Erwin Tinhof returned to the Burgenland in
1990 and has since followed a very individual path, both stylistically and
in his enthusiasm for niche varieties such as Neuburger. His wines are
often very stylish and made with a clear emphasis on structure and
balance over power. The Blaufränkisch Gloriette demonstrates this to
perfection: notes of wood, blackcurrant, and leather, with beautiful focus
and length. Also very good is the fruit-driven St Laurent classic. The
sweet wines are less constant in their quality but can also be excellent,
with almost infinite ageing potential.

ERNST TRIEBAUMER
Raiffeisenstrasse 9, 7071 Rust. Tel: 02685 528. Fax: 02685 60738. Website:
www.triebaumer.com. Vineyards: 11 ha. White grapes: Chardonnay, Welschriesling,
Pinot Blanc, Sauvignon Blanc, Furmint. Red grapes: Blaufränkisch, Cabernet
Sauvignon, Merlot.

Ernst Triebaumer may be commonly known by his initials, but there is
nothing alien about him. On the contrary, he seems as firmly rooted in
this part of the earth as his wines, which are among the finest in the country. It was not always clear that that would be so. A younger son of a small
grower, he was supposed to become a carpenter but, he says, he neither
liked getting up at four o'clock nor climbing around on roofs. After
coming to an agreement about the inheritance with his brother Paul and

expanding his share of the vineyards by buying other plots, he set about producing wines with an emphasis on biological methods, which at the time was most unfashionable. His 1986 Blaufränkisch, though, silenced his critics and made Austrian wine history, being one of the first indigenous reds of international calibre.

Triebaumer's top wine, Blaufränkisch Mariental, aged in mainly new barriques for fourteen to eighteen months, has long been regarded as a kind of gold-standard for Austrian reds: muscular (usually around fourteen degrees of alcohol) yet finely structured with berry and floral overtones supported by assertive tannins, it comes into its own only after some years of bottle age. The same is true for the fine Blaufränkisch Oberer Wald, and a delicately leather-scented blend with Cabernet Sauvignon and Merlot. His wood-aged Chardonnay Pankräften and Sauvignon Blanc Vogelsang are at times too opulent for my palate, but a series of often dazzlingly complex Ausbruch wines reveals Triebaumer once again as a master of his art.

GÜNTER TRIEBAUMER
Neue Gasse 18, 7071 Rust. Tel & Fax: 02685 6135. Website: www.triebaumer.at.
White grapes: Muskateller. Red grapes: Nebbiolo, Shiraz, Blaufränkisch.

Having taken over the estate from his father Paul (the brother of the more famous Ernst), Günter Triebaumer has thoroughly renovated the cellars, production methods, wine style, and marketing. Part of the distinctive character of his wines stems from his use of varieties such as Nebbiolo and Syrah (which he calls Shiraz, presumably to clarify his stylistic preference); the latter has lovely hints of nutmeg, violet, and eucalyptus. Among the indigenous varieties, there is a powerful and often port-like Blaufränkisch Reserve and a nicely delicate sparkling Moscato, made from Muskateller.

HERBERT TRIEBAUMER
Eisenstädter Strasse 10, 7071 Rust. Tel: 02685 528. Fax: 02685 60738.
Vineyards: 6 ha. White grapes: Gelber Muskateller, Grüner Veltliner. Red grapes: Blaufränkisch, Cabernet Sauvignon.

He spends most of his time working his father Ernst's vineyards, but Herbert Triebaumer also makes his own wines from his own vineyards. His Burgenland Rot (Cabernet Sauvignon/Blaufränkisch) has finesse, density, and deep aromas of summer fruit and leather. It has great style – and clearly shows paternal influence.

WENZEL

Hauptstrasse 29, 7071 Rust. Tel: 02685 287. Fax: 02685 2874. Vineyards: 11
ha. White grapes: Muskateller, Sauvignon Blanc, Welschriesling, Pinot Blanc, Pinot
Gris, Furmint. Red grapes: Blaufränkisch, Cabernet Sauvignon, Pinot Noir.

Michael Wenzel's family have been making wine in Rust since the
seventeenth century, and he clearly feels this tradition keenly.

Michael's father Robert, who has handed over the running of the
estate, was especially concerned with championing the Furmint and
Muskateller grapes, as well as Pinot Blanc. The son has set his sights on
excellence in all fields and is giving great attention to his red wines, the
best of which are Blaufränkisch Bankräften and Pinot Noir Kleiner Wald.
Among the dry whites, there is a delicate Gelber Muskateller and a meaty,
attractive Furmint. Excellence is attained with the Ausbruch wines Am
Fusse des Berges (Sauvignon Blanc/Pinot Gris/Welschriesling) and Saz
(Furmint/Grüner Veltliner), both wines of great complexity and purity
of fruit.

MIDDLE BURGENLAND (MITTELBURGENLAND)

Vineyards: 1,877 hectares.
Soils: gravel, sand, loam, crystalline deposits.
White grapes (18.3 per cent): Welschriesling, Pinot Blanc.
Red grapes (81.7 per cent): Blaufränkisch (52.2 per cent of total
plantings, and about two-thirds of all red grapes), Zweigelt, Cabernet
Sauvignon.

The Middle Burgenland, going southward along the Hungarian border, is
"Blaufränkischland" – the country of the Blaufränkisch vine. Its wines are
wonderfully generous and deep, often with succulent berry aromas and a
characteristic salty note. As in other red wine areas, vinification methods
have greatly advanced during recent decades and so there are few old
wines to illustrate ageing potential, but the new generation of
Blaufränkisch grown here has good to very good prospects for ageing.

Geologically speaking, this stretch of countryside was formed by
prehistoric rivers, which brought gravel with chalky and crystalline
deposits, together with sandy and marly layers. There is some basalt
around Oberpullendorf, but sandy loam, loam, and an occasional
inclusion of gravel predominate.

The area is protected from winds by the Ödenburg Mountains to the north and a chain of hills (the Bucklige Welt) directly to the west and the south. The Pannonian plains of Hungary to the east play a major role in the climate of the region, bringing with them stable, continental climatic conditions. However, in summer and autumn the influence of Lake Neusiedl twenty kilometres (twelve miles) away is still noticeable, especially around Deutschkreutz in the west, as the lake stores heat during the day and gives it off during the night.

This gently hilly area with its heavy soils and hot summers (an average maximum in August of 32°C/89.6°F) has moderate rainfall (an annual mean of 594 litres per square metre) and a pronounced variation between daytime and nighttime temperatures, and between summer and winter. Blaufränkisch was already planted here over a century ago, and many growers today have the great advantage of being able to work with vineyards that are eighty years old or more.

There are traditional *Rieden* here (Dürrau, Hochäcker, and Gfanger in Horitschon, Hochberg in Deutschkreuz), but wines are often blended or labelled by variety. Single-vineyard wines are gaining in importance, though traditionally they have less significance here than in the northern Burgenland. A recent initiative to strengthen the terroir idea has been launched by two growers, the brothers Roland and Heinz Velich, whose Moric project encompasses wines made from old vines in Neckenmarkt to the north and in Lutzmannsburg in the southern part of the region. Using only old Blaufränkisch vines vinified traditionally and without a marked new wood flavour, they have successfully shown the substantial differences in the terroirs of their two sites over several vintages.

Several growers here sell their best Blaufränkisch as "Juwel", a distinction awarded at a blind tasting held by local Blaufränkisch producers.

Top growers

ARACHON TFXT
Günster Strasse 60, 7312 Horitschon. Tel: 02610 42321. Fax: 02610 423214. Website: www.arachon.com. Vineyards: 29 ha under contract. Red grapes: Blaufränkisch, Cabernet Sauvignon, Merlot, Zweigelt.
A much-talked-about joint venture between some very different producers, Manfred Tement, F. X. Pichler, and the late Tibor Szémes, Arachon is an attempt to produce a no-expenses-spared red wine in an area where none of them owns vineyards. The result, made from grapes produced by

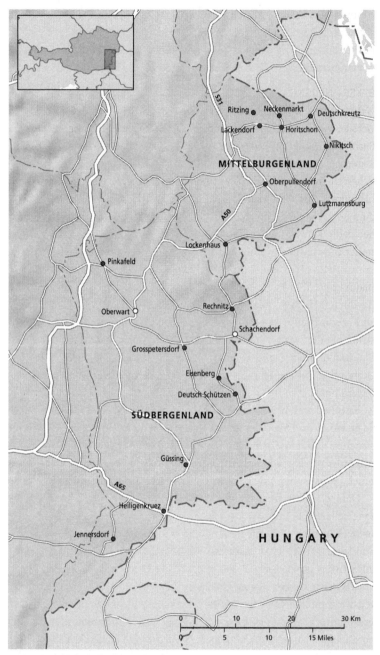

iii Middle & South Burgenland

contract growers, is an international, barrel-aged blend (Blaufränkisch/ Zweigelt/Cabernet Sauvignon/Merlot). I have always found it well made, but its circumspect winemaking-by-committee style inevitably entails a certain blandness.

BAYER–IN SIGNO LEONIS

Wirtschaftspark 5, 7311 Neckenmarkt. Tel: 02610 42644. Fax: 02610 42644. Website: www.weinfreund.at. Vineyards: none. White grapes (Thermenregion): Chardonnay, Pinot Gris. Red grapes (Middle Burgenland): Blaufränkisch, Cabernet Sauvignon, Zweigelt.

When the unstoppable wine entrepreneur Heribert Bayer started making his wines from bought-in grapes, it was thought by many to be a gimmick, another cult red surfing the trend. Now, ensconced in a decidedly glitzy winery complete with fountain and panoramic views set rather incongruously among industrial buildings, Bayer has silenced his critics with his red, In Signo Leonis, a sophisticated blend of Blaufränkisch, Zweigelt, and Cabernet Sauvignon. It has soft tannins, fine flavours of berries, cedar, and leather, is aged in new oak for two years, and is consistently one of Austria's classiest red blends. He also makes a string of other wines, among them In Signo Tauri, a good Pinot Noir; the Blaufränkisch In Signo Sagittarii, and the broad-shouldered Albatross (Rotgipfler, Pinot Gris, Chardonnay), made in the Thermenregion, Bayer's home.

Sails Red and Avantgarde Zweigelt are good entry-level wines. In Signo Sagittarii is an altogether different animal and its sophisticated tannin structure and raciness make it one of Austria's finest Blaufränkisch wines. Albatross is a big white blend with a good deal of new French oak – too much perhaps, but only time will tell as these are wines made to age.

Named after Bayer's star sign, In Signo Leonis is also constructed with long cellaring in mind, but is not, thankfully, packed with alcohol, oak, or overripeness. Instead, there are aromas of cedar and cigar, hyacinth and violet, and a tarry saltiness balancing the blackberry fruit, a most attractive combination.

Having started as a wine collector and consultant to various Austrian red-wine producers in the 1980s, Bayer aims for the depth and race of great Bordeaux, rather than maximum fireworks early on. With his combination of pragmatism and great ambition, Bayer has quickly succeeded in setting standards in this region, and will continue to do so.

GAGER

Karrnergasse 8, 7301 Deutschkreutz. Tel: 02613 80385. Fax: 02613 8038515. www.weingut-gager.at. Vineyards: 20 ha. Red: Blaufränkisch, Zweigelt, Cabernet Sauvignon, Cabernet Franc, Syrah, Rösler, Tannat.

Until 1999 Josef Gager's wine was only one (growing) part of a general farming concern. Today this estate is among the region's best. Gager and his son Horst only make red wines, every one of them a testimony to their passion for fathoming just what is possible in every vintage, a passion resulting in big, meaty wines, generous to a fault. With its punch and complexity, Cablot (Cabernet Sauvignon/Cabernet Franc/Merlot) is reminiscent of new-wave Bordeaux, while Quattro (Cabernet Sauvignon/Blaufränkisch/Zweigelt/Merlot) offers a more distinctively Austrian aromatic spectrum. Always adventurous, the Gagers are also responsible for two rarities: the opulent blend Tychoon, which includes some Rösler (an old Austrian grape), and Tannat (yes, the southern French one), as well as Austria's only totally convincing Syrah.

GESELLMANN

Langegasse 65, 7301 Deutschkreutz. Tel: 02613 80360. Fax: 02613 80315. Website: www.gesellmann.at. Vineyards: 28 ha. White grapes: Chardonnay. Red grapes: Blaufränkisch, Cabernet Sauvignon, Merlot, Zweigelt, St Laurent, Pinot Noir.

If the names on the bottles from this estate seem nothing short of eccentric, the wines themselves can certainly stand up in the face of international competition. Albert Gesellmann, who has taken over from his father Engelbert, spent a crucial apprenticeship at Stellenbosch in South Africa and Cuvaison in California and appears to have brought home with him the blessings of a southern sun.

Produced in exceptional years only, G (Blaufränkisch/St Laurent) shows a dazzling array of chocolate, dark berries, and deep, salty flavours – perhaps the future of reds in the region? The traditional flagship Opus Eximium (Blaufränkisch/Zweigelt/St Laurent) shows Gesellmann's great commitment to Austrian varieties and shines with beautiful definition and structure; a consistently elegant wine. Its "international" counterpart Bela Rex (Cabernet Sauvignon/Merlot) shows great race and potential and ages beautifully. Also fine are the complex Pinot Noir Siglos and the Syrah. With his subtle Chardonnay Steinriegel Gesellmann proves that great whites are possible, too, in this region.

HEINRICH

Karrnergasse 59, 7301 Deutschkreutz. Tel: 02613 89615. Fax: 02613 896154.
Website: www.weingut-heinrich.at. Vineyards: 30 ha. Red grapes: Blaufränkisch,
Cabernet Sauvignon, Syrah, Pinot Noir, Merlot, Zweigelt.

Until 1992, Johann Heinrich sold his wines in bulk, but with the
beginning of Austria's red wine renaissance he decided to bottle himself
and he has saved neither effort nor expense on his huge, state-of-the-art
winery. Today he works with his daughter Silvia, who gained experience
in Germany and Italy before returning home. The focus here is
Blaufränkisch, of course, though other varieties play a significant part.
The two top wines are Blaufränkisch Reserve Goldberg, a robust, dark
creation of character, tannic depth, and obvious oak influence, and
Terra O, a somewhat bewildering marriage of Blaufränkisch, Cabernet
Sauvignon, Pinot Noir, Merlot, Syrah, and Zweigelt with complexity and
length. Elegy (Cabernet Sauvignon/Merlot) is striving for a more
international style, and Pinot Noir Weisses Kreuz has buxom plum fruit
that make it interesting, but lacking in the elegance that would take it to
the next level.

IBY

Kirchengasse 4, 7312 Horitschon. Tel: 02610 422920. Fax: 02610 4229290.
Website: www.iby.at. Vineyards: 27 ha. Red grapes: Blaufränkisch, Zweigelt, Pinot
Noir, Cabernet Sauvignon.

Anton Iby, father and son, are driven by an almost maniacal perfectionism.
They are also open to international trends, as their computer-
controlled winery-with-laboratory demonstrates. Having said that, their
efforts are concentrated on creating wines with a uniquely Burgenland
character. This union of technology and terroir is not easy to achieve, and
while all the wines are very well made indeed, they can at times appear
almost too polished, and too reliant on oak aromas. The stylish
Blaufränkisch Chevalier carries its French ideal on the label, while the
smoky Quintus (Blaufränkisch/Zweigelt/Cabernet Sauvignon) is often
characterized by elderberry, wood and mulled-wine aromas. Top of the
bill is Blaufränkisch Dürrau, more concentrated and more powerful, with
often very attractive, mature tannins supporting clover and berry tones.

IGLER

Langegasse 49, 7301 Deutschkreutz. Tel: 02613 80365. Fax: 02613 896837.
Website: www.weingut-igler.at. Vineyards: 25 ha plus 5 ha. Red grapes:

Blaufränkisch, Cabernet Sauvignon, Pinot Noir, St Laurent.

Hans Igler was one of the red wine pioneers in this area. Today, the estate is led by his daughter Waltraud together with her husband, Wolfgang Reisner, and a comprehensive modernization of the cellars has allowed the wines to be vinified with even more precision than one had grown used to from this outstanding producer. Waltraud Reisner believes passionately in respecting nature while using technology well. Cold maceration and temperature-controlled fermentation is used for all wines. There is great stylistic coherence in this wide range of elegant, often complex offerings, centring on Blaufränkisch with some other varieties, notably a slender and cherry-fruited Pinot Noir and the famous Vulcano (Blaufränkisch/Cabernet Sauvignon/Zweigelt/ Merlot). The greatest wines are a well-defined Cabernet Sauvignon; Ab Ericio (Blaufränkisch/Merlot/ Zweigelt), a class act full of wonderful spice with hints of cherry and plum rounded off by lingering fruit; and the equally excellent Blaufränkisch Juwel, all finely wrought tannins, succulently integrated wood, and pure, deep fruit on the finish.

MARIA KERSCHBAUM

Dreifaltigkeitsgasse 30, 7322 Lackenbach. Tel: 02619 8505. Fax: 02619 8530. Website: www.weingut-kerschbaum.at. Vineyards: 6 ha. Red grapes: Blaufränkisch, Cabernet Sauvignon, Zweigelt.

A small producer who was little known until recently, Maria Kerschbaum produces wonderfully succulent, sappy wines whose dark, cherry fruit and dense aromas are winning admirers. Particularly good are Poesie (Blaufränkisch/Cabernet Sauvignon) with its rich liquorice notes, and the fine Blaufränkisch Juwel.

PAUL KERSCHBAUM

Hauptstrasse 37, 7312 Horitschon. Tel: 02610 2392. Fax: 02610 2340. Website: www.kerschbaum.at. Vineyards: 25.5 ha. White grapes: Pinot Blanc. Red grapes: Blaufränkisch, Zweigelt, Cabernet Sauvignon.

The introverted Paul Kerschbaum has been pursuing a personal vision of Middle Burgenland reds for well over a decade now, and his recent vintages show a fascinating depth of fruit. He has also had a comprehensive building programme, including new cellars. His Blaufränkisch Dürrau is imposing with great presence and length, while the addition of Zweigelt and Merlot to the Blaufränkisch makes Impresario softer and more flattering, with notes of bitter chocolate and dense red fruit. Both wines profit from some age. The velvety Blaufränkisch Juwel shows even more substance and spice combined with great persistence on the palate.

KIRNBAUER

Rotweinweg, 7301 Deutschkreuz. Tel & Fax: 02613 89722. Website: www.phantom.at. Vineyards: 18 ha. White grapes: Chardonnay. Red grapes: Blaufränkisch, Cabernet Sauvignon, Merlot, Zweigelt, Syrah.

A winery on the top of a hill announces Walter Kirnbauer and his wines. Everything here is designed to be both ultra-modern winery and visitor attraction, and the wines follow this contemporary, international approach. With its spicy nose, Das Phantom is a satisfying blend of Blaufränkisch, Merlot, Cabernet Sauvignon, and Zweigelt, while the Blaufränkisch Goldberg is all seductive fruit, without much depth. A surprise is a slightly chubby Syrah with spice and varietal character.

LEHRNER

Hauptstrasse 56, 7312 Horitschon. Tel: 02610 42171. Fax: 02610 42124. Vineyards: 18 ha. Red grapes: Blaufränkisch, Cabernet Sauvignon, Merlot, Zweigelt, St Laurent.

One of the most solid producers of the region, Paul Lehrner not only believes in keeping his prices very reasonable, but also produces wines of great generosity. Particularly recommendable are Paulus (Blaufränkisch/ Zweigelt/Cabernet Sauvignon) with its satisfyingly peppery, berry fruit, and the old-vine Blaufränkisch Steineiche.

MORIC

Kirchengasse 3, 7051 Grosshöflein. Tel: 0664 4003231. Website: www.moric.at. Vineyards: 15 ha. Red grapes: Blaufränkisch.

Begun only in 2000, this may turn out to be the most significant initiative in Austrian winemaking in recent years. It is the brainchild of the enterprising Velich brothers (see Neusiedlersee, above), whose great Chardonnays had already proved their credentials. Buying grapes from mainly very old (thirty-five to 100 years) Blaufränkisch vines, winemaker Roland Velich has created a portfolio of four wines with unmistakable terroir typicity, and in doing so has made some of Austria's finest reds. The yields are severely limited, and the wines are vinified with long maceration times of up to three weeks, the use of ambient yeast and, incredibly for an ambitious Austrian red, hardly any new wood and very light toasting. Named after the villages of Lutzmannsburg and Neckenmarkt, both in the south of the region, the two Alte Reben ("old vine") wines are both outstanding, the former being perhaps more approachable initially because of its creamy, berry fruit. The Alte Reben Neckenmart, however, is in a class of its own with immensely deep colour and profound notes of eucalyptus, dark berries, mint, and peppery spice, all supported by fine, mature tannins to give a wine of great length and greater potential.

UNITED VINEYARDS PFNEISL FAMILY

Karrnergasse 64, 7301 Deutschkreuz. Tel: 02613 802701. Fax: 02613 802704. Website: www.wine-pentagon.com. Vineyards: 103 ha. Grape varieties: Blaufränkisch, Cabernet Sauvignon, Merlot, Zweigelt, Syrah.

No, this is not a translation; this is the actual name of a winery whose international, Anglo-Saxon orientation has become a credo, and who has taken to aggressive marketing. One can only hope that Pentagon (Blaufränkisch/Cabernet Sauvignon/Merlot/Syrah/Pinot Noir) is named for its five varieties, but its style is recognizably modern and without edge: primary fruit, extract, and toasted aromas combining to flatter. The Shiraz is similarly fleshy, with berry aromas supported by sweet extract, which shows the handwriting of Australian flying winemaker Michael Gadd.

SZEMES

Weinhoferplatz 7, 7423 Pinkafeld. Tel: 0357 42367. Fax: 0357 4157. Website: www.szemes.at. Vineyards: 12 ha. Red grapes: Blaufränkisch.

Illa Szemes makes her wines on a négociant basis and has succeeded in creating consistent quality, particularly with her Blaufränkisch Imperial, a wine with clear barrique notes and attractive fruit.

TESCH

Herrengasse 26, 7311 Neckenmarkt. Tel: 02610 43610. Fax: 02610 42230. Website: www.tesch-wein.at. Vineyards: 11 ha. Red grapes: Blaufränkisch.

Neckenmarkt is emerging as one of the best terroirs in the Middle Burgenland, and long before the Velich brothers demonstrated this with their Moric project (q.v.), Josef Tesch had produced serious reds here. Titan combines Cabernet Sauvignon with Syrah and at times Blaufränkisch to give a broad wine often somewhat dominated by toasted aromas, while the Blaufränkisch Selection, made from sixty-year-old vines, is elegant and profound.

WELLANSCHITZ (DONATUS-WEINGUT)

Lange Zeile 28, 7311 Neckenmarkt. Tel: 02610 42302. Fax: 02610 42304.
Website: www.wellanschitz.at. Vineyards: 24 ha. Red grapes: Blaufränkisch,
Cabernet Sauvignon, Pinot Noir, Syrah.

Stefan, Georg, and Christine Wellanschitz are a formidable trio and their enthusiasm has made of this estate one of the most consistently original and fascinating in the area. Theirs are not wines made for maximum elegance and finesse, but their earthy aromas and sappy fruit make them a pleasure to drink. Only six wines are made here. The strongest are the cedar-spiced Blaufränkisch Altes Weingebirge, whose generous aromas remind one of the southern Rhône; the imposing Fraternitas (Blaufränkisch/Cabernet Sauvignon, in other years also Zweigelt and Syrah); and Blaufränkisch Well, a glorious blend of nutmeg, bramble, and walnut often with a touch of animal spice. All these wines are already drinkable during their youth, but will blossom if given some years of bottle age.

WENINGER

Florianigasse 11, 7312 Horitschon. Tel: 02610 42165. Fax: 02610 42150.
Website: www.weninger.com. Vineyards: 27 ha. Red grapes: Blaufränkisch, Merlot,
Cabernet Sauvignon, Zweigelt.

Franz Weninger combines seriousness with ambition and was one of the first to realize the potential of this region. Today he makes wine in both the Middle Burgenland and in Hungary and has secured himself a place among the elite of Austrian wine producers. Like the top wines of some of his colleagues, his Blaufränkisch Dürrau could in the past at times have been reproached for being a "tasting wine", made mainly to impress; but now he has sold his concentrator, taken to wooden fermenting vats, and uses less new wood than in the past. The effect of this change of heart is that his top wine is all harmony and maturity, still leaning toward over-ripe fruit, but carried by fine, ripe tannins. My personal favourite is often Veratina (Blaufränkisch/Merlot/Cabernet Sauvignon/Zweigelt), whose subtle, more elegant style allows for a play of smoky aromas and fruit notes strongly reminiscent of Left Bank Bordeaux First Growths. Also outstanding is the holly-scented Merlot, whose depth and style are immediately convincing.

WIEDER

Lange Zeile 76, 7311 Neckenmarkt. Tel: 02610 42438. Fax: 02610 42420.

Website: www.weingut-juliana-wieder.at. Vineyards: 20 ha. White grapes: Welschriesling. Red grapes: Blaufränkisch, Cabernet Sauvignon, Merlot, Zweigelt, Syrah.

Georg Wieder's wines trace a steady improvement in style and technique, which earns him a place in this guide. His Blaufränkisch wines as well as his Sempre (Blaufränkisch/Cabernet Sauvignon/Syrah) already show good structure and firm fruit, and the excellent Neckenmarkt vineyards may be able to yield yet greater qualities.

SOUTH BURGENLAND (SUDBURGENLAND)
Vineyards: 449 hectares.
Soil: slate, clay, loam.
White grapes (56.8 per cent): Welschriesling, Grüner Veltliner, Pinot Blanc, Muscat Ottonel.
Red grapes (43.2 per cent): Blaufränkisch, Zweigelt, Cabernet Sauvignon, Uhudler.

South Burgenland seems far away from everything, a remote region of idyllic hills, dark woods, and medieval castles, among which, incidentally, is Lockenhaus, the forbidding fortress in which the violinist Gidon Kremer holds his legendary music festivals. Sandwiched between Styria in the west and Hungary in the east, it has only a few pockets of vineyards spread over some twenty kilometres (twelve miles) on the eastern edge of the region, on the border with Hungary, mainly around the villages of Rechnitz, Eisenberg, Deutsch-Schützen, Eberau, and Heiligenbrunn in the very south. It is the smallest wine-producing region of the Burgenland, at least in terms of area under vine, and the climate and geology are quite different to the rest. This is Austria's highest wine-growing area. The hills rise up to almost 900 metres (2,953 feet) above sea level and in the higher parts, weathered blue slate makes up the majority of the soil, while deep clay and loam dominates in the valleys.

The south-facing Eisenberg was an iron ore mine in Roman times, and its ferrous inclusions in loam and slate soils impart a particular mineral depth and elasticity to its wines; it is one of the few genuinely recognizable red wine terroirs in the country, even if the only growers who currently vinify Eisenberg Blaufränkisch to a consistently excellent standard are the Krutzler brothers. As this small region has not yet exploited its undoubted potential, it is difficult to say as yet whether there are other outstanding terroirs waiting to be discovered.

The hills protect the vines from northerly winds while the woods on their summits cool the vineyards during the night. With around 750 millimetres (29.6 inches) annual rainfall, the South Burgenland is wetter than the rest of the Burgenland. The annual mean temperature of 9°C (48.2°F) is lower than that of the Middle Burgenland, and in this climate determined by hills, altitude, and the influences of the Pannonian plains, the Blaufränkisch wines can develop a unique character and concentration, with typical notes reminiscent of eucalyptus, dark berries, and tar.

A local rarity is the Uhudler, a rosé made directly from American rootstocks (*see* Grape varieties, Chapter Two) in the village of Heiligenbrunn. The only other Uhudler is made in neighbouring West Styria.

Top growers

KOPFENSTEINER

7474 Deutsch-Schützen 38. Tel: 03365 2236. Fax: 03365 22365. Website: www.kopfensteiner.at. Vineyards: 8 ha. White: Welschriesling, Pinot Blanc. Red: Blaufränkisch, Cabernet Sauvignon, Blauburger.

Thomas Kopfensteiner is one of the few ambitious growers in the region. His Blaufränkisch Weinberg shows mellow fruit with wood notes and the variety's characteristic pepper tone, while his Border (Blaufränkisch/ Cabernet Sauvignon/Merlot) offers morello cherries and extract sweetness supported by soft tannins.

KRUTZLER

Hauptstrasse 84, 7474 Deutsch-Schützen. Tel: 03365 2242. Fax: 03365 20013. Website: www.krutzler.at. Vineyards: 10 ha. Red grapes: Blaufränkisch, Zweigelt, Merlot, Cabernet Sauvignon.

The Krutzler winery is one of the most highly rated red wine producers in Austria. Erich and Reinhold Krutzler have redefined red wine from this part of the world, mainly with their great Perwolff (mostly Blaufränkisch/ Cabernet Sauvignon), one of the very few Austrian reds to have demonstrated excellence and consistency for a decade now. Most of the grapes for it come from the Eisenberg vineyard, and the style has always put the emphasis on elegance and structure over weight. A considered use of new oak gives these wines their profound and playful spice tones. It is without doubt one of Austria's great wines, at once unmistakably of the region and universal in its sophistication.

SCHIEFER
7503 Welgersdorf 3. Tel & Fax: 03362 2464. Website: www.weinbau-schiefer.at.
Vineyards: 5 ha. Red grapes: Blaufränkisch .

Uwe Schiefer produces some of Austria's most captivating Blaufränkisch, notably his outstanding Blaufränkisch Reihburg, with tarry, succulent, cherry and bramble fruit and ripe tannic backbone.

WACHTER-WIESLER
Hauptstr. 26, 7474 Deutsch-Schützen. Tel & Fax: 03365 2245. Website: www.wachter-wieser.at. Vineyards: 9 ha. Red grapes: Blaufränkisch, Zweigelt, Cabernet Sauvignon.

A traditional grower who also runs his own *Heurige*, Franz Wachter produces wines that are deeply rooted in their terroir. The Blaufränkisch Pfarrweingarten, with its bramble and clover spice, seems a textbook example of what this variety can do. Wachter also makes good Cabernet Sauvignon.

WALLNER
Deutschschützen, 7474 Deutschschützen. Tel & Fax: 03365 2295.
Vineyards: 8 ha. Red grapes: Blaufränkisch, Zweigelt, Cabernet Sauvignon, Merlot. White grapes: Welschriesling, Pinot Blanc.

Joseph Wallner produces a blend called Kentaur from Blaufränkisch, Cabernet Sauvignon, Merlot, and Zweigelt, with an elegant aromatic spectrum of cedar, leather, and brambles, remarkably Bordelais in style and with good ageing potential. Also good is the Blaufränkisch Reserve.

5

Lower Austria (Niederösterreich)
Part I: The Danube, including Vienna

Comprising places as different as the Wachau and the Thermenregion, Lower Austria is the country's largest wine-growing region. Its diverse climates and wines have led to several drafts and redrafts of area boundaries and their names in recent years, often motivated by local politics.

Lower Austria's climates are as varied as its wines, and they are all affected by the Danube. The main influence comes from the north and the west, and meets the continental Pannonian climate of Burgenland to the east. Climatic and geographic conditions are discussed in more detail in the individual area introductions.

In terms of style it appears sensible to group Lower Austria into three sub-sections. First come the Danube areas: the Wachau, Kamptal, and Kremstal are all based mainly on Grüner Veltliner and Riesling, as are the Traisental and Donauland. The moderating influence of the Danube is important for all of them. Styles range from the uncompromising mineral purity of the Wachau to the exuberant inventiveness of the young Donauland growers, who are not afraid of using oak and malolactic fermentation. In wine law, Vienna is a region by itself, but for the purposes of the book it appears sensible to discuss it in the context of the Danube areas. Wines here are still overwhelmingly simple, but the excellent Nussberg vineyard is yielding increasingly complex wines. Of growing significance is the *Gemischte Satz*, the mixed planting of several white varieties in one vineyard. Historically used to spread the risks of weather and disease, it has been found to be well adapted to conditions here.

The Weinviertel, about a hundred kilometres (sixty miles) across, is a universe of its own with several different climatic zones. The north is influenced by the proximity of forest, while the south is more similar to the neighbouring Donauland and Vienna. Grüner Veltliner is the lead grape here and the overwhelming majority of wines are very simple. Most grape-growers still operate mixed farms and low-density plantings with high-trained vines. While there are some producers making outstanding wines, the area still has a lot to prove.

Sandwiched between the south of Vienna, the Weinviertel, and the Burgenland, the Carnuntum and the Thermenregion are determined by very different climatic influences and soils. Many of the most ambitious wines grown in Carnuntum are red and based on Zweigelt and Blaufränkisch, but these wines have not yet been able to find a place among the country's best. It is unlikely that this is simply a question of terroir. Carnuntum, like the Donauland, is a region with rather artificial boundaries. Perhaps the key to the question is more likely to lie in the relative uniformity of vinification in this area, which makes it hard to distinguish individual styles and terroir.

To the west of the Carnuntum is Lower Austria's second-largest wine growing area, the Thermenregion, a historic region with a distinctive landscape and climate, successfully defending its unique varieties and styles. The luscious white varieties Zierfandler and Rotgipfler, with their floral spice and citrus tones, are the main white grapes here, and there is also a some good Pinot Noir.

WACHAU
Vineyards: 1,390 hectares.
Soils: primary rock, loess, gneiss, crystalline slate, sand.
White grapes (eighty-nine per cent): Grüner Veltliner, Riesling, Chardonnay, Pinot Blanc, Muskateller, Neuburger, Müller-Thurgau.
Red grapes (eleven per cent): Zweigelt, St Laurent, Blauer Portugieser. (Red grapes play no role in quality production here.)

This, Austria's best wine region, is also blessed with great natural beauty and charm. Set along the Danube, its steep, woody hills rise upward with a peculiar mixture of grace and dramatic sweep. Set into the hillsides are the Baroque towns of Loiben, Dürnstein, Weissenkirchen, Joching, and Spitz on one side of the river, and Mautern on the other.

A natural passageway between east and west, the Wachau has seen many migrations and its fair share of battles. The first evidence of human culture here, the Willendorf Venus, is a small stone figurine dating from 20,000 BC. The Celts probably began to produce wines in much of the Wachau. They were supplanted by the Illyrians, who in turn failed to stem the invasion of the Roman army. In 15 AD the Danube became the northern border of the Roman Empire, and the occupiers erected a permanent camp, Favianis, near where Mautern is now. The first evidence of wine production, grape-seeds excavated from tombs, also dates from Roman times.

The now-famous appellation "Vinea Wachau Nobilis Districtus" ("The Renowned District of the Wachau Vineyards") was recorded in a document by Leuthold I of Kuenring in 1285, and was adopted in 1984 as the name of a producers' association. The organization was founded by four Wachau growers: Wilhelm Schwengler (of Freie Weingärtner Wachau), Franz Hirtzberger, Franz Prager, and Josef Jamek. Today it has about 170 members and controls some eighty-five per cent of the area under vine.

At the beginning of the twentieth century, the Wachau was not especially known for great wines, but more for its orchards, especially apricots, cherries, and apples. It was not until the 1950s that the first great wines began to emerge from the ancient vineyards, partly, ironically, because the price of fruit fell and many growers turned to wine instead.

Understanding the wines, soils, and climate of the Wachau is a lifelong task and a source of endless discussions and research. Like all of eastern Austria, the Wachau is a meeting point of western European and Pannonian climatic influences. Atlantic air meets warm, continental currents flowing in from the eastern Pannonian Plains. The continental character of the climate (hot, dry summers, severe winters) is offset by the effect of the Danube, which balances out the differences of temperature to some extent. Nevertheless, big differences between day and night temperatures, especially during the weeks leading up to the harvest, intensify the aromas of the wine, particularly in the higher vineyards. The cool fruit and the exotic characteristics of Wachau wines are a result.

The steep hills are very important. Close to the banks of the Danube (at 250 metres/820 feet), the annual mean temperature is about 9°C (48.2°F). From 250 metres (820 feet) to 450 metres (1,470 feet) it is 8-9°C (46.4-48.2°F), and from 450 metres (1,470 feet) to 600 metres (1,970 feet) it is 7-8°C (44.6-46.4°F). Most of the best vineyards are situated around 400 metres (1,300 feet), though Toni Bodenstein's

iv Wachau

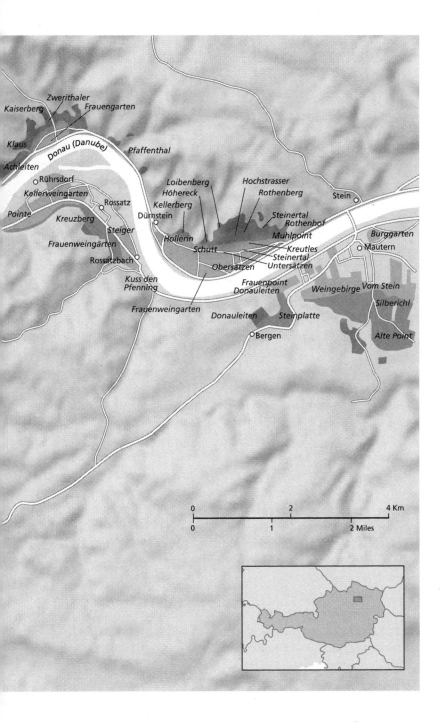

legendary Riesling Wachstum Bodenstein vineyard is at 600 metres (1,970 feet), which, he admits, made many colleagues doubt his sanity when he decided to recultivate it. They doubt no longer.

Annual rainfall in the Wachau is lower than in any other wine-producing area in Austria (500 millimetres/19.7 inches, with 580 millimetres/22.8 inches in Spitz, and 520 millimetres/20.5 inches in Loiben), and the terraces especially need irrigation during the summer. The vegetation period is around 245 days, less in the higher vineyards.

Around Loiben, the influence of the Danube is less strongly felt, making the vineyards sensitive to frost; while in the area of Wösendorf and Spitz, the "Spitz trench", a tributary valley leading north into the Waldviertel, assures a constant and regular flow of cool air. Toward Krems, where the valley opens up to the east, the arid Pannonian summers assert themselves slightly more than in the rest of the Wachau.

The key to the *Rieden* in the Wachau is, of course, the soil. Seen from the river, the soils very roughly follow an ascending order: loess and sandy soils near the banks of the Danube, larger loess deposits further up the hill, and finally weathered gneiss, granite, and slate soils in the top vineyards, which also tend to produce the best wines. These are the oldest rock formations in Austria. Toward the east of the region, near Krems, there are also some yellow loess, loamy soils around Weissenkirchen, and there is some slate in the westernmost corners. Yields on the highest vineyards tend to be lower than thirty hectolitres per hectare, and they require a disproportionate amount of work. While a vineyard with a light incline might take 300 to 400 hours of labour per hectare per year, the upkeep of the terraces and the strenuous (and overwhelmingly manual) work on the slopes pushes this figure up to 2,000 hours.

The terraced vineyards of the Wachau have never taken to the Lenz Moser training system as it is almost impossible to use any kind of machine here. Within the terraces, the number of vines per hectare is between 7,000 and 7,500 compared to fewer than 5,000 in vineyards organized according to Lenz Moser.

The Wachau is the only wine-growing area in Austria with a sense of and a passion for terroir and a *cru* structure similar to that of Burgundy, up to and including the near-mysticism attached to some of the more famous vineyards. Going from east to west on the right, northern bank of the Danube, the best sites of the Wachau include Schön and Kalkofen, both of which face southwest. The soils here are weathered granite and slate, and these vineyards have a particular mesoclimate that derives from the Spitzer Graben, the Spitz Trench. Some of the finest *Rieden* of the Wachau can be found in Spitz itself. These are Tausendeimerberg, or Burgberg, a hill rising just behind the town with steep, south-facing terraces of crystalline soils on Paleocene para gneiss; Hochain and the famous adjacent Singerriedl, again with weathered gneiss and brown soil rich in silicates, a vineyard that benefits from maximum exposure to the sun and renowned for its finely-chiselled Rieslings; Rotes Tor just to the south of the Singerriedel, and Steinborz, a miniature plateau. Another outstanding *Ried* is Honivogl at the foot of the Singerriedl, with crystalline soil overlaid by brown soil.

At Wösendorf and Weissenkirchen, eight kilometres (five miles) downstream, the main *Rieden* are Hochrain and Kollmitz, characterized by deep para gneiss soils with a top layer of sandy loess; Pichlpoint; and Ritzling with loamy sands on weathered granite. The Hinterseiber and Vorderseiber are further up the hill and characterized by para gneiss again. To the east of Weissenkirchen, the Ried Achleiten is renowned for its distinctive "*stinkerl*", a "stink" or mineral note shared by many of the wines grown on it. The stone walls of the terraces date back to the twelfth century. At the top of the hill, the soils are made up mainly of Gföhl gneiss. At the lower end, dark, often amphibolitic stones with slate emerge from the rock. Next to Achleiten is the almost equally famous Ried Klaus, again mainly gneiss and some slate, and a famous Riesling vineyard.

Following the river, we come to the charming village of Dürnstein with its ruined castle on the hill above it. Here, Hollerin and Kellerberg are particularly fine. Both situated at the southeastern side of the hill, their soils are dominated by weathered gneiss and sand for the former, and crystalline gneiss and slate for the latter, which also benefits from the immediate influence of the wooded hilltops surrounding it. The Loibenberg, under vine since the fourteenth century, rises up to a height of 420 metres (1,380 feet) and has soils ranging from weathered gneiss and slate to sandy loam and some loess in the east. The Mühlpoint nearby has similar soils, while up the hill the Ried Steinertal is purely crystalline, a small, sheltered spot. The Ried Schütt was mentioned first in 1379. It demarcates the border between Dürnstein and Loiben and is separated into two vineyards, the Dürnsteiner Schütt, with weathered gneiss and sand soils and a distinctive mesoclimate, and Loibner Schütt, which faces southwest.

The village of Mautern on the south side of the Danube has conditions that are considerably different, and its vineyards are much flatter than the terraced hills across the river. The Ried Burggarten, once, apparently, the site of Charlemagne's camp, is slowly being eaten up by building. Its soils are gravel and sand. The Silberbühel, below the magnificent Göttweig Abbey, has some crystalline soils and gravel, mostly covered by sandy loess. At its foot the Ried Vom Stein, a former gravel pit, is planted exclusively with Riesling.

The Wachau is a white-wine area par excellence, and the undisputed leaders are Riesling and Grüner Veltliner, which here can produce intensely concentrated and powerful wines with enormous ageing potential. Other common varieties are Chardonnay (in the Wachau called Feinburgunder), Müller-Thurgau, Muskateller, Pinot Blanc, and Sauvignon. Muskateller and Pinot Blanc in particular can evolve into beautifully elegant wines.

The Wachau classification

Priding itself on its special status as an area of great tradition and great wines, the Wachau operates its own system of wine classification, which specifies not only grape variety, year, and often site, but also three steps of quality. Steinfeder, named after a plant growing in the vineyards, denotes the simplest, lightest wines with low alcohol (up to eleven degrees), best drunk young. The second step is Federspiel, named after a device used in falconry to lure the hawk back to the glove. These wines have about twelve degrees of alcohol, are more substantial, and need to age for about two years. The third and highest step is named after the little emerald-green lizards that sun themselves between the vines in summer: Smaragd. Elsewhere in Austria, these wines would be called Auslese. They are made from the best and ripest grapes and can have very considerable alcohol levels. They are made to last and should be given plenty of time. At their best, they are among the greatest white wines made anywhere in the world.

Top growers

ALZINGER

Unterloiben 11, 3601 Dürnstein. Tel: 02732 77900. Fax: 02732 77950.
Website: www.alzinger.at. Vineyards: 8.5 ha. White grapes: Grüner Veltliner,
Riesling, Chardonnay.

Leo Alzinger still seems surprised by his good fortune. Like many others
in the area, his parents sold their wine in the barrel, and it took courage
and vision to change. After three decades of immensely careful and
detailed work Alzinger is now one of the greatest white-wine
producers. What distinguishes his wines and often makes them
unmistakable is a crystalline, mineral clarity, and this is achieved with the
simplest means: low yields (but not too low, to avoid extreme alcohol
levels), a gravity-driven winery to avoid pumping, reliance on ambient
yeasts, fermentation in large barrels for the top Veltliners and in steel
tanks for all other wines, and long lees contact. Perhaps Alzinger's
greatest terroir is the Steinertal, which produces Riesling of world-class
eloquence and depth, and a Grüner Veltliner whose concentration and
style astonish with every vintage. Other great wines come from the
Loibenberg, whose often floral character is transformed into elegance and
depth in Alzinger's hands, and from the Rieden Hollerin, Mühlpoint,
Höhereck, and Hochstrasser. All are wines of impeccable character and
balance, and great ageing potential. Like several other great producers in
the area, Alzinger is also already sharing with the next generation, in this
case his capable son Leo, whose stylistic ideas follow those of his father.

BÄUERL

Loiben 28, 3601 Dürnstein. Tel: 02732 75555. Fax: 02732 755554. Website:
www.baeuerl.at. Vineyards: 3.3 ha. White grapes: Riesling, Grüner Veltliner, Gelber
Muskateller.

With under four hectares Wolfgang Bäuerl is one of the smallest
independent producers in the area, but he has proved himself to be one of the
most consistently interesting. Not all his wines play in the top league, but
his classy wines from the Kellerberg show him to be a master of his craft.

JOHANN DONABAUM

Laaben 15, 3620 Spitz. Tel & Fax: 02713 2488. Website: www.weingut-
donabaum.at. Vineyards: 4.5 ha. White grapes: Grüner Veltliner, Riesling,
Neuburger.

The winery of Johann Donabaum, one of the Wachau's most talented young producers, is a kilometre away from the Danube in a side valley. His location in the Spitzer Graben, the Spitz Trench, means that some of his vineyards have cooler nights than those directly adjacent to the river. Still in his twenties, Donabaum worked with F. X. Pichler before taking over the family winery, and he has instantly become one of the region's finest producers. His Riesling Offenberg is utterly individual with its delicate, bewitching notes of white blossoms, a wine of great refinement and immense potential. Very fine also are his lovely and long Grüner Veltliner Spitzer Point and his fine Grüner Veltliner Berglage Loiben. Donabaum also makes an excellent Neuburger Biern, a brilliant rarity combining opulence and concentrated fruit.

SIEGHARDT DONABAUM

Zornberg 4, 3620 Spitz. Tel: 02713 2287. Fax: 02713 22874. Website: www.donabaum.com. Vineyards: 10.5 ha. White grapes: Grüner Veltliner, Riesling, Neuburger, Gewürztraminer.

One of the most dependably fine producers in Spitz, Sieghardt Donabaum clearly puts elegance before power for his series of Smaragd wines, whose creamy, precise fruit comes from great attention to detail and long yeast contact. Particularly fine are his Grüner Veltliner Atzberg Smaragd with its often exotic aromas, and the Riesling Tausendeimerberg Smaragd, a wine of exceptional transparency.

FREIE WEINGÄRTNER WACHAU

3601 Dürnstein 107. Tel: 02711 371. Fax: 02711 313. www.fww.at. Vineyards: 400 ha. Grapes: all varieties grown in Lower Austria.

This 700-producer cooperative controls roughly a third of the Wachau's vineyard area is slowly recovering from a very fraught recent history. Previously fêted as "the world's best cooperative" by the press, internal politics led to the departure of the very successful and ambitious team of directors, a disastrous step followed by several wilderness years marked by bad structural investments and plummeting wine qualities. Roman Horwarth and Heinz Frischengruber, recently employed to stop the rot and re-establish the FWW among the region's best, are facing a challenge. The first two vintages under their control indicate a consolidation and give reason for hope. The 2004 series already showed good aromatic profiles in the top wines (sold as Domäne Wachau) from the famous *Rieden* Kellerberg, Tausendeimerberg, Achleiten, and Kollmitz.

GRITSCH

Viessling 21, 3620 Spitz. Tel & Fax: 02713 8478. www.josef-gritsch.net.

Vineyards: 4 ha. White: Riesling, Grüner Veltliner, Gelber Muskateller.

Patient and consistent work have earned Josef Gritsch a place among the Wachau's best. Showing the typically clear minerality of the Spitz terroir, his wines can tend toward the one-dimensional, but his crystalline Riesling Bruck Smaragd and his fine Grüner Veltliner Schön Smaragd are wonderfully expressive. Gritsch also produces an outstanding, opulent Gelber Muskateller with some residual sugar.

HIRTZBERGER

Kremser Strasse 8, 3620 Spitz an der Donau. Tel: 02713 2209. Fax: 02713 220920. Website: www.hirtzberger.com. Vineyards: 20 ha. White grapes: Grüner Veltliner, Riesling, Pinot Blanc, Pinot Gris.

Franz Hirtzberger's enthusiasm and persistent application have helped make him one of the most influential personalities of the Wachau, and one of Austria's finest wine producers. Hirtzberger's winemaking style is marked by his constant search for ultimate expressiveness and aromatic complexity, necessitating risky late-harvesting and often resulting in high alcohol levels. The extract and structure of these wines, however, transform them into miracles of depth, marrying a taste for extremes with the mineral Spitz terroir. Only in a few very hot vintages have I thought that things might have been carried too far.

Among the Smaragd wines, there is a series of classic names: Grüner Veltliner Rotes Tor, dense and elegant with mineral notes on the length; Grüner Veltliner Axpoint, more concentrated and with fine quince aromas; Grüner Veltliner Honivogl, a great wine made to be laid down but already showing exceptional complexity and structure. Riesling is represented with the delicately mineral Setzberg, the aristocratic and mineral Hochrain, and Singerriedel, a great wine of incredible clarity, depth, and complexity. There are also a fine Neuburger and a Pinot Gris Smaragd, which add often exotic notes.

HÖGL

Viessling 31, 3620 Spitz/Donau. Tel: 02713 8458. Fax: 02713 8454. Website: www.weingut-hoegl.at. Vineyards: 5.5 ha. White grapes: Riesling, Grüner Veltliner, Gelber Muskateller.

Finding Josef Högl's estate is a bit of a challenge. His tiny farm is tucked away in the Spitzer Graben. Here, seemingly, presentation is nothing, wine is everything. Formerly sorcerer's apprentice to F. X. Pichler, Högl creates wines of great concentration and clarity in a cellar that is hewn right into the mountain. The style of his wines is determined by their location and the greatest among them sparkle with crystalline depth. Reliably outstanding are the mineral Grüner Veltliner Ried Schön Smaragd and the Riesling Ried Bruck, a miraculous and complex expression of the slate soils of this terroir.

HÖLLMÜLLER

Weinbergstrasse 46, 3610 Joching. Tel & Fax: 02715 2380. Website: www.gruener-veltliner.at. Vineyards: 6 ha. White grapes: Riesling, Grüner Veltliner, Gelber Muskateller, Pinot Blanc.

Alois Höllmüller has the courage to swim against the tide. Instead of trying to produce prestigious Smaragd wines by waiting until the required sugar levels are attained on the vine, he prefers creating wines with less alcohol but more filigree fruit, and he closes them with plastic corks. As the Vinea Wachau allows only natural cork for Smaragd wines he is not allow to declare his more powerful wines as such and has taken himself out of this classification system. His most brilliant, most precise wines are usually found among the lighter styles, such as his fine Grüner Veltliner X Large, or his Riesling Pichlpoint X Large.

HOLZAPFEL

3610 Joching 36, Tel: 02715 2310. Fax: 02715 23109. Website: www.holzapfel.at. Vineyards: 9.5 ha. White grapes: Riesling, Grüner Veltliner, Pinot Blanc.

Karl Holzapfel not only inhabits one of the most beautiful buildings in the Wachau (which also houses a good restaurant), but he also has vines in the famous Achleiten vineyard. His Grüner Veltliner and Riesling are perfect examples of clean, well-made Wachau fruit, with lovely, elegant structure, though they are not as mighty and perhaps as complex as other wines from this *Ried*. Particularly fine is his Grüner Veltliner Smaragd Achleiten and an unusual wine, the Pinot Blanc Hippolyt, with its creamy pear fruit and length.

HUTTER

St Pöltener Str. 385, 3512 Mautern. Tel: 02732 83004. Fax: 02732 83004. Website: www.hutter-wachau.at. Vineyards: 11 ha. White grapes: Riesling, Grüner Veltliner, Pinot Gris. Red grapes: Zweigelt, St Laurent.

Fritz Hutter's winery is in Mautern, on the "other" bank, the southern bank of the Danube, opposite the town of Krems, but his vineyards are situated mainly in and around Loiben. His wines are often a little more down-to-earth than others from this terroir, but at their best they show beautifully clear and generous fruit. His Riesling Smaragd Loibenberg, for instance, is almost the definition of the terroir with its aromas of peach and peach blossoms, while his Grüner Veltliner Gärten Loiben, an assemblage of several smaller vineyards, excels at distilling the floral tones so associated with Loiben.

JÄGER

3610 Weissenkirchen 1. Tel: 02715 2535 Fax:02715 2534. Vineyards: 6 ha.
White grapes: Riesling, Grüner Veltliner, Gelber Muskateller.

In their historic cellars the Jägers, father and son, are making wines that have for some time been among the secrets of the Wachau. Their wines from Ried Achleiten in particular, such as the fine Grüner Veltliner, can show great concentration and mineral depth. The Riesling, too, offers elegant, peach fruit and complex aromas. These wines do not necessarily advertise their virtues while they are young, but they promise much for those patient enough to wait.

JAMEK

Joching 45, 3610 Weissenkirchen. Tel: 02715 2235. Fax: 02715 2222. Website: www.weingut-jamek.at. Vineyards: 25 ha. White grapes: Grüner Veltliner, Riesling, Chardonnay, Muskateller, Pinot Blanc.

Josef Jamek, the octogenarian *eminence grise* of the Wachau with his short-cropped hair, his moustache, and his ceremonious courtesy, is a relic of the Habsburg era, as well an important local personality who has made a huge contribution to Wachau wine. After the war he helped to save the entire area from being flooded by a planned hydro-power plant. When he took over the family estate, there was no world-famous Wachau wine, and the region was seen as a rural appendage to Krems. If things are different today, it is in no small part thanks to Jamek's efforts, often in concert with Franz Hirtzberger's father, Franz senior.

Today the Jamek estate is run by his daughter and son-in-law, Jutta and Hans Altmann, and the cellarmaster and oenologist is Volker Mader.

During the last few years, I have not been totally convinced by the Jamek wines. They are consistently close to the top, but never quite there. Their style tends toward residual sugar and, at times, a hint of botrytis, and it is perhaps this rather old-fashioned idea of Wachau wines that causes my reservations. Despite this caveat, Jamek's Grüner Veltliner Achleiten Smaragd is a wonderfully mineral wine with great length. Also fine are the Riesling Klaus Smaragd and the Riesling Freiheit Smaragd.

KARTÄUSERHOF

Kremser Strasse 6, 3610 Weissenkrichen. Tel: 02715 2374. Fax: 02715 237. Website: www.stierschneider.at. Vineyards: 8 ha. White grapes: Riesling, Grüner Veltliner, Gelber Muskateller, Sauvignon Blanc, Pinot Blanc. Red grapes: Zweigelt, Pinot Noir.

A mid-sized producer, Karl Stierschneider has made himself a name for well-crafted, individual wines topped off by the occasional gem. His finest wines come from the Ried Achleiten, from where he vinifies delicately mineral Grüner Veltliner and a Riesling pure and focussed enough to cut glass.

KNOLL

3101 Unterloiben 10. Tel: 02732 79355. Fax: 02732 793555. Vineyards: 13.5 ha. White grapes: Grüner Veltliner, Riesling, Chardonnay, Muskateller.

Few great winemakers have a style so individual that their signature is immediately apparent in a wine, and the publicity-shy Emmerich Knoll is one of them. There is a floral elegance to his wines, combined with great, mineral definition and a positively Baroque interplay of aromas that is quite unmistakably Knoll.

Emmerich Knoll's views are those of a far-sighted traditionalist. He consciously relies on his instincts rather than on technology (too much of which makes wines anonymous, he says), and the cellar is still dominated by large barrels, many of which are embellished with traditional wood carvings. Steel tanks are standing alongside. Knoll does not believe in interventionist winemaking, and if some of his wines stop fermentation while they still have some residual sugar, he accepts this as a vintage characteristic.

The ageing potential of his wines proves him right. After five years or so, they open up new depths and an entirely new aromatic spectrum, which, in the case of the Veltliners, can be strongly reminiscent of the best Puligny-Montrachets. His reference collection of old wines, by the way, is famous in itself and reaches back into the mists of Austrian wine-making. Occasional vertical tastings show beautiful and perfectly structured wines made long before that 1985 watershed, and an evolution that seems endless.

Speaking of ageing, one caveat is to be noted here: always emphasizing delicate fruit, Knoll's wines are particularly bedevilled by cork problems. He has spared neither cost nor effort to combat this, but so far it remains a serious issue, and it is to be hoped that alternative closures will soon find their way onto his bottles.

Knoll makes Rieslings from *Rieden* Loibenberg and Schütt, and his Grüner Veltliners are some of the best made from this grape. Other varieties, such as Chardonnay and Muskateller, are dismissed as toys, with which he enjoys experimenting. These are terroir wines, and as many vineyards are planted with both Riesling and Grüner Veltliner, they offer comparisons between terroirs and varieties. Schütt and Loibenberg, for instance, both Riesling Smaragd, form a complementary couple: Schütt is the more assertive, dense, fragrant, and deep with wonderfully pure length; the Loibenberg opens up an incredible array of floral, feminine aromas but reveals an underlying structure every bit as impressive. The Grüner Veltliner Loibenberg Smaragd shows the blossom notes of this terroir, but in addition to this spice, ripe fruit, and mature acidity. The same variety on Ried Schütt shows more concentration and deep, focussed fruit with a majestic length. Also fine are the wines from Ried Pfaffenberg, a vineyard across the border in the Kremstal. In particularly great years, Knoll produces a Vinotheksfüllung, a selection of the best grapes. He has moved away from botrytis in his dry wines, and has always made outstanding sweet wines.

Emmerich Knoll's son, also called Emmerich, is now increasingly working with his father and is bringing his own ideas into the process.

LAGLER

Rote Tor Gasse 10, 3620 Spitz an der Donau. Tel: 02713 2516. Fax: 02713 25164. www.weingut-lagler.at. Vineyards: 13 ha. White: Grüner Veltliner, Riesling, Neuburger, Pinot Blanc, Chardonnay, Sauvignon Blanc.

Karl Lagler is one of the most consistent growers in Spitz, and his wines are continuing to rise in quality. His finest, from the *Rieden* Steinborz, Tausend-Eimer-Berg, and Hartberg, are beautifully crafted and concentrated, and not least among them is a remarkable Sauvignon Blanc. Best of all are the Riesling and Grüner Veltliner Smaragd from the Steinborz, both showing exceptional mineral depth and beautiful purity.

LEHENSTEINER

3610 Weissenkrichen 7. Tel: 02715 2284. Fax: 02715 22844. Vineyards: 7.5 ha. White grapes: Riesling, Grüner Veltliner.

Andreas Lehensteiner has attracted attention with some finely judged wines emphasizing finesse and purity over concentration and power. From his vineyard on the Ried Achleiten he produces wines that convince where some more overwhelming Wachau wines fail: with harmony and clarity.

NIKOLAIHOF

Nikolaigasse 3, 3512 Mautern. Tel: 02732 82901. Fax: 02732 76440. Website: www.nikolaihof.at. Vineyards: 20 ha. White grapes: Riesling, Grüner Veltliner, Frühroter Veltliner, Chardonnay, Pinot Blanc, Neuburger.

The Nikolaihof is one of a handful of good producers on the "wrong", southern side of the Danube. Founded in 985 as a feoff of the diocese of Passau, it is one of the most traditional estates of the Wachau. Christine Saahs cultivates vineyards on both banks of the river, notably the Ried Steiner Hund near Krems, officially just beyond the border of the Wachau, on which she grows her finest Riesling. All vineyards are tended according to Biodynamic principles, and even in illness-prone years they appear to be at least as healthy as neighbouring plots.

On the Danube's southern bank, roughly opposite Krems, the *Rieden* Vom Stein and Im Weingebirge produce fine Riesling and Grüner Veltliner respectively on gravel and sandy loam. Sometimes these do not have the focus and elegance of "proper" Wachau wines from the primary rock to the north, but they often show stunning complexity and their ageing potential is considerable. The most astonishing wine I have drunk in the Wachau for a long time was Riesling Vinothek 1990, a wine that was matured in a large wooden barrel for fourteen years before being bottled. Its aromas had imperceptibly melted into one another to become a bewitching display of fruit, almond, extract sweetness, and beautifully oxidative depth. A great wine.

2005 was the first vintage pressed with a restored 300-year-old tree press, and the creamy, complex style of the Nikolaihof wines is aided by long lees contact. Outstanding are the slightly metallic Riesling Steiner Hund and the Grüner Veltliner Im Weingebirge, also vinified in large wooden casks, a wine with immense, quiet depth and outstanding ageing potential.

FRANZ XAVER PICHLER

3601 Oberloiben 27. Tel: 02732 85375. Fax: 02732 8537511. Website: www.fx-pichler.at. Vineyards: 13 ha. White grapes: Grüner Veltliner, Riesling, Sauvignon Blanc, Muskateller.

Like his wines, F. X., as he is called, combines a penchant for the monumental with quiet authenticity. Lionized around the world for his great Rieslings and Grüner Veltliners, he is keenly aware that greatness is born in the vineyard. When it became technically possible to make wines with hitherto unheard-of concentration and overwhelming, overripe exoticism he made them to perfection and seduced the world. Then, as they were winning top scores, he silently evolved and created a style marked by elegance, depth, and an almost monastic concentration on the essential.

His Federspiel wines are excellent, but he comes into his own with his Smaragds, which are a masterclass in terroir expression. Among the Veltliners, the special bottling "M" (for "Monument"), a selection of the best grapes from different vineyards, is almost too dense and overpowering, a wine that needs time. Outstanding also is his mineral Kellerberg with its opulent, yet razor-sharp fruit. His Steinertal shows profound definition, like pure granite with all the flowers that grow on top of it. As might be expected, the Loibenberg is much more beguilingly floral and has the elegance of a dancer.

RUDI PICHLER

Wösendorf 38, 3610 Weissenkirchen/Wachau. Tel: 02715 2267. Fax: 02715 22674. Vineyards: 9 ha. White grapes: Grüner Veltliner, Riesling, Chardonnay, Pinot Blanc, Roter Veltliner.

Having unjustly suffered the fate of being "the other Pichler" for a long time, Rudi has now established himself as one of the finest Wachau winemakers. The Rieslings especially are very fine, powerful wines with wonderfully concentrated fruit and rock-solid structure. Unlike many of his Wachau colleagues, Rudi Pichler is willing to experiment and to bring in modern technology such as temperature-controlled fermentation. Some wines go from steel into small new oak barrels, but they are never overwhelmed by the wood. Barrel-aged Grüner Veltliners with residual sugar are a great rarity in the Wachau, but here they work astonishingly well and demonstrate that this grape is capable of immense transformations and seemingly limitless quality. Rudi Pichler has vineyards in the best terroirs around, among them Hochrain (which produces a stunning Grüner Veltliner) and Achleiten. His finest wines, though, come from the Ried Kollmütz, where he grows a Grüner Veltliner whose complexity and mineral purity are phenomenal.

PRAGER (BODENSTEIN)

3610 Weissenkirchen 48. Tel: 02715 2248. Fax: 02715 2532. Website: www.weingutprager.at. Vineyards: 14 ha. White grapes: Riesling, Grüner Veltliner, Chardonnay, Sauvignon Blanc.

No producer has impressed me more with the consistent excellence of his wines than Toni Bodenstein at Prager. A biologist, geologist, and historian (and the author of several books), he brings considerable intellectual baggage to winemaking. His work in the vineyards is led by a meticulous understanding of soils and their geological origins, while his biological research has taught him to understand the systemic nature of climate and winemaking.

This has led to projects such as Arche Noah ("Noah's Ark"; *see* Chapter Two), a vineyard that preserves the genetic variety of Austrian vines, which is, he believes, threatened by modern cloning methods. He has also instituted new practices like allowing the leaves to partially overhang the grapes to protect them from sunburn; important, he believes, in view of rising global temperatures. Even in hot vintages like 2003 he makes delicate mineral wines with beautiful acidity.

All Prager wines are marked by attention to terroir, structure, and transparency, characteristics that have given him an international fan base. His Grüner Veltliner Smaragd Zweritaler shows perfectly focussed minerality and elegance combined with great length. Grüner Veltliner Achleiten Smaragd is more concentrated, and transforms this unique terroir into a wine of great honeyed clarity, fruit, and depth, good in its youth and even better with age. His Rieslings show their origins and vintage even more clearly. The Kaiserberg has great mineral concentration and fine apricot notes, a textbook Wachau Riesling of great class. Even clearer and more polished, Ried Klaus plays off precise fruit notes against mineral structure, while the Riesling Steinriegl is all complexity and finely modulated precision. Flinty, complex, and long, the Riesling Achleiten teases out a different tone from the vineyard than the Grüner Veltliner. Finest, however, is probably the Riesling Wachstum Bodenstein, the producer's pet project, grown on a vineyard previously thought too high to produce good wine, it is a Riesling of immense floral eloquence and minerality, sophisticated and long, as close to perfection as a bottle can be.

SCHMELZ

Weinbergstrasse 14, 3610 Weissenkirchen. Tel: 02715 2435. Fax: 02715 24354. Website: www.schmelzweine.at. Vineyards: 10.5 ha. White grapes: Grüner Veltliner, Riesling, Sauvignon Blanc, Neuburger, Gelber Muskateller.

Johann Schmelz was cellarmaster for Jamek before starting out on his own, and now he has emerged as one of the Wachau's finest producers. Finely chiseled aromas are a characteristic of all his wines, beginning with the relatively simple (and cheap) Federspiels, which already show beautiful minerality and refinement. The Smaragd wines have more density without trying to overwhelm. The greatest among them is certainly the Riesling Dürnsteiner Freiheit, a wine of exceptional finesse and mineral depth, supported by residual sugar. Also fine are the cooly mineral Grüner Veltliner Höhereck, the dense and crystalline Grüner Veltliner Pichl Point, and the deep, steely, and lovely Rielsing Steinriegl.

SCHNEEWEISS

3610 Weissenkirchen 27. Tel: 02715 2227. Fax: 02715 222727. Website: www.wachauerwein.at. Vineyards: 5 ha. White grapes: Riesling, Grüner Veltliner, Neuburger, Gelber Muskateller.

After a lean patch, Peter Reiter, Anton Schneeweiss's son-in-law, has revived this estate and restored not only its good reputation, but also expectations for its future. The wines can show density and plenty of clean fruit, and the vines, in *Rieden* like Vorderseiber, Steinriegl, Ritzling, and Achleiten, should allow them to go on to even greater things.

PAUL STIERSCHNEIDER-URBANUSHOF

3601 Oberloiben 17. Tel: 02732 72750. Fax: 02732 72728. Vineyards: 5 ha. White grapes: Grüner Veltliner, Riesling, Gelber Muskateller, Sauvignon Blanc, Chardonnay.

In the family since 1696, the Urbanushof produces expressive wines known for rich extract even in the lighter examples. Small yields and *Rieden* such as Loibenberg and Frauenweingarten are key for good quality. Paul Stierschneider also produces a Wachau rarity, an exemplary Sauvignon Blanc Klostersatz. Best among the other wines on his list is perhaps his Riesling Rothenberg Smaragd.

TEGERNSEEHOF

Unterloiben 12, 3601 Dürnstein. Tel: 02732 85362. Fax: 02732 85320.
Website: www.tegernseehof.com. Vineyards: 25 ha. White grapes: Grüner Veltliner,
Riesling, Chardonnay, Sauvignon Blanc.

The Tegernseehof is one of the largest Wachau producers in private hands. Martin Mittelbach, the son and heir of the estate, recently carried out an ambitious renovation and improvement programme, which included the rebuilding of several hectares of terraced vineyards. It is obvious that this producer is reaching for the very top, even if its style is, to my mind, veering too much toward overripeness, exotic fruit, and correspondingly high alcohol.

The Grüner Veltliner Höhereck shows elegance and honeyed fruit, while the austerely mineral Riesling Steinertal and the clean, mineral Riesling Kellerberg play on pure, stone-fruit aromas. The Riesling Creation is an extreme wine whose high alcohol and residual sugar I find less harmonious, while the opulent Grüner Veltliner shows a more coherent picture and has considerable ageing potential.

WESS

Kellergasse, 3601 Unterloiben. Tel: 02277 73099. Fax: 02277 73099. Website:
www.weingut-wess.at. Vineyards: 5 ha. White grapes: Riesling, Grüner Veltliner.

Rainer Wess is a novelty in the Wachau: a high-quality négociant without vineyards of his own who only started in 2003. Before beginning his current venture he was one of the directors of the Freie Weingärtner Wachau. It is still to early to judge the long-term performance and over-all quality of his wines, but he proved his credentials while with the FWW. The first wines under his own name are very promising indeed, and he has a rapidly expanding export list. The Riesling and Grüner Veltliner Pfaffenberg, and the Grüner Veltliner Loibenberg show particular clarity and fine fruit; an excellent beginning.

KAMPTAL

Vineyards: 3,869 hectares.
Soil: primary rock, loam, loess, slate.
White grapes (eighty-four per cent): Grüner Veltliner, Riesling, Chardonnay, Pinot Blanc.
Red grapes (sixteen per cent): Zweigelt, Pinot Noir, Cabernet Sauvignon, Cabernet Franc, Merlot.

The Kamptal is the valley of the river Kamp, a few kilometres east of the Wachau. The first mention of wine-growing here was in 1082, when the area was owned by the bishops of Passau, in Bavaria. Its centre is the beautiful Baroque town of Langenlois, which also claims to have the highest number of vineyards within its confines – a claim which is, incidentally, disputed by Gols in the Burgenland.

The situation of the Kamptal, between the Pannonian Plains and the forested Waldviertel, determines the climate. Protected from north winds by the foothills of the Manhartsberg and the hills of the Weinviertel, the south-facing vineyards on the gentle slopes of the Kamptal have excellent conditions. The average annual temperature is 9°C (48.2°F), with a vegetation period of about 234 days and annual mean rainfall of about 580 millimetres (22.8 inches) per year, significantly more than the Wachau. There is a danger of late frosts in May for all vineyards, and of frosts in spring and autumn for the lower ones. Hail in early summer is another hazard, but September usually marks the beginning of a dry period spanning the entire harvest season, until November.

Geologically, Langenlois is at the meeting point of several formations. The subsoil is largely gneiss and crystalline slate, overlaid by maritime sediments, such as sands and clays. Other influences are the slow south-ward shift of the bed of the river Danube, which has deposited gravel throughout the region, and loess dating from the last ice age. This gives a soil profile of loess and crystalline soils on hills and hillsides, and gravel with loam and sand in lower areas.

By far the most important *Ried* is to the northeast of Langenlois: the Heiligenstein ("Rock of Saints"), which has undergone a remarkable change of name. During the Middle Ages it was known as Hellenstein ("Hell Rock"), possibly because of the scorching heat in the vineyards during the summer. A geographical anomaly, the Heiligenstein is a cone of primeval rock that has pushed through the surrounding area. Its soils consist of weathered crystalline rock, volcanic rock, and desert sands. The southern parts are called Zöbinger Heiligenstein. The entire hill has now been declared a natural monument, and officials seem to be especially concerned about the rare grasses that grow here. There are plans to plant more grass on the Heiligenstein – for the first time in 250 million years. Apart from rare grasses, though, Riesling from here is wonderfully expressive.

The Ried Letten, adjacent to the Heiligenstein, was originally called

KAMPTAL Vineyards

- under 200 metres
- 200 – 300 metres
- over 300 metres

Reising

Gleßeln

Irrblin

Reith

Schontal

Schiltern   Anger

Tanzer

Seeber

Mitelberg

Loiser Heide

Haid

Käferberg

Loiser Berg

Decha

Auf der
Setz

Steinhaus

Pfeifenberg

Liss

Leimer

Dorner

Neuberg

Lengenfeld

Kittmannsberg

Sauber

Wechselberg

Sand

Fuchsloch

Zeiselberg

Kremsfeld

Kremsfeld

Friesenrock

Kremsfeld

Stratzing

0   2   4 Km

0   2 Miles

tiefern

Rosenberg

m Renner

Schönberg

Loischl

Obernholz

Steinfeld

Schnauterin

uchtal

Wolfsgraben

Saß

Obritzberg

Kirchholz

Elsarn

Pfaffenberg

ogelberg

Ringerin

Sandgrube

Stangl

Bieckenweg

Zöbing

chelberg

Steinwand

Grub

Wechselberg

Reith

Antenau

ogerl

laseln

Heiligenstein

Placher
Point

Groisl

Oberhasel

Lamm

Lammberg

Oberhasel

Mitternhasel

Galsberg

Strass im Strassertale

Unterhasel

Wolfsgraben

Langenlois

Galgenberg

Satzen

Spiegel

Stein

anzuan

Gobelsburg

Hadersdorf

Landstraß

Hutweg

Engabrunn

Steinsatz

Badfield

Horstadt

Wohra

Redling

Gobelsberger
Haide

Gedersdorf

v Kamptal

Red Letten because the iron content coloured the soil orange. Apart from Grüner Veltliner, this is also a preferred site for Pinot Blanc and Pinot Noir. Today it is usually called Kammerner Heiligenstein and vinified together with other sub-vineyards of the Heiligenstein proper. Ried Grub runs along the hillside. A natural plateau, this site was used 15,000 years ago as a campsite by mammoth and reindeer hunters. Whether the prehistoric bones add anything to the quality of loess is not clear, but the position of the vineyard, protected from three sides against cold winds, benefits the wine.

Underneath the *Rieden* Heiligenstein and Letten is Ried Lamm, which has recently distinguished itself with some outstanding Grüner Veltliners and Rieslings. The plot is called Lamm not because it used to be a feeding ground for lambs, but because of the deep loam (spelled like the English "loam" in Kremstal dialect and pronounced with an audible "a") which makes up its soil.

On the southern side of Langenlois lies the Gobelsburg, a charming Baroque castle belonging to Zwettel Abbey, and an excellent wine estate. To the west of the Gobelsburg, the *Rieden* Thal, Hofstatt, Spiegel, and Pazaum (Innere, Mittlere, and Obere) are situated on a hill, partly with black soil on loam and loess.

The Loiser Berg and the smaller Vogelsang lie to the west of Langenlois. A flat hill, this vineyard can be cool, moist, and windy, but the southerly exposure and the absence of frost compensate for this. Its weathered, crystalline soils are ideal for Riesling, and very good for Grüner Veltliner and Pinot Blanc.

The largest vineyard area is the Schilterner Berg, directly north of Langenlois. Some excellent vineyards are to be found here. Ried Steinmassel (formerly a quarry), is a protected basin sunk into the surrounding countryside. The quarrying has exposed the crystalline slate subsoil, which is very suitable for Grüner Veltliner and Riesling. The *Rieden* Käferberg and Dechant, near the top of the hill, are large vineyards with heavy, brown, loess soils on primary rock, used especially for Pinot Noir and Merlot, but also for Grüner Veltliner. Other *Rieden* here are Hoheneck, Fahnberg, Hozweg, Bockshörndl, Frau Point, Vögerl, Hofstatt, Schenkenbichl, and Tagler.

A few kilometres east from Langenlois we come to Strass im Strassertal, another old winemaking village. Loess, brown, and black soils dominate here, and the best vineyard is the Ried Gaisberg to the east, close to the Heiligenstein. It benefits from the crystalline soils of the Heiligenstein, but is more overlaid by brown earth and loess. The Wechselberg to the north of the village and the *Rieden* close to it also benefit from crystalline soils with loess and loam, and some brown earth in the lower parts. The Ried Hasel to the east of the village is very varied in its exposition, but the loess, gravel, and black earth that make up its soil help to produce consistently interesting wines. There are other wine-producing villages, notably Lengenfeld, Schönberg, and Haderstdorf, but these are not yet consistently producing very interesting wines.

Kamptal wines can be very distinguished indeed, more opulent and perhaps broader than those of the Wachau, but also more varied in style. The main grape varieties are Grüner Veltliner and Riesling, with Neuburger, and, increasingly, more international ones such as Chardonnay, Pinot Blanc, and even Sauvignon Blanc. There is some red wine being made here, too: Zweigelt of course, but also surprisingly good Pinot Noir.

In Langenlois, visitors can go to the Loisium, a wine museum, visitors' centre, and "cellar world". It may not change the quality of Kamptal wines, but it can be a useful point of departure for the uninitiated.

Top growers

AICHINGER

Hauptstrasse 15, 3562 Schönberg am Kamp. Tel: 02733 8237. Fax: 02733 76458. www.wein-aichinger.at. Vineyards: 12.5 ha. White grapes: Grüner Veltliner, Riesling, Sauvignon Blanc, Traminer. Red grapes: Zweigelt.

Anna and Josef Aichinger run this "gourmet *Heurige*" and wine estate: they are respectively a chef and a sommelier. Their wines have established an excellent reputation independently of the *Heurige*, the Grüner Veltliner being rated especially highly. Aichinger wines are frequently slightly sweeter than other Kamptal wines, but the sugar is well integrated. Particularly fine are the Grüner Veltliner Alte Reben, a harmonious wine with tones of citrus and boiled sweets; Riesling Schönberg, whose intense minerality and apricot fruit make it my particular favourite; and the spicy Grüner Veltliner Renner with its grapefruit tones.

ALLRAM

Herrengasse 3, 3491 Strass. Tel: 02735 2232. Fax: 02735 22323. Website: www.allram.at. Vineyards: 14 ha. White grapes: Grüner Veltliner, Riesling,

Chardonnay, Gelber Muskateller, Pinot Blanc, Pinot Gris. Red grapes: Zweigelt, St. Laurent.

Choosing wild-yeast fermentation and long lees contact can make a producer less commercially competitive because wines are not necessarily ready when customers want them. Erich Haas has made this choice, and his wines show beautiful individuality and expressiveness in return, particularly the classy Grüner Veltliner Gaisberg, a complex, honeyed wine with citrus and cedarwood on the nose; the fine, mineral, and dense Riesling Heiligenstein, reminiscent of fresh almonds, peach, and white blossoms; or the imposing Chardonnay Strasser Wechselberg with its aromas of dried apricot and quince.

ANGERER

Schickenberggasse 4, 3552 Lengenfeld. Tel: 0676 3655787. Fax: 02719 8424. Website: www.kurt-angerer.at. Vineyards: 33 ha. White grapes: Grüner Veltliner, Riesling. Red grapes: Zweigelt, Cabernet Sauvignon, St Laurent, Merlot.

Grüner Veltliner specialist Kurt Angerer is a newcomer to the wine scene, and he has already secured himself a place among the most interesting and innovative producers of the area. His wines are like their creator: charming, uncompromising, and a little pugilistic. His Grüner Veltliner Unfiltriert ("unfiltered") is a massive wine, vinified in new oak, high in alcohol, and releasing a range of fascinating aromas. Named after its loamy soils, the Grüner Veltliner Loam (which is local dialect, not a nod to his export market) presents soft, generous fruit and fine length. In some vintages, I have been very impressed by the Grüner Veltliner Spies, a wine of wonderfully earthy complexity and great length. The Riesling Donatus is beginning to look very good.

BRANDL

Heiligensteinstrasse 13, 3561 Zöbing. Tel: 02734 26350. Fax: 02734 26354. Website: www.weingut-brandl.at. Vineyards: 8 ha. White grapes: Grüner Veltliner, Riesling, Gelber Muskateller.

With only eight hectares in production, Günther Brandl is among the very smallest producers in the area, and he likes it this way. "I don't need a Mercedes," he says. "I get to see my kids every night, and if I were to expand that wouldn't be possible." Working with his father Johann, Brandl uses international experience, notably in South Africa, to innovate carefully and evolve his style toward more precise, purer aromas. The result is an exceptional series of wines. Topping the bill are two wines harvested in November, the Novemberlese. The Grüner Veltliner has wonderfully rich and deep fruit, almost imperceptible residual sugar, and aristocratic Kamptal aromas: a long and great wine and one of the best bargains to be had in Austria. Veering toward ripe peach and exotic fruits, the Riesling Novemberlese is equally outstanding.

BRÜNDLMAYER

Zwettler Strasse 23, 3550 Langenlois. Tel: 02734 2172. Fax: 02734 3748. www.bruendlmayer.at. Vineyards: 70 ha; 30 ha under contract. White: Grüner Veltliner, Riesling, Pinot Gris, Chardonnay, Pinot Blanc.
Red: St Laurent, Cabernet Sauvignon, Merlot, Pinot Noir, Zweigelt.

With a combination of superb winemaking skill, great personal charm, and fine business sense, Willi Bründlmayer has established himself as one of the wine world's premier personalities. At university, he wanted to become a research scientist, but a family emergency brought him back to his father's winery and he has never regretted staying.

Bründlmayer uses neither herbicides nor artificial fertilizers but pays the greatest possible attention to detailed canopy management and the control of yields as well as to the ecological balance of his vineyards, one of which is lyre-trained: the greater leaf surface is more laborious to look after but it also gives the wines significantly more concentration, Bründlmayer finds. All grapes are harvested in small boxes.

In the cellar, too, Bründlmayer goes his own way. When most of his colleagues imported Allier oak barrels by the truckload, he got together with a local cooper and had him make up barrels from Austrian, Russian and French oak as well as from acacia and other woods in order to see which ones would really be most suitable for his purposes. He still works with local craftsmen, using both acacia, and French and Austrian oak, which he matches to the characteristics of individual wines and vintages. Blessed with a combination of open mindedness, respect for tradition and a willingness to innovate where necessary, he continues to experiment both in the cellar and the vineyard, constantly redefining and modifying his technique, while remaining always true to his underlying ideal of individuality, elegance, and clarity.

Bründlmayer's beautiful, traditional cellar is complemented by a large hall of tanks and presses agleam with steel and the newest technology. Ably assisted by his cellarmaster Josef Knorr, he uses ambient yeasts, either strains frozen from previous vintages or samples taken from small, preharvested lots of grapes. These are fermented and then injected into other musts to start fermentation. Gentle presses and careful treatment of the unfiltered must are further hallmarks of this winery.

Not a single mediocre wine leaves the Bründlmayer estate, and from the simple Leicht & Trocken ("Light and Dry") up to the heavy guns, the white wines set a yardstick for every vintage. Bründlmayer also produces good red wine, but even his most careful Pinot Noir or Cabernet finds it impossible to compete with the Rieslings and Veltliners.

There is a large range of wines, so I will mention only the top flight. Grüner Veltliner Alte Reben ("Old Vines") is matured in new oak barrels, but being rich in extract the wine is not overwhelmed by the wood: it is a deep and powerful wine with many layers of gradually evolving fruit aromas. The Grüner Veltliner Ried Lamm, aged in large acacia barrels for nine months and always harvested late, is more baroque in its aromatic profile: it offers a bewildering array of finesse, spice, and ripe fruit notes, even if at up to 14.5 degrees of alcohol it can be almost overwhelming. Also very fine is the creamy Grüner Veltliner Käferberg, equally powerful, though less marked by wood and with profound grapefruit and tobacco notes.

Grown on the primary rock soils of the Kamptal's most famous vine-yard, the Riesling Zöbinger Heiligenstein is aged for up to one year in large vats and shows a wonderfully aristocratic aromatic profile of yellow blossoms and mineral profundity. Two wines still exceed it in density and refinement: the miraculously concentrated Riesling Heiligenstein Lyra (from the lyre-trained vines) and the Riesling Heiligenstein Alte Reben, one of the world's great Rieslings. All of these wines are made to improve with age, and vertical tastings back to 1947 (when winemaking here was not what it is today) have borne out the extraordinary potential of these wines. The Bründlmayer list is rounded off by a very interesting, cool and elegant Chardonnay, a classic-method sparkling wine, and several reds. The Pinot Noir Cecile is in a simpler mould than the great whites, while Anselm (St Laurent/Zweigelt) shows good, deep, berry fruit and smoky aromas; it is one of the Kamptal's best reds. Whenever possible, Bründlmayer also makes sweet wines, which can be phenomenal.

EHN

Bahnstrasse 3, 3550 Langenlois. Tel: 02734 2236. Fax: 02734 22364. www.ehnwein.at. Vineyards: 12 ha. White: Grüner Veltliner, Riesling, Gelber

Muskateller, Sauvignon Blanc, Gemischter Satz. Red: Zweigelt.

Brother-and-sister team Ludwig and Michaela Ehn run this consistent, and consistently interesting, estate in the middle of Langenlois. Their Grüner Veltliner Titan shows intense minerality and beautifully integrated wood, while the Riesling Heiligenstein Reserve is dense and well-defined, with complex aromas and good length. Perhaps the finest wine is the Jubliäumswein, a fragrant *Gemischter Satz* with a beautiful play of aromas, individual and long.

EICHINGER

Langenloiser Strasse 365, 3491 Strass. Tel: 02735 56480. Fax: 02735 56488.
Website: www.weingut-eichinger.at. Vineyards: 8 ha. White grapes: Grüner
Veltliner, Riesling, Roter Veltliner, Chardonnay.

Birgitt Eichinger's finely wrought wines are becoming more and more interesting, and she has produced several series notable for their elegance and stylish fruit. Next to a beautiful Riesling Heiligenstein with complex stone-fruit and holly aromas and perfectly judged balance, she makes very good Chardonnay, particularly Strasser Gaisberg, ripe with stewed-apple tones and lively acidity, and Strasser Stangl, a denser, even more complex wine. The Grüner Veltliner Gaisberg, too, shows classic fruit and fine structure.

SCHLOSS GOBELSBURG

Schlossstrasse 16, 3550 Gobelsburg. Tel: 02734 2422. Fax: 02734 24220.
Website: www.gobelsburg.at. Vineyards: 38 ha. White grapes: Grüner Veltliner,
Riesling. Red grapes: Zweigelt, Pinot Noir, St Laurent, Merlot.

Schloss Gobelsburg is a beautiful baroque castle belonging to the monastery of Zwettl. It has an eighteenth-century feel to it, especially in the upper floors, which double as a museum. As befitting a castle, it has a long and varied history leading back to Celtic settlements in the area. It has been associated with wine production since 1074, and was taken over by the Zwettl Abbey in the late seventeenth century after the then-owner had ruined himself with an ambitious (and charming) renovation programme; he joined the order on condition that it took over his debts together with his possessions.

During the twentieth century, there was a good spell followed by a steep decline, which was halted in 1996 when Michael Moosbrugger together with Willi Bründlmayer leased the castle and vineyards. Moosbrugger is not from a wine-growing family. He studied philosophy and music until he was forced to help in the family hotel after the death of his father. It was here that his fascination with wine began, a fascination which led him first to Lausanne, and then be an assistant at the Salomon and Jamek estates. When Gobelsburg announced that it was looking for a new winemaker, he knew that his chance had come.

Today this is an exemplary estate, and Moosbrugger's constant quest for perfection and for rediscovering forgotten winemaking knowledge also make him one of the most interesting winemakers to talk to about the Kamptal, and about winemaking. There is a discreet opulence in all these wines, particularly in the case of the Veltliners. The Grüner Veltliner Renner is long and dense with notes of grapefruit and black pepper. It serves as an introduction to the great Veltliners of the estate, Lamm and Grub, both complex and as rich in aromas as an oriental spice shop. The former wine is perhaps more elegant and expressive, the latter often needing more time to open up. Among the Veltiners, the Heiligenstein, with its delicate, mineral aromas, is a good foil to the Riesling Alte Reben, a dazzling wine with amazing concentration and length. In recent vintages, Moosbrugger has enlarged his repertoire with a fascinating glimpse back into history. His Riesling and Grüner Veltliner Tradition are made with techniques that could have been used around 1800. The wines develop an outstanding richness of secondary aromas and a towering individuality. They often have some residual sugar as the fermentation stops by itself. They can be oxidative because they are vinified in large wood, but these are wines fascinating not just for their historical interest, but for their quality.

HIEDLER

Am Rosenhügel 13, 3550 Langenlois. Tel: 02734 2468. Fax: 02734 24685. www.hiedler.at. Vineyards: 25 ha. White grapes: Grüner Veltliner, Riesling, Sauvignon Blanc, Chardonnay, Pinot Blanc. Red grapes: Pinot Noir.

With immense patience and energy, Ludwig and Maria Angeles Hiedler have built up their family estate to be among Austria's finest. A perfectionist who will take considerable risks to get the best possible quality and maturity, Ludwig is determined to tease out all the expression and variety his outstanding terroirs can offer. He uses industrial yeasts which, he believes, have a smaller and more controllable influence on aroma. The greatest of his wines is his Grüner Veltliner Maximum, which has wonderful depth and delicacy; its fine floral and mineral notes make one forget its power. The Grüner Veltliner Thal Novemberlese shows great aromatic precision and concentration, but often needs some bottle age to open up fully. The deep and mineral Riesling Heiligenstein can seem almost austere in its aromatic transparency, while the Riesling Maximum has the same concentration underlaid with even greater minerality. Both improve with age. Also fine is the Pinot Blanc Maximum with its ringingly pure pear and apple notes.

HIRSCH

Hauptstrasse 76, 3493 Kammern. Tel: 02735 2460. Fax: 02735 36089. Website: www.weingut-hirsch.at. Vineyards: 25 ha. White grapes: Grüner Veltliner, Riesling.

Hannes Hirsch is one of Austria's cosmopolitan young winemakers and has spent time working vineyards in California, Australia, Chile, New Zealand, and South Africa. This openness has led him to concentrate on Austrian classics: he produces only Grüner Veltliner and Riesling, and those only in three variations each.

Careful thought has been invested in every detail here, from the high density of vines (5,500 per hectare) and vineyard work according to organic principles, to picking in small boxes, exclusive reliance on natural yeasts, slow vinification, bottling only in July to give the wines time to develop, and a total changeover to screwcaps to guarantee aromatic purity. This last decision caused something of a scandal in Austria, but the results are entirely convincing. As for the analytical details of the wines (something of a fetish with some wine-lovers) Hirsch cheerfully admits that he has no idea. "I don't have a laboratory and I don't look at the official analyses," he comments. "Either the wine is good or it isn't, no matter how much residual sugar or acidity it has."

The rocky soils of the Lamm, Gaisberg, and Heiligenstein vineyards find expression in the aromatic purity of three single-vineyard wines. Grüner Veltliner Lamm can be austerely mineral in its youth, but its immense, pure length shows it to be a wine of great potential that needs bottle age. The elegant, delicately honeyed Riesling Gaisberg shows great mineral length, while the Riesling Heiligenstein is a masterpiece of purity and complexity, whose great length plays with aromas of stone-fruit and spring blossom. It is a wine that will only open up fully several years after bottling.

JURTSCHITSCH (SONNHOF)

Rudolfstrasse 39, 3550 Langenlois. Tel: 02734 21160. Fax: 02734 211611.
Website: www.jurtschitsch.com. Vineyards: 60 ha plus bought-in grapes. White
grapes: Grüner Veltliner, Riesling, Chardonnay, Pinot Blanc, Sauvignon Blanc. Red
grapes: Pinot Noir, Zweigelt, Merlot.

Led by the inseparable Jurtschitsch brothers, this estate is one of the
major players in the area, and was the first to cultivate its vineyards
organically: it started during the 1970s. It is famous for its old and
cavernous cellars, but recent investments have made sure that work
above ground is very modern, allowing cellarmaster Paul Jurtschitsch to
do everything necessary for reaching the qualities required. The
assortment of wines produced here is very impressive and reaches from
simple drinking wines to top growths.

The aristocratic Riesling Alte Reben has fine, floral aromas, and ages
well. The Grüner Veltliner Spiegel plays on the typical aromas of grapefruit, oriental spice, and caramel and shows beautiful purity on the
length. Also very well made, the Grüner Veltliner Schenkenbichl is built
around citrus, pepper, and eucalyptus, with a fine finale.

LEITHNER

Walterstrasse 46, 3550 Langenlois. Tel: 02734 2552. Fax: 02734 25524.
www.thomas-leithner.at. Vineyards: 10 ha. White grapes: Grüner Veltliner, Riesling,
Traminer, Neuburger, Chardonnay. Red grapes: Zweigelt.

Thomas Leithner is the great-nephew of the famous Dr Zweigelt, whose
eponymous newly bred variety conquered Austria in the inter-war years.
Leithner has made it his mission to make fine wine from this grape, and
his Hommage is a great success, a plummy but elegant wine with aromas
of cedar and red fruit, generous and with fine length. Among the whites,
his Grüner Veltliner Privat excels with its fine, racy nose, attractive grapefruit tones, and good, generous structure.It is a big-boned wine that bears
its weight well.

LOIMER

Haindorfer Vögerlweg 23, 3550 Langenlois. Tel: 02734 2239. Fax: 02734
22394. Website: www.loimer.at. Vineyards: 28 ha. White grapes: Grüner Veltliner,
Riesling, Chardonnay, Pinot Blanc, Pinot Gris. Red grapes: Cabernet Sauvignon,
Pinot Noir.

During the late 1990s, Loimer was known for his incredibly rich and
exotic, overripe wines, at times kissing the fifteen-degree mark in a wild,

alcoholic embrace that sent the critics into ecstasies. I myself was never taken with this style, and it is a welcome surprise to see that his ideals have evolved. Now ensconced in a hyper-modern black cube in the middle of his organically tended vineyards – the new structure is built over the old cellars and is gravity-fed – Loimer is making wines that establish him in the international class.

He has vineyards in several important *Rieden*, such as Käferberg, Seeberg, Spiegel, Steinmassl, and Dechant. Despite his fine and complex Grüner Veltliner Käferberg, he is revealing himself as a Riesling expert. The delicate and multi-faceted Seeberg is full of aromatic finesse and elegance, but it is the bewitching Riesling Steinmassl that really shows his art, with its subtle nose of white flowers and fresh rhubarb, mineral purity on the palate, and honeyed gracefulness on the finish. In addition to this, Loimer also makes an outstanding blend of Chardonnay and Pinot Blanc that shows luscious marzipan and mature fruit combined with a sophisticated caramel undertones. In a joint venture with some Thermenregion friends, he also produces a pure, wood-aged Chardonnay Loimer and Friends, which shows outstanding fruit and a creamy structure that promise a long life. Another wine that has evolved in leaps and bounds from its rustic beginnings is the now highly polished Pinot Noir, whose autumnal elegance and notes of clover, berries, and dry leaves are a wonderful portent.

RABL

Weraingraben 10, 3550 Langenlois. Tel: 02734 2303. Fax: 02734 230310.
Website: www.weingut-rabl.at. Vineyards: 55 ha. White grapes: Grüner Veltliner, Riesling, Chardonnay, Sauvignon Blanc, Gelber Muskateller, Traminer. Red grapes: Zweigelt, Merlot.

Rudolf Rabl's wines have, in recent years, seen a considerable rise in quality. The flinty, almost Chablis-like Grüner Veltliner Spiegel is an interesting and attractive wine with citrus and mineral tones. The Riesling Vinum Optimum shows good, fresh peach and exotic tones, an elegant wine that is a little tight in youth. More successful is the fine Traminer Auslese, almost too opulent and floral, with notes of bitter almond. The sweet wines lack sophistication, as does the estate Zweigelt.

SCHNEIDER-COBANESHOF

Weinstrasse 37, 3550 Gobelsburg. Tel: 02734 25640. Fax: 02734 25644.
Website: www.fescherkampl.at. Vineyards: 8 ha. White grapes: Grüner Veltliner,

Riesling, Chardonnay. Red grapes: Pinot Noir.

One of the growing number of organic producers in Austria, Gerald Schneider is beginning to make a name for himself with wines like his delicate Riesling Heiligenstein, whose generous tones of white blossoms and peach gives it the edge over the Grüner Veltliner Steinsetz, an equally well-crafted, but more rustic wine.

STEININGER

Walterstrasse 2, 3550 Langenlois. Tel: 02734 2372. Fax: 02734 237211. Website: www.weingut-steininger.at. Vineyards: 22 ha. White grapes: Grüner Veltliner, Riesling, Sauvignon Blanc, Pinot Blanc, Chardonnay, Traminer. Red grapes: Zweigelt, Merlot, Pinot Noir.

Karl Steininger makes a series of typically regional wines, among which are the intense and floral Grüner Veltliner Grand Grü and the Grüner Veltliner Novemberlese, a wine of aristocratic elegance and beautiful length. His Riesling Novemberlese, too, shows an attractive marriage of elegance and generosity. Steininger's main claim to fame, however, is his range of sparkling wines, from the peach and rose-scented Riesling to a Grüner Veltliner that beautifully reinterprets the grape, a baroque and lovely Traminer, a creamy Burgundersekt (Chardonnay/Pinot Blanc/Pinot Noir) and, recently, an animating Cabernet Sauvignon rosé.

TOPF

Placher Kellergasse 420, 3491 Strass im Strassertal. Tel: 02735 2491. Fax: 02735 249191. Website: www.weingut.topf.at. Vineyards: 29 ha. White grapes: Grüner Veltliner, Riesling, Sauvignon Blanc, Chardonnay, Traminer. Red grapes: Zweigelt, Cabernet Sauvignon, Pinot Noir.

For over a decade now, Johann Topf has continuously invested everything it takes to make great wine from new, high-density vineyard plantings to renovations in the winery. These gradual changes were accompanied by a rise in quality, and his elegant, mineral Riesling Wechselberg Spiegel demonstrates that his efforts have paid off. Notable among his other wines are Grüner Veltliner Ofenberg, with dense, varietal fruit and good persistence on the palate, and the Grüner Veltliner Alte Reben Hasel, powerful, compact, and vinified in new oak.

WEIXELBAUM

Weinbergweg 196, 3491 Strass im Strassertal. Tel: 02735 2269. Fax: 02735 226916. Website: www.vinoweix.at. Vineyards: 15 ha. White grapes: Grüner

Veltliner, Riesling, Sauvignon Blanc, Chardonnay, Pinot Blanc, Müller-Thurgau. Red grapes: Blauer Portugieser, Zweigelt.

A traditional producer, Heinz Weixelbaum concentrates on producing good, clean, terroir wines. His best come from the Gaisberg, adjacent to the Heiligenstein. Concentrated and with notes of Christmas spice and mature fruit, his Riesling Gaisberg is a fine and individual representative of this grape. From the same vineyard, his Grüner Veltliner Wahre Werte is generous and animatingly spiced. Good, too, is the Pinot Blanc Gaisberg with lovely tones of green apple and boiled sweets.

KREMSTAL
Vineyards: 2,176 hectares.
Soils: primary rock, loess, sand, gravel.
White grapes (eighty-six per cent): Grüner Veltliner, Riesling, Chardonnay, Roter Veltliner, Müller-Thurgau, Neuburger.
Red grapes (fourteen per cent): Zweigelt, Pinot Noir.

The picturesque town of Krems is situated by the banks of the Danube on the eastern edge of the Wachau, and it marks the beginning of the Kremstal to the east and northwest. Krems is one of the oldest documented Austrian settlements, mentioned first, as "*urbs chremisa*", in 995 AD, and has always played an important role in winemaking and the wine trade. During the Middle Ages, three-quarters of the population of the town lived off their vines. A number of fine Gothic and baroque buildings bear testimony to its wealth. A school of viticulture was founded here in 1975 and is still carrying on with its work.

In terms of climate and soil, the Kremstal, a slice barely fifteen kilometres (nine miles) wide, is very similar to the Kamptal, with loam and loess soil, and some sand and gravel, with large gravel deposits in lower vineyards. Chalky loess terraces are another characteristic of the area.

Protected by hills and by the Waldviertel to the northeast, the Kremstal benefits from warm, Pannonian air in summer, while the same weather systems can bring cold air in the winter, pushing temperatures very low, especially away from the river banks. Annual mean temperatures are around 9.6°C (49.2°F), while the annual mean rainfall increases as one goes up the hills, from just under 520 millimetres (20.5 inches) by the river to 750 millimetres (29.5 inches) on the hilltops. The

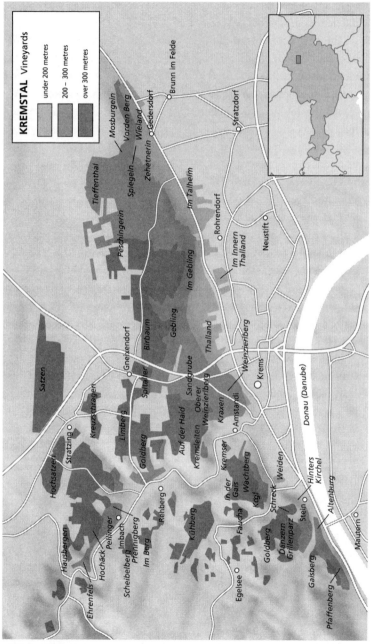

vi Kremstal

meeting of continental and Pannonian climates can produce great differences in weather between individual hills and vineyards.

The best vineyards around the city of Krems are Pfaffenberg to the east, part of which officially belongs to the Wachau, though the soil is identical on both sides. Most of the wines grown on this site are still bottled anonymously by the region's big cooperative, the Winzer Krems.

Steiner Goldberg and Steiner Hund are on opposite sides of the same hill. While Goldberg is dominated by sandy soils on crystalline sub-soil, Ried Hund has more sandy loess. The Kremstaler Kreuzberg is known for its Grüner Veltliner, which grows on gravel and crystalline soil.

The Rieden to the northeast of Krems are not as distinguished, and usually larger. Two of the most important ones are Thalland and Weinzierlberg, both dating back to the Middle Ages. Thalland has black earth on loess and gravel, while Weinzierl is dominated by loam, loess, gravel, and even clay. The Sandgrube is not, as the name would suggest, exclusively sandy, but is dominated by loam, gravel, and loess.

Rohendorf, away from the Danube and toward Langenlois, is home to the gigantic Lenz Moser winery. The village has some good vineyards, especially Rohrendorfer Gebling with weathered terraces, loess, and gravel. Ried Paschingerin has loess soil, as does Thalland.

Senftenberg is directly to the north of Krems. The vineyards are largely cultivated by part-time wine-growers, with one glorious exception: Martin Nigl, who makes some very remarkable wines here. Loam, loess, and gravel dominate, with some weathered crystalline rock soil. Good vineyards are Ehrenfelser, Emmerlingtal, Gartl, Stratzingbach, Hochäcker, Kremsleithen, Pellingen, and Rammeln.

About a third of the Kremstal vineyard is on the southern bank on the Danube, around the villages of Furth, Thallern, and Hollenburg. Most of these are at the foot of the hilly landscape which blends into the Traisental. Loess soils tend to make up the best vineyards, though there are also sandy soils, gravel, and loam. The more distinguished Rieden in this area are Spiegeln, Vordern Berg, Kogl, and Hochrain.

Top growers

BUCHEGGER

Weinbergstrasse 9, 3494 Gedersdorf. Tel & Fax: 02735 8969. Website: www.buchegger.at. Vineyards: 9 ha. White grapes: Grüner Veltliner, Riesling,

Chardonnay. Red grapes: Zweigelt, Merlot, Cabernet Sauvignon.

Walter Buchegger makes some of Lower Austria's most stylish wines. His Riesling Moosburgerin achieves a mineral density and floral expressiveness that is little short of miraculous, especially as there are few other distinguished wines from this *Ried*. Also excellent, with elegance and complexity, are his Grüner Veltliner Pfarrweingarten and the stunning Grüner Veltliner Reserve Leopold, a wine of ringing complexity and deep mineral aromas, sold only under screwcap and in magnums.

DOCKNER

Ortsstrasse 30, 3511 Furth-Höbenbach. Tel: 02736 7262. Fax: 02736 72624. Website: www.dockner.at. Vineyards: 30 ha. White grapes: Grüner Veltliner, Riesling, Chardonnay, Pinot Gris, Sauvignon Blanc, Gelber Muskateller. Red grapes: Zweigelt, St Laurent, Cabernet Sauvignon, Merlot, Pinot Noir.

Dockner father and son, both called Josef, are constantly improving the wines on this traditional estate and in recent years several have been very good. The intensely floral Riesling Rosengarten Reserve is a particular favourite. Also very interesting are the generous and well-balanced Chardonnay Vollmondlese, and a beautifully multi-layered Grüner Veltliner Lusthausberg.

FORSTREITER

Kirchengasse 7, 3506 Krems-Hollenburg. Tel: 02739 2296. Fax: 02739 22964. www.forstreiter.com. Vineyards: 14 ha. White: Grüner Veltliner, Riesling, Chardonnay, Gelber Muskateller. Red: Zweigelt, St Laurent.

A very reliable and consistent producer, Meinhard Forstreiter makes Grüner Veltliners with traditional, clear pepper and citrus fruit. Particularly good are the punchy Grüner Veltliner Tabor and Grüner Veltliner Schiefer, whose slate soils shine through their mineral backbone.

HAGEN

Seilerweg 45, 3503 Krems-Rehberg. Tel: 02732 78160. Fax: 02732 78164. Website: www.weingut-hagen.at. Vineyards: 13 ha. White grapes: Grüner Veltliner, Riesling, Pinot Blanc, Chardonnay. Red grapes: Zweigelt.

The Kremstal needs young and ambitious producers like Anton Hagen, who is transforming this traditional estate into a provider of increasingly good wines. His Grüner Veltliner Alte Reben shows astonishing mineral complexity and fine herbal notes, while his Riesling Pfaffenberg is one of the few to extract the minerality and floral grace this terroir has to offer, a wine of great potential and cut-glass fruit, as well as a bargain.

WEINGUT DER STADT KREMS

Stadtgraben 11, 3500 Krems. Tel: 02732 801440. Fax: 02732 801442. Website: www.weingutstadtkrems.at. Vineyards: 30 ha. White grapes: Grüner Veltliner, Riesling, Pinot Blanc, Chardonnay. Red grapes: Zweigelt.

When in 2003 the Freie Weingärtner Wachau made the mistake of parting with its team of directors, the Weingut der Stadt Krems, a traditional producer of modest wines, had the great good sense immediately to engage Fritz Miesbauer to breathe new life into its 550-year-old estate. Miesbauer embarked on an extensive programme of renovations and changes in working practice, which began to show results with the 2005 vintage. While it is impossible to work miracles overnight, I have been impressed by the purity and clarity of individual wines; they are a great improvement on previous years. The late-harvest Grüner Veltliner Wachtberg shines with perfect varietal fruit, and the Riesling Kögl demonstrates great style and mineral depth, as does the more elegant Riesling Grillenparz.

MALAT

3511 Palt 27. Tel: 02732 82934. Fax: 02732 8293413. Website: www.malat.at. Vineyards: 38 ha. White grapes: Grüner Veltliner, Pinot Blanc, Riesling, Chardonnay. Red grapes: Cabernet Sauvignon, Merlot, Pinot Noir, St Laurent.

Gerald Malat is a pioneer in the Kremstal and has probably created more new wine styles more successfully than anyone else in the area. He produces a bewilderingly large array of wines, mirroring his taste for going to the edge of the possible, both in the vineyard and the cellar. His Riesling Das Beste is dense and exotic in character, not a typical Riesling by any means, but an attractive wine. Its twin brother Grüner Veltliner Das Beste shows more depth with fine apple and citrus flavours, and good length. Also very interesting is Sauvignon Blanc Brunnenkreuz, a wine with filigree gooseberry fruit and beautiful persistence. By comparison, Malat's red wines seem more rustic and frequently overoaked. Best of the bunch is the warm Cabernet Sauvignon with its mulled-wine aromas and berry tones.

MANTLERHOF

Hauptstrasse 50, 3494 Brunn im Felde. Tel: 02735 8248. Fax: 02735 824833.

Website: www.mantlerhof.com. Vineyards: 14 ha. White grapes: Grüner Veltliner, Riesling, Roter Veltliner, Chardonnay.

Sepp Mantler's intellectual tastes let him engage in intense debates about the minutiae of winemaking, and his restless spirit expresses itself in his always beautiful and often individual wines. His Roter Veltliner was a little on the reductive side when I last tasted it, but his fresh and intriguingly spiced Grüner Veltliner Spiegel is always one of the finest wines in the area. The citrus, fragrant Riesling Zehentnerin and the more playful Riesling Tiefenthal, floral with honeysuckle and apricot on the nose, are also fine. All of Mantler's wines are very attractively priced, and his passion for old wines, backed up by a cellar of old Mantler vintages, demonstrates that his are wines made to age gracefully.

MAYR (VORSPANNHOF)

Herrengasse 48, 3552 Dross bei Krems. Tel: 02719 2342. Fax: 02719 23424. Website: www.vorspannhof-mayr.at. Vineyards: 10 ha. White grapes: Grüner Veltliner, Riesling, Sauvignon Blanc, Chardonnay, Gelber Muskateller.

Tucked away in the village of Dross (not otherwise known for great wines) Anton Mayr and his daughter Silke create excellent wines full of character and individuality, and at very reasonable prices. The finest among them is perhaps the Riesling Marthal, a wine of substance, fragrant and playful in its aromatic spectrum, with lovely mineral notes and elegant, mature acidity. Also very beautiful is the Grüner Veltliner Loiser Weg, a wine characterized by herbaceous tones and elegant, balanced fruit. Grown on loess soils, it is a little fatter than examples from more stony soils, but this ample structure suits it perfectly. Deeper and more concentrated, the Grüner Veltliner Gebling shows pure fruit. Also recommendable are the ripe, exotic though more rustic Sauvignon Blancs.

SEPP MOSER

Untere Wiener Strasse 1, 3495 Rohrendorf bei Krems. Tel: 02732 70531. Fax: 02732 70510. www.sepp-moser.at. Vineyards: 23 ha in Rohrendorf, 28 ha in Apetlon, Neusiedlersee. White grapes: Grüner Veltliner, Riesling, Chardonnay, Sauvignon Blanc, Pinot Blanc, Muskat Ottonel. Red grapes: Zweigelt, Merlot, Cabernet Sauvignon, Cabernet Franc.

Niki Moser heads one of the largest independent estates in the region (even if half of his land is around Apetlon, in the Burgenland) on which he produces a series of wines that is always reliable and can, in individual cases, be exceptional. Among the Kremstal wines, his Riesling Gebling shows pure varietal fruit and good concentration while his Sauvignon Blanc Atrium has beautifully mature fruit. From the Burgenland, Banfalu (Zweigelt/Merlot/Cabernet Sauvignon/Cabernet Franc) shows good berry fruit and smoky aromas typical of that region.

LENZ MOSER

Lenz-Moser-Strasse 1, 3495 Rohrendorf. Tel: 02732 85541. Fax: 02732 85900. Website: www.lenzmoser.at. Vineyards: 2,500 ha, most under contract. Grape varieties: all major Austrian grapes.

If the Lenz Moser winery is mentioned here, it is only that, with 3,000 grape producers and 2,000 hectares under contract, and with 16 million bottles produced each year, it is by far the largest player in the country. Unfortunately, the drive for top quality that has seized much of Austrian wine has yet to reach this house, which continues to produce a large variety of mass-market wines without exploiting the enormous potential of its vineyards. For their price, these wines are perfectly acceptable and competently made, but there is no discernable ambition to excel.

NIGL

Kirchenberg 1, 3541 Senftenberg. Tel: 02719 2609. Fax: 02719 26094. Website: www.weingutnigl.at. Vineyards: 25 ha. White grapes: Grüner Veltliner, Riesling, Chardonnay, Müller-Thurgau, Sauvignon Blanc. Red grape: Zweigelt.

With immense determination and great skill, Martin Nigl has transformed his family's small, traditional estate into the Kremstal's premier producer of great wine. On his steep Senftenberg vineyard in the far north of the region, where the climate is already influenced by the cool Waldviertel, Nigl manages to capture a crystalline mineral depth that so far eludes other producers. Two Grüner Veltliners and two Rieslings serve as an illustration of what this region as a whole may be able to attain. The Grüner Veltliner Senftenberger Piri shows flinty depth and aromas of plum and quince, combined with immense length, while the Grüner Veltliner Privat is even more concentrated, deep, and wonderfully elegant, though it needs some bottle age to unlock its full range of aromas. Among the Rieslings, Kremsleiten has an almost austere minerality with classic notes of apricot and orange peel, profound, elegant, and long. The complex and imposing Riesling Privat is more mature in its aromatic spectrum and seems the perfect expression of its granite-rich terroir. The Gelber Muskateller and the gooseberryish Sauvignon Blanc are charming in their fruit-driven elegance. The Zweigelt Eichberg shows classic structure and spicy fruit, a fine wine from a region not known for its reds.

PROIDL

Oberer Markt 5, 3541 Senftenberg. Tel: 02719 2458. Fax: 02719 24584.
Vineyards: 16 ha. White grapes: Grüner Veltliner, Riesling, Müller-Thurgau. Red grapes: Cabernet Sauvignon, St Laurent, Zweigelt.

Not many winemakers openly admit to not liking wine-tasting, but Franz Proidl is never one to care about appearances. What he does care about passionately, though, are the wines and vineyards of Senftenberg. Proidl has a somewhat eccentric but successful approach to winemaking, which involves letting the fermentation take care of itself and accepting the fluctuations in vintage character and quality that entails. In so doing he produces wines of exceptionally individual character, understandably often with some residual sweetness, among which are a fine Riesling Ehrenfels with honeyed fruit and beautiful mineral notes, a fine, elegant Riesling vom Urgestein, and a very lovely, succulent Riesling Hochäcker.

SALOMON (UNDHOF)

Undstrasse 10, 3504 Krems-Stein. Tel: 02732 83226. Fax: 02732 8322678.
Website: www.undhof.at. Vineyards: 25 ha. White grapes: Grüner Veltliner, Riesling, Traminer.

Until the return of Berthold Salomon, a former wine merchant and director of the Austrian Wine Marketing Board, to the family estate, the Undhof was known for solid but rarely spectacular wines. Salomon (who also produces wine in Australia and divides his time between the two sides of the globe) is a force of nature and under his guidance working processes have been revised and quality is improving rapidly. Pure and fragrant, the Grüner Veltliner Lindberg takes its inspiration from a Wachau Smaragd, while the Riesling Kögl Reserve shows lovely notes of green apple. Finest of all, the Riesling Pfaffenberg is a wine of mineral clarity, white peach aromas, and great persistence on the palate.

SCHMID

Obere Hauptstrasse 89, 3552 Stratzing bei Krems. Tel: 02719 8288. Fax: 02719 8218. Website: www.j-schmid.at. Vineyards: 10 ha. White grapes: Grüner Veltliner, Riesling, Gelber Muskateller, Chardonnay. Red grapes: Zewigelt.

Josef Schmid is one of the more ambitious producers in the Kremstal hinterland, and the clear, mineral purity of his wines makes them stand out.

Deep and long, the Grüner Veltliner Reserve shows all the classic aromas, while the Grüner Veltliner Galgenberg is more fragrant, with aromas of roses and delicate acidity. Also very good are the Riesling Weinzierlberg, a well structured, mineral wine with typical varietal fruit; and the house's top wine, Riesling Sunogeln, elegant and with green-apple aromas.

TRAISENTAL

Vineyards: 683 hectares.
Soils: loess, loam, gravel, granulite and chalky conglomerates.
White grapes (eighty-six per cent): Grüner Veltliner, Müller-Thurgau, Chardonnay, Pinot Blanc, Riesling, Neuburger.
Red grapes (fourteen per cent): Blauer Portugieser, Zweigelt, Blauburger.

Until 1995 Traisental was part of the Traismauer-Carnuntum region, which later became Donauland-Carnuntum – a series of changes that testifies to administrative helplessness when it comes to grouping together Lower Austria's large and varied wine areas, with their relatively few estates. About 700 growers cultivate as many hectares of land, few with very interesting results. Indeed, only three per cent of the growers in Traisental, bottle their own wines.

The Traisental is a valley along the river Traisen, south of the Danube and north of the town of St Pölten. Most of the vineyards are situated in a band along the Hollenburger Wald on the west side of the village of Nussdorf, which was first mentioned as a wine-growing village in 1083. The soils on the right bank of the river are dominated by loess and loam, while the left bank toward the Dunkelsteiner Wald also has some areas of granulite and chalky conglomerates.

Almost two-thirds of the wines are Grüner Veltliner, with only about fourteen per cent red varieties planted. The climate is very similar to that of the Donauland, unsurprisingly, as the area is only ten kilometres (6.2 miles) long and is a direct continuation of the Donauland. Pannonian influences prevail, while the Danube exercises a regulatory influence on the north of the area. It is bordered to the west by the Dunkelsteiner Wald, a wooded region blocking the way of the warm, Pannonian air and therefore forming a natural bar to wine production to the west. Annual rainfall is around 520 millimetres (20.5 inches).

That it is possible to produce excellent wines in this area is demonstrated by Ludwig Neumayer, the one grower from here to have attracted attention over the last few years. His estate is in Inzersdorf, where loam and loess dominate the soil.

Top grower

NEUMAYER

Inzersdorf ob der Traisen 22, 3130 Herzogenburg. Tel & Fax: 02782 82985. Website: www.weinvomstein.at. Vineyards: 8 ha. White grapes: Grüner Veltliner, Pinot Blanc, Riesling, Sauvignon Blanc, Chardonnay. Red grapes: St Laurent, Pinot Noir.

While his colleagues in the Traisental are still struggling, Ludwig Neumayer has established himself as one of Austria's best producers. He manages to make white wines that can give the best Wachau estates a run for their money. They seem to be almost exclusively a product of Neumayer's intelligence, will, and determination. It is therefore hardly surprising that the wines themselves are eccentric, such as a barrique-aged Grüner Veltliner, a beautifully complex wine made partly from over-ripe grapes.

His best wines are called Der Wein vom Stein ("wine from the rock"), a refreshing change from the more fanciful designations found elsewhere. The Grüner Veltliner is mighty and complex, almost overpowering when young, with notable oak, and often made as a Spätlese. The Riesling has deep fruit notes and good mineral characteristics, a particular achievement in this area. The Riesling Rothenbart is if anything slightly deeper and more complex than its colleague Vom Stein, while the Sauvignon Blanc vom Stein shows beautiful complexity and berry fruit.

DONAULAND

Vineyards: 2,732 hectares.
Soils: loess, gravel, loam.
White grapes (eighty-three per cent): Grüner Veltliner, Riesling, Pinot Blanc, Roter Veltliner.
Red grapes (seventeen per cent): Zweigelt, Blauer Portugieser, Blauburger.

Named almost by default, and successor to various other administrative districts, the Donauland is the stretch of land separating Vienna from the

Kamptal and Kremstal on the north bank of the Danube, and from the Traisental on the south bank.

Klosterneuburg, with its splendid monastery, its vineyards and its school of viticulture, is the most important town in the region. Indeed, the influence of the Klosterneuburg school on Austrian wine is difficult to overestimate. Not only was Austria's most popular red grape, the Zweigelt, developed here, but the know-how acquired here by young growers travels into every corner of the country and has only recently been rivalled, if not superseded, by expertise brought back from abroad. A large proportion of young, aspiring growers still spend the last few years of their schooling at Klosterneuburg.

In terms of winemaking the Donauland falls into three parts. First of these is the Wagram on the north bank of the Danube, which has soils that are almost pure loess on gravel, with some pockets of loam and gravel near the surface. The Wagram hills and the foothills of the Manhartsberg open up the region to the influence of the continental, Pannonian climate, tempered by the proximity of the river Danube, which acts as a regulating influence on temperature and humidity.

Grüner Veltliner and Roter Veltliner especially take to these conditions very well. Most growers here cultivate vineyards as a part of mixed agri-culture, and there is a particularly strong trend toward organic practices. Some of the country's most innovative wines have come out of here recently, especially oak-aged Veltliners of great complexity, produced by an enthusiastic and talented group of young growers. These wines are often more rounded and more floral than the Grüner Veltliners of neighbouring Kamptal, and more complex than those of the Weinviertel; they make the Donauland one of the country's most dynamic regions.

In the eastern corner of the area, Klosterneuburg benefits from a protected climate. Weathered sandstone, loess, and loam determine the soil, and it has more chalky soils than the north bank. Mainly Riesling and Pinot Blanc are grown here. The Grossriedental, toward the Kamptal in the northwest, is famous for its Eiswein.

Top growers

BAUER

Neufang 52, 3483 Feuersbrunn am Wagram. Tel: 02738 2556. Fax:02738 77075. Website: www.josefbauer.at. Vineyards: 12 ha. White grapes: Grüner

Veltliner, Welschriesling, Riesling, Pinot Blanc, Chardonnay. Red grapes: Zweigelt, Blaufränkisch, Cabernet Sauvignon, Merlot.

Josef Bauer produces good, reliable Rieslings and Grüner Veltliners, the pick of them all being his Grüner Veltliner Spiegel Alte Reben, with its good, peppery fruit and hints of exotic aromas.

EHMOSER

3701 Tiefenthal 9. Tel & Fax: 02955 70442. Website: www.weingut-ehmoser.at. Vineyards: 10 ha. White grapes: Grüner Veltliner, Pinot Blanc. Red grapes: Zweigelt, St Laurent.

Only a few years ago, the young Josef Ehmoser burst onto the wine scene with one of Austria's most individual and intriguing Grüner Veltliners, Aurum, harvested in November and partly fermented in barrique. It's a daring, thoroughly successful wine marrying wood notes and Christmas spices and showing great ageing potential. He also makes a good Grüner Veltliner Hohenburg and an interesting Pinot Blanc.

FRITSCH

Oberstockstall 24, 3470 Kirchberg am Wagram. Tel: 02279 50370. Fax: 02279 503719. Website: www.fritsch.cc. Vineyards: 13 ha. White grapes: Grüner Veltliner, Riesling, Chardonnay, Pinot Blanc. Red grapes: Zweigelt, Blaufränkisch, Cabernet Sauvignon, Merlot.

Karl Fritsch is one of the most dynamic young winemakers in this young, dynamic region. His Grüner Veltliners, especially, have attracted attention with their minerality and distinctive profile. The best of the bunch is the elegant Grüner Veltliner Schlossberg, followed by Grüner Veltliner Steinberg, which puts more emphasis on classical fruit. The red wines, too, are getting better every year, especially the stylish, nervy Pinot Noir "P" and the blend Foggatal (Zweigelt/Cabernet Sauvignon/Merlot), which shows well-rounded, smooth fruit and an accomplished use of oak.

LETH

Kirchengasse 6, 3481 Fels am Wagram. Tel: 0238 2240. Fax: 0238 224017. Website: www.weingut-leth.at. Vineyards: 38 ha. White grapes: Grüner Veltliner, Riesling, Sauvignon Blanc, Gelber Muskateller, Roter Veltliner. Red grapes: Zweigelt, Pinot Noir, Cabernet Sauvignon.

The largest producer in the area, Franz Leth makes a range of impeccable wines with a heavy emphasis on whites, the best of which are called Lagenreserve. Among these the Grüner Veltliner Scheiben, partly vinified in new oak, is wonderfully individual and stylish and is characterized by deep, mineral fruit, creamy texture, and great potential. Also fine are the precise Grüner Veltliner Brunnthal and the Riesling Wagramterrassen, with elegant notes of peach and persistence on the palate. A rarity and regional speciality, Leth's Roter Veltliner offers more charming, exotic fruit, while the Sauvignon Blanc presents crystalline varietal flavours. Well-crafted red wines round off the series, most interesting among them being the deep, leather and plum Zweigelt Gigama and an elegant Pinot Noir, which is somewhat oak-dominated in its youth but whose fine tannins and extract give it good ageing potential.

WINZERHAUS OTT
Neufang 36, 3483 Feuersbrunn. Tel: 02738 2257. Fax: 02738 2257.22.
Website: www.ott.at. Vineyards: 16 ha. White grapes: Grüner Veltliner, Riesling, Sauvignon Blanc.

Bernhard Ott makes no compromise in his search for the perfect Veltliner. Among his well-focused range, the Grüner Veltliner Rosenberg always shows a wonderfully tender, floral note underlaid by mineral structure, while the Fass 4 is a more ample, rounder wine with almost baroque richness. Another facet of this grape is shown in Der Ott, a wine with wonderfully elegant spice and fine acidity.

SÖLLNER
Hauptstrasse 34, 3482 Gösing am Wagram. Tel: 02738 3201. Fax: 02738 3220.
www.weingut-soellner.at. Vineyards: 11 ha. White grapes: Grüner Veltliner, Riesling, Roter Veltliner. Red: Zweigelt, St Laurent.

The pioneers of Biodynamic agriculture in the area, Daniela Vigne and Toni Söllner believe in natural vinification and make most of their wines in large wooden barrels, without filtration. They produce a range of deeply satisfying wines with clear varietal fruit, the finest of which are the Grüner Veltliner Fumberg Reserve and the appealing Roter Veltliner Reserve, all herbaceous spiciness and delicate fruit.

WIMMER-CZERNY
Obere Marktstrasse 37, 3481 Fels am Wagram. Tel: 02738 2248. Fax: 02738 2244. Website: www.wimmer-czerny.at. Vineyards: 12 ha. White grapes: Grüner Veltliner, Riesling, Pinot Blanc, Traminer, Roter Veltliner. Red grapes: Zweigelt, Blaufränkisch, St Laurent.

Hans Czerny has changed over to organic production, and is one of the most reliable winemakers in the area: his Grüner Veltliners, fermented only with ambient yeasts, always show clear varietal character and good structure. The fine, creamy texture of the Grüner Veltliner Felser Berg Reserve makes it my consistent favourite among his wines.

VIENNA

Vineyards: 679 hectares.
Soils: slate, gravel, loam, loess.
White grapes (eighty-five per cent): Grüner Veltliner, Riesling, Pinot Blanc, Chardonnay, Welschriesling, Gemischter Satz, Müller-Thurgau, Neuburger, Sauvignon Blanc, Traminer, Frühroter Veltliner, Sylvaner, Muskat-Ottonel, Muskateller, Ritgipfler, Scheurebe, Roter Veltliner, Bouvier, Zierfandler.
Red grapes (fifteen per cent): Zweigelt, Pinot Noir, St Laurent, Blauburger, Blauer Portugieser, Cabernet Sauvignon, Blaufränkisch, Merlot, Syrah.

In Austrian wine law, Vienna forms an independent region, on a par with Lower Austria, the Burgenland, Styria, and the Bergland Österreich. However, for reasons explained in the introduction to this chapter, I will consider it along with the other regions of the Danube.

The city's wine pedigree is impeccable. The Celts made wine in their settlement of Vedunia, and the Romans did the same in their military port of Vindobona. Ever since then, wine has been made, sold, and drunk in Vienna, although in the reorganization of the city after the Turkish siege in 1683 the sale of wines was largely pushed out to the periphery.

Then in 1784 Emperor Joseph II officially recognized the local custom by which growers sold their home-produced wine and food in small inns called *Heurigen*, most of which are scattered around the wine-growing areas in the outskirts of the city. As the name *Heurige* ("this year's") suggests, the wines sold in these places are largely from the current vintage, though an "Alter", "last year's" wine, is usually also available. Traditionally (and despite the English saying that good wine needs no bush), the sign of a *Heurige* is a bunch of fir branches hung above the door. This also explains their alternative name, *Buschenschank*.

The custom is said to go back to Charlemagne, and it is still one of the best-loved aspects of life in the city. Today, many of these *Heurigen* are tourist traps to which people are delivered by the busload to be filled up with cheap wine and pushed out for the next lot, but it is still possible to find small, beautiful *Heurigen* used only by locals. Wine is sold by the jug or the glass and can at its best be utterly enchanting: greenish-gold, fresh and crisp, a wine that, to me, seems to capture women and song in a glass.

The Viennese have always liked their wine. During the Middle Ages, they drank up to six times more than they do now, which means that the average annual consumption in the city was well above 200 litres. In 1815 the annual consumption was eighty-seven litres per head. With rising taxes and the phylloxera catastrophe, wine consumption and cultivation in the capital collapsed dramatically, and at the end of the nineteenth century, the people of Vienna had more than halved the amount of wine they drank per year. This figure has declined even further: today Austrians drink around thirty litres of, mainly Austrian, wine per head per year. The nation has definitely sobered up.

The climate of Vienna is influenced by two things in particular: the Pannonian Plains in the east, and the river Danube. The river is an important tempering factor and protects against late frosts and other extremes of the Pannonian climate, which makes itself strongly felt here: summers are hot while winter temperatures are consistently around freezing point. The annual vegetation period is 255 days, and the annual mean rainfall around 660 millimetres (twenty-six inches).

Vienna has vineyards to the north of the city and in small parts of the south. Most are in the historic eighteenth and nineteenth districts, and across the Danube, in the twenty-first district.

The area under vine today is less than half what it was until 1950. Now, however, new vineyards are being planted again. Wines are still not commonly identified with *Rieden* here, though some individual vineyards have been known since the Middle Ages. The best vineyards in Vienna are situated on the hills to the north of the city, in and around the suburbs of Stammersdorf and Döbling.

Close to Stammersdorf, north of the Danube, the Bisamberg hill offers the best location for wine-growing on black earth, loess, and lighter sedimentary soils. The best-known *Rieden* here are Herrenholz, Kirchberg, Hochfeld, and In den Rothen, whose warmer mesoclimate suits Riesling.

Just to the north of the historic city centre are the suburbs of Döbling and Grinzing, where most Viennese wine is grown. With its panoramic view, the Kahlenberg is not only famous for its wines, but also for its walks and the many *Heurigen* here. The chalky Nussberg is the neighbouring hill, and its slightly steeper slopes as well as its immediate proximity to the heat-reflecting Danube make it Vienna's best vineyard. The neighbouring *Rieden* Burgstall and Collin have more loamy and sandy soils, as have the *Rieden* Preussen, Rosengartl, and Schoss. In Grinzing, Hungerberg, Reisenberg, and Schenkenberg, all sandy loam, and the more heavy, stony Sommereck and Steinberg are also good terroirs.

The majority of the wines grown around Vienna are produced for *Heurige* consumption and the emphasis is on uncomplicated wines for early drinking. A quarter of the total production is Grüner Veltliner. Some younger growers have broken out of the straightjacket of *Heurige* production and, even though they still operate *Heurigen*, they are producing much more ambitious wines, which are at times aged in oak for greater complexity. Riesling and Chardonnay have most potential here, as Grüner Veltliner tends to become too broad in its aromas. An old custom that has recently been rehabilitated (especially by Fritz Wieninger) is the planting of mixed vineyards, the *Gemischter Satz*, which can produce wines of astonishing complexity and individuality.

Top growers

EDLMOSER

Maurer Lange Gasse 123, 1230 Wien. Tel & Fax: 01 8898 680. Website: www.edlmoser.at. Vineyards: 9 ha. White grapes: Riesling, Pinot Blanc, Goldburger, Gelber Muskateller, Chardonnay. Red grapes: Zweigelt, Cabernet Sauvignon, St Laurent, Syrah.

Michael Edlmoser is determined to make his estate one of the country's finest. He has worked for Emmerich Knoll in the Wachau and at Hall Crest Vineyards in California, and is not afraid to innovate. His varietal whites are simple but clean. His sophisticated use of oak is demonstrated by his Chardonnay Grande Reserve, which is inching its way year by year toward a real expression of terroir. His St Laurent Grande Reserve is elegant and attractively earthy. Riesling Privat is a very floral wine with some residual sugar and very good ageing potential. Also very good is his Cabernet Sauvignon, an elegant wine made along international lines.

WIENINGER

Stammersdorfer Strasse 80, 1210 Wien. Tel: 01 290 10 12. Fax: 01 2901 01 23. www.wieninger.at. Vineyards: 25 ha. White: Grüner Veltliner, Chardonnay,

Riesling, Bouvier, Pinot Blanc, Sauvignon Blanc, Welschriesling, Gemischter Satz. Red: Cabernet Sauvignon, Merlot, Zweigelt, Pinot Noir.

Almost singlehandedly, Fritz Wieninger has woken Vienna's vineyards out of their *Heurige* slumber and proven that it is possible to create wines of international standing here. With irresistible dynamism, he has spent the last decade building himself a new winery, buying up good vineyards on and around the Nussberg, and creating series after series of outstanding wines. His most individual wine is in a local tradition: Nussberg Alte Reben is from a vineyard planted as *Gemischter Satz*, a mixed planting of Pinot Blanc, Neuburger, Grüner Veltliner, Welschriesling, Sylvaner, Zierfandler, Riesling, and Traminer. This system was originally used to spread the risk of frost or other dangers, and Wieninger creates deep and intriguing wines from old, mixed Nussberg vineyards. His Riesling Nussberg is attractively soft with a fine green-apple note, while Chardonnay Tribute and Select are more international in style. Wieninger is also a champion of Pinot Noir, which he vinifies into dense and generous wines with good ageing potential.

ZAHEL

Maurer Hauptplatz 9, 1230 Wien. Tel: 01 8891 318. Fax: 01 8891 310. Website: www.zahel.at. Vineyards: 7 ha. White grapes: Grüner Veltliner, Chardonnay, Riesling, Bouvier, Pinot Gris, Gelber Muskateller, Sauvignon Blanc, Orangetraube, Gemischter Satz. Red grapes: Cabernet Sauvignon, Merlot, Zweigelt, Pinot Noir.

Brothers Alfred and Richard Zahel have invested a great deal to lift the quality of their wines above that necessary for their beautiful *Heurige*, and they are now beginning to reap the rewards, especially with their expressive Riesling Nussberg and the *Gemischte Satz* Nussberg Grande Reserve. Their red wines, such as the buxom Antares Grande Reserve (St Laurent/Zweigelt/Cabernet Sauvignon/Merlot) and the St Laurent Reserve, are not yet stylistically quite as well defined.

6

Lower Austria (Niederösterreich), Part II

WEINVIERTEL

Vineyards: 15,892 ha.
Soil: loess, loam, primary rock, black earth.
White grapes (seventy-nine per cent): Grüner Veltliner, Neuburger, Müller-Thurgau, Pinot Blanc, Ruländer, Traminer, Welschriesling, Roter Veltliner, Frühroter Veltliner
Red grapes (twenty-one per cent): Blauer Portugieser, Zweigelt.

The Weinviertel has no less than a third of Austria's entire area under vines: this is the the country's largest wine region, with almost 16,000 hectares of vineyards in all. The landscape here can be very pleasant: softly rolling hills stretching in all directions, and with vineyards and woodland punctuated by small towns and villages with lovely rustic or baroque architecture. Small wonder, then, that it has become a favourite retreat for writers and artists.

The Weinviertel stretches over most of northeast Austria, right up to the Slovak border. There are plenty of reliable producers here. The best are often distinguished by their ability and diligence, rather than by their terroir, though there are some pockets with distinctive soils and mesoclimates that are particularly suited to certain vines and styles.

The geology of the Weinviertel (which simply means "Wine Region") is diverse. There is loess and black soil, mainly planted with Grüner Veltliner and Müller-Thurgau; pure loess for a variety of whites and reds, and loam, thought to be particularly suited to Pinot Blanc and Traminer. Sandy soils are less popular with the growers here, while chalky soils are planted with Pinot Blanc, Neuburger and Zweigelt, especially in the Mailberg region. There are some primary rock soils as well, which are planted mainly with Grüner Veltliner, Welschriesling and, alas, Blauer Portugieser.

The climate in the Weinviertel is more middle than eastern European and is influenced by the wooded hills surrounding the vineyards. The climate overall is cooler and more moderate than in the regions where the Pannonian influence prevails: the Pannonian influence is broken by the hills of Slovakia. With an average rainfall of about 500 millimetres (19.7 inches) per annum (only 400 millimetres/15.7 inches around Retz and Wolkersdorf) it is one of the driest wine areas in Europe. The mean temperature, however, is lower than that of the Kamptal, Kremstal and Wachau to the east: 6-7°C (42.8-44.6°F). At 180 days the vegetation period can be considerably shorter than those of other areas. The extent of the region, however, means that mesoclimates create conditions under which very different wines can ripen.

One such mesoclimate distinguishes the Mailberg area, a small pocket situated in a valley in the north-centre of the Weinviertel. This cauldron-shaped valley with sand and loess soils allows some interesting reds to ripen on the southeast-facing hillsides. Because of the enclosed nature of the valley, daytime temperatures are higher than those of surrounding areas, while at night cool air comes streaming down from the wooded top of the Buchberg in the west. The growers of this area, incidentally, market their wines under the English designation "Mailberg Valley", a very New World approach.

A notable feature of the Weinviertel are its Kellergassen ("cellar streets"), roads lined with facades of wine cellars that look very much like stuccoed, baroque houses built into the hillsides; little towns, all the inhabitants of which live in bottles. These can be enormously atmospheric places, conjuring up images of a lost world.

The town of Retz, with real, live inhabitants, is the local centre: a charming, 700-year-old town with some beautiful buildings and a labyrinthine system of cellars and vaults criss-crossing under the foundations to a total length of twenty-six kilometres (sixteen miles).

These cellars are not only ideal storage space for wines, they have also provided a network of escape routes during the town's numerous periods of occupation: by the Swedes in the Thirty Years' War, the Prussians in the eighteenth century, Napoleon's army in the nineteenth, and the Germans and Russians in the twentieth century.

The soils around Retz, mainly weathered gneiss and granite, and one of the lowest annual rainfalls in Austria, make the area ideal for light, aromatic wines, seventy per cent of which are white.

Apart from these specific districts, the wines of the Weinviertel can be divided broadly between east and west. The West (around the towns of Retz, Horn, Hollabrunn and Korneuburg) is mainly planted with indigenous vines such as Grüner Veltliner, Müller-Thurgau, Welschriesling, Frühroter Veltliner, and smaller amounts of Pinot Blanc, Chardonnay, and Riesling, as well as with the field blend known as *Gemischter Satz*. Among the reds, which are very much in the minority, there is Blauer Portugieser, Zweigelt and Blauburger, and, more recently, Cabernet Sauvignon.

The eastern Weinviertel (around Mistelbach and Gänserndorf), produces mainly light, fresh and acidic wines, vinified predominately from Grüner Veltliner, but also Welschriesling, Müller-Thurgau, Pinot Blanc, Frühroter Veltliner, and Riesling. There are some climatically protected "red islands", especially the slightly warmer, bowl-shaped area around Mailberg, in which Blauer Portugieser and Zweigelt are grown. Welschriesling is also used as a basic wine for Sekt, especially by the Viennese firms of Schlumberger and Kattus.

The DAC initiative (*see* Chapter One) has brought some much-needed dynamism to this region.

Top Growers

DIEM
Obere Hauptstrasse 28, 2223 Hohenruppersdorf. Tel: 02574 8292. Fax: 02574 8904. Website: www.wein-diem.at. Vineyards: 9 ha. White grapes: Grüner Veltliner, Riesling, Pinot Blanc. Red grapes: Zweigelt, Blauburger, St Laurent.
Good, long-lived Pinot Blanc and Zweigelt are made on this well-known estate. His Grüner Veltliner, too, shows beautifully clean fruit and animating Veltliner spice.

FIDESSER
2051 Platt 39. Tel & fax: 02945 2592. Website: www.fidesser.at. Vineyards: 9 ha. White grapes: Grüner Veltliner, Riesling, Sauvignon Blanc, Weisser Veltliner, Gelber Muskateller. Red grapes: Pinot Noir, Zweigelt.

These are surprisingly well-defined wines with pleasantly articulated fruit. The Grüner Veltliner and Sauvignon Blanc Ausserm Holz especially are worth looking out for. A friend of rare grapes, Rudolf Fidesser also produces an elegant Weisser Traminer (*see* Roter Traminer, Chapter Two) and a Gelber Muskateller which can be outstanding.

SCHLOSSWEINGUT GRAF HARDEGG
2062 Seefeld-Kadolz 1. Tel: 02943 2203. Fax: 02943 2210. Website: www.grafhardegg.at. Vineyards: 43 ha. White grapes: Grüner Veltliner, Riesling, Pinot Blanc, Viognier. Red grapes: Merlot, Zweigelt, Cabernet Sauvignon.

To find an estate of true international ambition among a multitude of correct but often unexciting neighbours comes as a surprise, but a welcome one. Winemaker Peter Malberg searches for structure and distinction to match that of the architecture of the yellow, moated Habsburg baroque castle that is Schloss Hardegg.

There is not a single bad wine among the many and often eccentric offerings here, beginning with the classic Grüner Veltliner in several variations (very good: Alte Reben) to much less obvious choices. Among the latter are one of Europe's best Viogniers, cooler and more balanced than many from Condrieu, and a very decent Syrah. Among the reds, there is an elegant if perhaps somewhat reserved Merlot and a good Pinot Noir. Another surprise is the outstanding Riesling Mailberger Hochlüssen, a sweet wine reminiscent of the Mosel, and very successful indeed.

MINKOWITSCH
2261 Mannersdorf an der March 64. Tel & fax: 02283 2583. Website: www.roland-minkowitsch.at. Vineyards: 8 ha. White grapes: Grüner Veltliner, Riesling, Chardonnay, Gewürztraminer. Red grapes: Zweigelt.

Roland Minkowitsch is one of the few Austrian growers still to use an old tree press. He also ages all his wines in barrels, both large and, in the case of his Chardonnay, small and new. The results are are beautifully dense and fruity wines with considerable individuality. I was especially taken by a marvellously rich Gewürztraminer Auslese and Spätlese. An old-fashioned wine in the best sense, his Riesling "de vite" is also fine, with harmonious interplay between fruit and acidity.

PFAFFL
Hauptstrasse 24, 2100 Stetten. Tel: 02262 673423. Fax: 02262 673421. Website: www.pfaffl.at. Vineyards: 45 ha. White grapes: Grüner Veltliner, Riesling,

Chardonnay, Sauvignon Blanc, Welschriesling. Red grapes: Cabernet Sauvignon, Zweigelt.

Known as "Herr Veltliner", Roman Pfaffl is the pioneer of high quality wines in the Weinviertel and a driving force behind the Weinviertel DAC initiative. It took hard work for him to get to this position, and nobody would have predicted it when, in 1979, he took over a farm with a little less than one hectare under vine. He increased the vineyards and improved his wines year by year and slowly began to be recognized as one of the better growers of the area. With the 1997 vintage, he managed to break through into the top rank with Veltliners which had not only the distinctive pepper note (the "*Pfaffl-Pfefferl*") so much associated with this wine, but also the depth to support it.

Looking at the range, one is reminded of a child in a toy shop: so many different varieties, vineyards and vinifications are on offer, every one of them showing a distinctive personality. The finest of the Veltliners is Hundsleiten-Sandtal, a sophisticated wine vinified in oak, but never dominated by wood aromas which simply coax it towards a more ample, generous expression. The Riesling Terrassen Sonnleiten offers fine aromas of stone-fruit and great persistence on the palate, while the elderflower-scented Sauvignon Blanc offers more seductively opulent tones. Also skillfully vinified in oak, the Chardonnay Rossern shows a hint of butter-scotch over tight, well-defined fruit. Pfaffl also produces several red wines, amongst which the fine Heidorn, a blend of Cabernet Sauvignon and Zweigelt, and Excellent (Zweigelt/Cabernet Sauvignon), an elegant and often deep wine.

POLLERHOF

Winzerstrasse 48, 3743 Röschnitz. Tel & fax: 02984 3995. Website: www.pollerhof.at. Vineyards: 10 ha. White grapes: Grüner Veltliner, Riesling, Traminer, Gelber Muskateller. Red grapes: Zweigelt.

Erwin Poller's cellar in a quiet side street of the calm village of Röschnitz may be traditional, but he travelled widely before returning to make wine on the family estate. He has made a name for himself with his often intriguing and individual wines, amongst which are an excellent Gelber Muskateller, a sappy and attractive Traminer, and a mineral, expressive Grüner Veltliner Königsberg, the best wine produced here. Always looking for new possibilites, Erwin Poller has also begun to produce

Gamay, which so far is blended with Syrah, Zweigelt, and Cabernet Sauvignon into Church Hill.

PRECHTL

2051 Zellerndorf 12. Tel: 02945 2297. Fax: 02945 2240. Website: www.prechtl.at. Vineyards: 9 ha. White grapes: Grüner Veltliner, Sauvignon Blanc, Welschriesling, Chardonnay. Red grapes: Zweigelt.

Erwin Prechtl has a passion for the Weinviertel and its wines and consistently produces pure and elegant Grüner Veltiners, particularly from the Altenberg vineyard. The vines are over seventy years old.

SALOMON

2162 Falkenstein 24. Tel & fax: 02554 85437. Website: www.weingut-salomon.at. Vineyards: 9 ha. White grapes: Grüner Veltliner, Riesling, Chardonnay, Sylvaner, Muskat Ottonel, Welschriesling, Neuburger.

An old estate producing consistently good Grüner Veltliner, Riesling, and Sylvaner. The vineyards benefit from the distinctive climate around Falkenstein, a valley surrounded by forests which shield the vineyards from cold winds. Not to be confused with the Undhof Salomon (q.v.), or with Fritz Salomon of Gut Oberstockstall (not profiled in this book).

SCHWARZBÖCK

Hauptstrasse 58, 2102 Hagenbrunn. Tel: 02262 672740. Fax: 02262 672257. Website: www.schwarzboeck.at. Vineyards: 11 ha. White grapes: Grüner Veltliner, Riesling, Pinot Blanc, Chardonnay. Red grapes: Zweigelt.

Young and ambitous, Rudolf Schwarzböck produces Grüner Veltliner that is often distinguished by its clear and concentrated fruit, particularly in the single vineyard wines Sätzen-Fürstenberg and Kirchberg. Riesling Aichleiten shows finesse and elegance. He also makes several reds.

SETZER

3472 Hohenwarth 28. Tel: 02957 228. Fax: 2288 Website: www.weingut-setzer.at. Vineyards: 15 ha. White grapes: Grüner Veltliner, Riesling, Pinot Blanc, Roter Veltliner. Red grapes: Merlot.

Far off the beaten track, Hans and Ulrike Setzer are among the producers who demonstrate the potential of the Weinviertel. Their wines are powerful and made without compromise, like their flagship Grüner Veltliner 8000, so named because the vineyard is planted with eight thousand vines per hectare and kept to a minimal yield. This is a wine rich in extract and with ringingly pure fruit. They also make very good Sauvignon Blanc and an attractively elegant Riesling.

STUDENY

2073 Obermarkersdorf 174. Tel: 02942 8252. Fax: 02942 8220. Website: www.studeny.at. Vineyards: 14 ha. White grapes: Grüner Veltliner, Riesling, Sauvignon Blanc, Pinot Blanc. Red grapes: Cabernet Sauvignon.

Herbert Studeny is one of the young generation of producers who have travelled widely (in his case internships in Alsace, Napa Valley, and Australia) and have come home with a head full of new ideas which have dynamized an otherwise solid but unexciting estate. The Grüner Veltliner Atschbach shows great clarity and some complexity thanks to long lees contact, while the polished character of the Sauvignon Blanc is reminiscent of a New World wine.

WEINRIEDER

2170 Kleinhadersdorf, Untere Ortsstrasse 44. Tel: 02252 2241. Fax: 02252 3708. Website: www.weinrieder.at. Vineyards: 15 ha. White grapes: Grüner Veltliner, Riesling, Chardonnay, Pinot Blanc, Welschriesling. Red grapes: St Laurent.

Pure and classic varietal fruit is the hallmark of this consistent producer. His Grüner Veltliner Schneiderberg is always one of the most rounded and well-made in the region, largely thanks to rigorous selection and late harvesting. He also makes very good Pinot Blanc and a Chardonnay Hohenleiten with good, clear fruit. The best wine from this estate, however, is his beautiful Riesling Eiswein, whose pure and fine varietal aromas combine concentration and nobility, a wine that effortlessly competes with much more famous names.

ZULL

2073 Schrattenthal 9. Tel: 02946 8217. Fax: 02946 8214. Website: www.winezull.at. Vineyards: 17 ha. White grapes: Grüner Veltliner, Riesling, Welschriesling, Chardonnay. Red grapes: Zweigelt, Cabernet Sauvignon, Merlot, Pinot Noir.

Werner Zull and son Philipp are among the region's most enthusiastic producers of reds. A large range of very approachable wines is on offer, amongst which a good Grüner Veltliner DAC and a sappy Zweigelt Schrattental.

THERMENREGION

Vineyards: 2,332 ha.

Soils: chalky loam in the northwest; gravel, clay, sand.

White grapes (sixty-one per cent): Pinot Blanc, Neuburger, Zierfandler, Rotgipfler.

Red grapes (thirty-nine per cent): Blauer Portugieser, Zweigelt, Pinot Noir, Cabernet Sauvignon.

Just south of Vienna, the Thermenregion got its name from the many spas (*"Thermen"*) which could be found here, though the Viennese still call it, less ceremoniously, "Südbahn", or "southern railway", as the old railway tracks run through here. The Viennese often take the Thermenregion as a natural extension of their city and go to a *Heurige* in, say, Baden or Gumpoldskirchen, instead of choosing the nearer ones in the suburbs.

This charming landscape has a great vinous history. There has been a continuous wine culture here since the twelfth century (the Freigut Thallern, Austria's oldest surviving wine estate, was founded by Cistercian monks in 1141). During the eighteenth and nineteenth century especially, the best wines for Vienna's tables came from the Thermenregion and were usually referred to by their town of origin, for example "Vöslauer" or "Gumpoldskirchner". This village identity and the intimate connection with the Cistercian order are two of several similarities with the Côte d'Or, with which the region shares not only one geographic latitude (47°) but also similar climatic conditions. Red grapes were planted here experimentally during the second half of the nineteenth century.

The stars here are the white grapes Zierfandler and Rotgipfler, two varieties of unclear origin, both probably crossings of a Traminer vine and Roter Veltliner. They are usually vinified in oak and develop characteristic aromas of mandarin, marzipan, and roses. They can be very powerful, easily with fourteen degrees of alcohol or more, and while the wood can overwhelm their delicate fruit, in good hands oak and grape can be married gloriously well. Vinified on its own and without pronounced wood tones, Zierfandler can develop a range of fine and delicate aromas reminiscent of Mosel Riesling. Confusingly, blends of Zierfandler and Rotgipfler are known as Spätrot Rotgipfler. Both varietals are demanding in terms of soil and attention, but this weakness is often turned into a strength, as these aromatic and thin-skinned berries can be vinified into outstanding nobly-rotten sweet wines when conditions allow.

In terms of climate as well as geography the Thermenregion is on the border between Lower Austria and the Burgenland. The Vienna Woods protect it from cold northerly winds so that it has a typically Pannonian climate of hot summers, cold winters, and an annual mean temperature of 10°C (50°F). In warm years grapes can suffer heat damage especially in the south, and growers have to be careful not to produce wines with low acidity. The annual rainfall is around 650 millimetres (25.6 inches), and the vegetation period is about 230 days. The southern, dryer part of the region, also called Steinfeld, has soils dominated by layers of sand and clay on chalk with large deposits of gravel, a constellation especially suitable for red wines. This region is extremely vulnerable to spring frosts.

In the north there is a higher ground water level. Porous loam soils in the lower parts give way to the weathered volcanic rock that marks the soils of the Vienna Woods. The maritime origin of the low-lying soils is demonstrated by the frequent finds of fossilised coral, seashells, and so on, especially in the area around Sooss.

To the southeast the vineyards are dominated by a chain of hills of which the Anninger, 674 metres (2,210 feet), is the highest. Around Gumpoldskirchen in the north, the south-facing hillsides with their chalky and rich soils are good for more demanding white varieties such as Pinot Blanc, Chardonnay, and Traminer, as well as Zierfandler, Rotgipfler and Neuburger, the latter of which can be both powerful and complex. Closer to Bad Vöslau and Tattendorf in the south, poorer, more gravelly soils create perfect conditions for reds, mainly (still, alas) the unexciting Blauer Portugieser, but increasingly also Zweigelt, St Laurent and Pinot Noir.

Faced with stiff competition from big Austrian Chardonnays and Sauvignon Blanc, these individual and fascinating wines have fallen out of fashion a little in recent years, but they form an important aspect of the country's wine landscape and heritage. Less touched in the explosion of new styles than other regions, the "Südbahn" had also begun to look a little safe and traditional; pretty, but a little dull. A new generation of ambitious and able wine-growers has started to dynamize the region again, created new wine styles and revived the virtues of the old ones. Today, Thermenregion wines are becoming an exciting prospect once again.

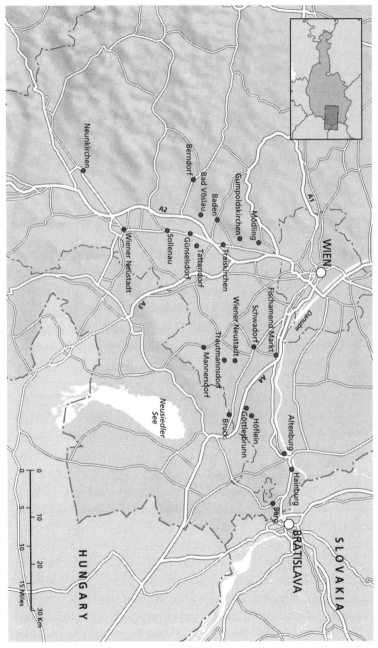

vii Thermenregion & Carnuntum

Top Growers

ALPHART

Wiener Strasse 46, 2514 Traiskirchen. Tel: 02252 52328. Fax: 02252 523284.
Website: www.alphart.com. Vineyards: 10 ha. White grapes: Grüner Veltliner,
Riesling, Rotgipfler, Zierfandler, Chardonnay, Neuburger. Red grapes: Zweigelt,
Pinot Noir, St Laurent.

Karl Alphart concentrates on the indigenous Zierfandler, Rotgipfler, and
Neuburger. His wines are usually ample and generous, notably the citrus-
scented Neuburger and the excellent Rotgipfler Rodauner with its playful
aromas of banana, marzipan, and orange peel.

AUMANN

Oberwaltersdorfer Strasse 105, 2512 Tribuswinkel. Tel: 02252 80502. Website:
www.aumann.at. Vineyards: 7 ha. White grapes: Grüner Veltliner, Riesling,
Sauvignon Blanc, Zierfandler, Chardonnay, Neuburger. Red grapes: Zweigelt, Pinot
Noir, St Laurent.

Leopold "Leo" Aumann is a young and ambitious grower whose wines
have started to attract attention. His mighty Chardonnays are still lacking
in sophistication, but the Rotgipfler Flamming shows beautiful Alsace
vendange tardive character and thrives on being vinified in used barriques.
Aumann has also made the red varieties his own. There is very decent
Pinot Noir and St Laurent, as well as a very interesting blend called
Harterberg (Cabernet Sauvignon/Merlot/Zweigelt), a robust wine
showing ample, velvety fruit with notes of smoke and eucalyptus. His
Zweigelt Reserve is also very good.

BIEGLER

Wiener Strasse, 2352 Gumpoldskirchen. Tel: 02252 62196. Fax: 02252
621964. Website: www.weingut-biegler.at. Vineyards: 8 ha. White grapes: Grüner
Veltliner, Riesling, Rotgipfler, Zierfandler, Chardonnay. Red grapes: Zweigelt, Pinot
Noir.

Beautifully situated in a Renaissance house in Gumpoldskirchen, the
quiet and thoughtful Manfred Biegler has one of the best *Heurige* in the
area. He makes a wide, very traditionally oriented selection of wines, but
it is the local heroes Zierfandler and Rotgipfler that really shine. His
Zierfandler shows good structure with notes of citrus peel and quince,
while his Rotgipfler Reserve is full of aromas of candied fruit, mandarin,
and hazlenut, often supported by some residual sugar. Perhaps the most

convincing and bewitching are the nobly-sweet and late-harvest wines from Rotgipfler, which combine creamy complexity and ageing potential.

FISCHER

Hauptstrasse 33, 2500 Sooss, Tel: 0225 87130. Fax: 0225 82666. Website: www.weingut-fischer.at. Vineyards: 17 ha. White grapes: Grüner Veltliner, Riesling, Rotgipfler, Zierfandler, Welschriesling, Chardonnay, Pinot Blanc, Neuburger. Red grapes: Zweigelt, Blauer Portugieser, Pinot Noir, Cabernet Sauvignon, Merlot, St Laurent.

Christian Fischer produces both red and white wines, but it is the reds that steal the show, and particularly his beautifully earthy Pinot Noir Premium. Also very good are Gradenthal (Zweigelt/Cabernet Sauvignon/ Merlot) with notes of forest fruits, and a broad-shouldered Cabernet/ Merlot blend.

JOHANNESHOF REINISCH

Im Weingarten 1, 2523 Tattendorf. Tel: 02253 81423. Fax: 02253 81924. Website: www.j-r.at. Vineyards: 30 ha. White grapes: Chardonnay, Pinot Blanc, Riesling, Sauvignon Blanc. Red grapes: Cabernet Sauvignon, Merlot, Pinot Noir, St Laurent, Zweigelt.

Trained in California, Johannes Reinisch has striven to replicate his American experience, not only in terms of cellar technology, but also by building a state-of-the-art winery right in the middle of the Thermenregion. From belfry and to large, brick cellars with 350 barriques, from inbuilt romanticism to indirect lighting to *Heurige*, this is about as perfect as an architect can design it.

The mainly red wines are all accomplished, particularly the Pinot Noir Grande Reserve, a wine with velvety tannins, firm, mature fruit and considerable ageing potential. A fine, tarry St Laurent and an elegant Merlot/Cabernet Sauvignon Reserve with elegant fruit reminiscent of St-Emilion are also among the producer's best.

KRUG

Kirchenplatz 1, 2352 Gumpoldskirchen. Tel: 02252 62247. Fax: 02252 62244. Website: www.krug.at. Vineyards: 12 ha. White grapes: Rotgipfler, Zierfandler, Chardonnay, Pinot Gris. Red grapes: Zweigelt, Blauer Portugieser, Pinot Noir, Cabernet Sauvignon, St Laurent.

With his assertively modern vinification and his memorably Picasso-like labels, Gustav Krug has decided to follow an individual route. Often international in orientation and with plenty of new wood on the nose, his wines can succeed, especially the generous Rotgipfler Rasslerin and the Zierfandler Sonnberg, all caramel and appealing, soft, citrus fruit. Krug also has ambitions for his reds, particularly his Cabernet Sauvignon Privat, a wine with often medicinal tones, strongly influenced by barrique.

SCHNEIDER

Badnerstrasse 3, 2523 Tattendorf. Tel & fax: 02253 81020. Website: www.tattendorf.at/schneider. Vineyards: 8 ha. White grapes: Chardonnay, Pinot Blanc. Red grapes: Pinot Noir, Cabernet Sauvignon, Merlot, St Laurent.

One of the region's smaller producers, Erich Schneider's St Laurent Reserve is among the best representatives of this variety in the area. He also produces a good if somewhat rustic Pinot Noir Reserve.

SPÄTROT

Jubiläumstrasse 43, 2352 Gumpoldskirchen. Tel: 02252 61164. Fax: 02252 62129. Website: www.spaetrot.com. Vineyards: 15 ha. White grapes: Rotgipfler, Zierfandler, Weisser Riesling, Pinot Gris, Muskat Ottonel, Neuburger. Red grapes: Zweigelt, Blaufränkisch.

Concealed behind this name, and the historic facade of the cellars, are Johann and Johanna Gebelshuber, two young winemakers who some years ago took on the challenge of running Gumpoldskirchen's unremarkable cooperative, which processes grapes from roughly a third of the region's vineyards. Driven by the couple's energy and expertise, the cooperative is producing increasingly interesting wines. Vinified in large wooden barrels, the Zierfandler/Rotgipfler Reserve shows beautifully precise fruit with flavours of clementine and rose petals lingering on the palate for a considerable time. The Rotgipfler Privat is also beautifully structured, less opulent than some, but all the more elegant and with very good ageing potential. Pursung top quality in a cooperative is never easy, but the Gebelshubers have already shown that they intend to settle only for the best.

STADLMANN

Wiener Strasse 41, 2514 Traiskirchen. Tel: 02252 52343. Fax: 02252 56332. Website: www.stadlmann-wein.at. Vineyards: 12 ha. White grapes: Zierfandler, Rotgipfer, Pinot Blanc, Riesling, Neuburger, Muskat Ottonel, Grüner Veltliner.

If there is one wine that has consistently demonstrated the potential of Zierfandler for serious, ageworthy wine, it is surely Johann Stadlmann's outstanding Zierfandler Mandelhöh, a wine with impeccable structure and aromas of citrus and quince, great depth, and ringing clarity. Old vintages show a transformation into a Loire-like, creamy complexity. Another fine wine and a hint to all chefs is Asia Edition, whose exotic citrus and mango tones lend themselves to Asian cuisine. Stadlmann is the seventh generation of his family to run the estate, and has found a happy balance between local tradition and carefully innovative winemaking. He is one of the region's key wine personalities.

THIEL (KREMSMÜNSTERHOF)

Badener Strasse 11, 2352 Gumpoldskirchen. Tel & fax: 02252 62372. Website: www.weingut-thiel.at. Vineyards: 10 ha. White grapes: Riesling, Rotgipfler, Zierfandler, Chardonnay. Red grapes: Zweigelt, Pinot Noir.

It is rare for a grower in this region to produce an exceptional Riesling, but in 1997 Richard Thiel managed to do just that. Amid an enormous range of wines, the Rotgipfler Grand Select stands out with its lovely opulence and mature fruit.

ZIERER

Badner Strasse 36, 2352 Gumpoldskirchen. Tel: 02252 62169. Fax: 02252 607165. Website: www.weingut-zierer.at. Vineyards: 9 ha. White grapes: Riesling, Zierfandler, Rotgipfler, Welschriesling, Chardonnay, Pinot Blanc. Red grapes: Zweigelt, Pinot Noir.

Among all Thermenregion producers, Harald Zierer is perhaps the most Alsacien in style and orientation. His Rotgipfler Grande Reserve dazzles with notes of clover, orange and cinnamon – Christmas in a bottle. The top Zierfandler, also called Grande Reserve, is more floral with nutty, woody aromas. Also excellent is the Zierfandler/Rotgipfler Sonnenberg, an often distinctly *vendange tardive*-like blend of great finesse and length.

CARNUNTUM

Vineyards: 892 ha.
Soil: sand, loam, gravel, loess.
White grapes (sixty-six per cent): Grüner Veltliner, Welschriesling, Pinot Blanc, Chardonnay.
Red (thirty-four per cent): Blaufränkisch, Zweigelt, Cabernet Sauvignon, St Laurent.

Carnuntum is a somewhat artificial administrative entity, named after the capital of the Roman province which existed here 2,000 years ago. Situated on the banks of the Danube, Carnuntum was the largest city in the Roman border colony, and was an important trading point on the amber road. Some 70,000 people lived there, compared to 1,200 today. Relics like a triumphal arch and an amphitheatre still testify to this part of the region's past. The modern Carnuntum is a wedge between the Weinviertel to the north, delineated by the river Danube, and the Neusiedlersee region to the south, and reaches some fifty kilometres (thirty-one miles) from Vienna to the Slovak border.

In terms of wine production the most important area of Carnuntum is the four-kilometre (2.5-mile) stretch between Göttlesbrunn and Höflein which contains the majority of forward-looking winemakers. The vineyards in the second area, to the east, near Prellenkirchen, are mainly cultivated by part-time growers and *Heurige* producers. Wine of distinction is a rarity there.

The geology of the area is dominated by the changing course of a prehistoric river, which deposited gravel along its path. This was partly overlaid by loess during the ice ages. The soils are deep and fertile, with some loam and sand.

Climatically, the Leitha mountains in the west and the Vienna Woods to the northwest shield the area from the influence of moderate, Atlantic weather systems, while the Danube, marking the area's northern border, acts as a natural climate barrier, especially in summer. Pannonian influences prevail, leading to hot summers and cold winters. During summer nights cool air comes from the Vienna Woods; those same woods, however, can lead to a shortage of rain, as the clouds from the west often shed their load over the hills. Another problem is the northerly wind, which pushes down winter temperatures as low as -20°C (-4°F), leading to frost damage to the vines. Only the vineyards around Göttlesbrunn are protected from this by the Alstenberg and Schüttenberg hills. It is in this red wine enclave that the most interesting wines are to be found.

The ambitious growers here are acutely aware that Carnuntum's wines are still lacking in regional identity, and a group of red-wine-makers is now working with Australian oenologist Forbes MacGregor to push quality and style. An increased reliance on Zweigelt and St Laurent as is certainly a step in the right direction. In the short term this concerted effort has led to wines more determined by solid, modern winemaking and frequent tastings among colleagues than by terroir, but this is definitely an area to watch.

Top Growers

ARTNER
2465 Höflein, Dorfstrasse 93. Tel: 02162 631. fax: 02162 66255. Website: www.artner.co.at. Vineyards: 13 ha. White grapes: Welschriesling, Grüner Veltliner, Gelber Muskateller, Chardonnay, Sauvignon Blanc. Red grapes: Zweigelt, Syrah, Merlot, Cabernet Sauvignon, Blaufränkisch.
Ambitious Hannes Artner is distinguishing himself with interesting reds, among them a successful Syrah and a good blend, Amarok.

GLATZER
2464 Göttlesbrunn, Rosenbergstrasse 5. Tel: 02162 8486. Fax: 02162 8901. Website: www.weingutglatzer.at. Vineyards: 16 ha. White grapes: Grüner Veltliner, Pinot Blanc, Sauvignon Blanc. Red grapes: Zweigelt, St Laurent, Blaufränkisch.
Modern, satisfying wines from a well-regarded estate. The Grüner Veltliner usually emphasizes exotic notes, while the Zweigelt Dornenvogel shows good berry fruit. The dense St Laurent Altenberg is one of one of the new generation, one to watch.

GRASSL
Am Graben 4 and 6, 2464 Göttlesbrunn. Tel & fax: 02162 8483. Website: www.weingut-grassl.com. Vineyards: White grapes: Chardonnay, Grüner Veltliner. Red grapes: Zweigelt, Cabernet Sauvignon, Blaufränkisch, St Laurent.
Like other good producers in the area, Hans Grassl and his son Philipp are putting their faith in red wines, with several new vineyards planted. Their blend Bärnreiser (Zweigelt/Merlot/Cabernet Sauvignon), fermented in wooden vats, shows good, foresty fruit and soft tannins, while the substantial St Laurent Reserve is nicely balanced with earthy, tarry fruit.

GERHARD MARKOWITSCH
Pfarrgasse 6-8, 2464 Göttlesbrunn. Tel: 02162 8222. Fax: 02162 822211. Website: www.markowitsch.at. Vineyards: 26 ha. White grapes: Chardonnay, Grüner Veltliner, Sauvignon Blanc. Red grapes: Blaufränkisch, Cabernet Sauvignon, Merlot, Pinot Noir, Zweigelt.
The enthusiastic Gerhard Markowitsch is the driving force of the region, and in his avant-garde winery he is pursuing a powerful, concentrated style without compromise. At the head of the fray, the prestige blend

Rosenberg (Zweigelt/Merlot/Cabernet Sauvignon) presents dense, wooded and chocolatey notes but is often dominated by high alcohol. Redmont (Zweigelt/Cabernet Sauvignon/Syrah) is a New World wine with plenty of punch, and with its plump, wooded fruit the Pinot Noir goes in the same direction. All these wines are well made, but one cannot help thinking that cellar techonology and new oak, while adding to their sweetness and density, have taken off the edge off what individuality they might otherwise have had. Markowitsch also makes a good, internationally-styled Chardonnay.

NETZL

2464 Göttlesbrunn, Rosenbergstrasse 17. Tel: 02162 8236. Fax: 02162 8214. Website: www.netzl.com. Vineyards: 15 ha. White grapes: Red grapes:

Good, solid reds here, especially the blends Anna Christina (Zweigelt/ Cabernet Sauvignon/Merlot) and and Edles Tal (Zweigelt/Merlot), both with plenty of wood and soft fruit.

PITNAUER

Weinbergstrasse 4-6, 2464 Göttlesbrunn. Tel: 02162 8249. Fax: 02162 8217. Website: www.pitnauer.com. Vineyards: 17ha. White grapes: Pinot Blanc, Chardonnay. Red grapes: Zweigelt, Cabernet Sauvignon, Merlot.

A red wine specialist, Hans Pitnauer interest in Bordeaux varieties is evident from his well balanced Franz Josef (Cabernet Sauvignon/Zweigelt) and his Quo Vadis (Merlot/Cabernet Sauvignon/Zweigelt), which to me seems, like many wines in the area, a little high on the wood. The Zweigelt Bienenfreser has received the same treatment, and is round and smoky with good but not overcharged structure.

7

Styria (Steiermark)

With its undulating hills, slim poplar trees swaying in the wind, and intensely atmospheric sunsets, this is one of the most beautiful wine-growing regions in the world. To the east the hills are enveloped in dense forest and are reminiscent of a different period of European history. Particular landmarks are the rattling windmill wheels, or *Klapotetz*, which are designed to scare off birds feasting on the grapes.

Styria's benefactor was the legendary and somewhat tragic Archduke Johann (1782-1859), the *enfant terrible* of the Vienna court, who horrified the imperial family by marrying a commoner, the daughter of a post-master. Practically exiled from court, he put his energies into developing the education and the economic base of the area. His special enthusiasm was viticulture, and on his initiative the first systematic research into and classification of Styria and its wines were undertaken. His research estate near Marburg (now Maribor) is now in Slovenia.

Shortly after Johann's death, oidium and phylloxera, the wine plagues of the nineteenth century, swept across the principality. Vineyards had to be pulled out, an action at times protected against rebellious growers by the army. The replanting of the Styrian vineyards, however, benefited the area considerably, as only varieties of high quality were allowed to be planted and some other, less viable grapes vanished from the map.

Today all is calm. Strolling through the vineyards it is still difficult to know when one is in Austria, or Slovenia, or Hungary. The people claim to have little in common with their neighbours, and often profess never to have met even those who live literally across the road.

Styrian vineyards are often situated on very steep slopes with inclines of up to sixty degrees. Working these vineyards is as arduous as it is perilous, but the results are often very impressive. While Styria enjoys the warmest summers in Austria, hail can be a major hazard.

Styria is extremely rural. Graz is the only city and Vienna seems much more than just 300 kilometres (200 miles) away. Styrian viticulture can be very traditional and quite unexciting, especially as many growers sell their wines through their own *Heurigen* to tourists with fairly undemanding palates. (Many growers also have sidelines such as fruit schnapps, which is often excellent, and the ubiquitous pumpkin-seed oil.) Those few who have broadened their horizons to the outside world, however, are producing wines which have gained a worldwide reputation.

Different conditions shape different wines, and Styria, though mainly a white-wine country, is for once not dominated by Grüner Veltliner. The main variety here is Welschriesling, with Pinot Blanc and Chardonnay (here called Morillon) in hot pursuit. There is some Zweigelt here, and also Müller-Thurgau, Sauvignon Blanc, Schilcher, Traminer, Muskateller, Ruländer, Pinot Gris, St Laurent, and Riesling.

In recent years especially, Chardonnay and Sauvignon Blanc have made the name of the region, though the white Pinot varieties can also be very successful, and it seems to me that Pinot Gris is generally underestimated. Most growers vinify their wines in two distinct styles, the "classic", involving steel tanks and no malolactic fermentation, and a more international line with oak ageing. Both can be very successful, though nowadays the best wines are usually made in the international style.

Despite its small production, Styria covers a large area and is usually considered in three parts.

SOUTH STYRIA (SÜDSTEIERMARK)
Vineyards: 1,741 hectares.
Soils: slate, sand, marl.
White grapes (eighty-three per cent): Welschriesling, Chardonnay, Sauvignon Blanc, Pinot Blanc, Müller-Thurgau.
Red grapes (seventeen per cent): Zweigelt, Blauer Wildbacher, Blauer Portugieser, Cabernet Sauvignon.

This is the most significant of the three Styrian wine-growing areas.

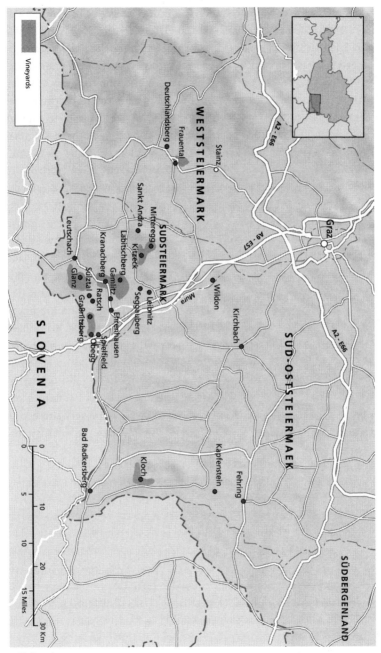

viii Styria

Wine has been grown here since the fourth century BC, and even at the end of the nineteenth century, the Lower Styria of the Habsburg Empire had some 35,000 hectares under vines, some of which are now in Slovenia. Southern Styria is the farthest corner of modern Austria, and for a long while few people saw much incentive for moving and working here. It is only recently that the potential has been unlocked once more.

These new Styrian wines have taken the wine world by storm with their character, depth, and sophistication. Vinified with or without oak, Chardonnay (always called "Morillon" in Styria) and Sauvignon Blanc, plus the occasional Pinot Blanc, can be great and opulent wines. Sauvignons are by turns intensely varietal with tones of green peppers and gooseberry, or profoundly complex wines aged in wood. The Chardonnays are unlike any other European example: more muscular than burgundy, they are more New World, comparable perhaps to the best of New Zealand. Usually high in alcohol (around fourteen degrees), their dense structure effortlessly supports their power. With a little age these wines become increasingly complex.

Made for finesse rather than power, Gelber Muskateller can be marvellous here: light, rose-scented, and delicious. Around the southern village of Klöch with its volcanic soils, there is a small Traminer enclave, and this aromatic grape, too, can create bewitching wines with tones of nutmeg and exotic flowers.

South Styria is on the rim of a hill formation made from gneiss and glimmer slate. It was never heavily overlaid by glaciers during the ice age, so rivers formed the face of the landscape and its soil, depositing chalk, sand, clay, and loam sediments and cutting regular valleys.

The climate is influenced not only by the Pannonian, but also by southern European weather systems, and with 800 to 1,000 millimetres (31.5 to 39.4 inches), the annual rainfall is double that of the Burgenland. On these hills, the middle and high vineyards are the best, as they escape the constant danger of frost damage in the valleys, while the hilltops are exposed to cold winds. The very bottoms and tops of the hills are often used for orchards. The vegetation period here is 240 days, with an annual mean temperature of 9.2°C (48.6°F).

The most northerly pocket of the region, Kitzeck, has a little more than 100 hectares of mainly slate soil, with Riesling, Pinot Blanc, Pinot Gris, and Welschriesling growing in vineyards such as the Annaberg,

Altenberg, Einöd, Gauitsch, Langriegel, and Trebien. Neighbouring St Andrä has thirty-six hectares of vineyards, among them the Harrachegg, the chalky Sausaler Schlössl (which was an experimental vineyard during the nineteenth century), and the Wilhelmshöhe, a high, south-facing *Ried* on which Chardonnay, Sauvignon Blanc, Sylvaner, and Zweigelt grow on weathered primary rock.

Travelling south from Kitzeck, we find the largest area under vine in Southern Styria, 350 hectares to the south of Gamlitz. The south slope of the Kranachberg (406 metres/1,330 feet), contains some hundred individual *Rieden*, and varies from sandy soils to chalk to marl. Sauvignon Blanc, Pinot Blanc, and Pinot Noir are the most important varieties here. The Pfarrweingarten, south of Gamlitz, with loamy sands on a coral base, and the Sernauberg, with loamy sand and gravel on coral deposits, and the Karnerberg are also important *Rieden*.

Part of another larger area of *Rieden*, the Czamillonberg is one of the finest in the area. Sauvignon Blanc, Chardonnay, and Muskateller ripen on this south-facing vineyard with its silicate deposits and brown sediment soil.

The easternmost corner of South Styria, between the villages of Spielfeld and Ratsch, contains a concentration both of excellent vine-yards and distinguished growers. Some of the very best wines of Styria are made here. The area, site of the eleventh-century Ehrenhausen castle, rises between 360 and 470 metres (1,180 and 1,540 feet) above sea level and has about eighty hectares of vineyards, many of them very steep. Like most vineyards here, the Nussberg faces south. Its chalky, marl soils with silicates and sand are an ideal foundation for Chardonnay, Sauvignon Blanc, Pinot Blanc, Welschriesling, Muskateller, and Pinot Gris. The graphite and marl soils of the Untere Anzried are used to grow Sauvignon Blanc and Morillon, the great successes of the area.

With the *Rieden* Zieregg, Grassnitzberg, and Hochgrassnitzberg, we come to some of the "*grand crus*" of Styria. Zieregg is an enclosed *Ried* of some twelve hectares, stretching seamlessly into Slovenia. Drainage has been installed at huge cost to prevent erosion. The soil of the best, upper, part is made up of fossil chalk on a marl subsoil that comes to the surface in places. The Grassnitzberg is composed of several soils and microclimates and is composed of low parts, southeast facing hill-side, and some northeast facing plots. It, too, is dominated by fossil chalk at the top, turning into loam and sand as one goes down the hill. The Hochgrassnitzberg is an enclosed hillside with sandy loam and weathered fossil chalk up to one metre (three feet) down. It faces south and southwest. Obegg, a neighbouring *Ried*, is made up of sandy and chalky soil.

Top Growers

GROSS

Ratsch an der Weinstrasse 26, 8461 Ehrenhausen. Tel: 03453 2527. Fax: 03453 2728. Website: www.gross.at. Vineyards: 22 ha. White grapes: Chardonnay, Muskateller, Pinot Blanc, Pinot Gris, Sauvignon Blanc, Traminer. Red grape: Zweigelt.

Without a doubt, Alois Gross is one of the magicians of the Austrian wine scene. His wines are often described as reticent and philosophical, two adjectives that also apply to their creator; they open up only gradually in a slow evolution of bewitchingly fine aromas.

Tucked into in the Styrian hills, his ultra-modern winery breathes the same quiet elegance, while the vineyards are immaculate. Gross is a fanatic for quality and to him that translates into painstaking care of the vines: in some vineyards up to five passes through the vines were necessary in the difficult 2004 vintage – a huge additional workload.

Vinification follows the principle of not too much oak or too many other strong influences. Relatively cool, temperature-controlled fermentation in steel is the rule, with ageing, for the top, single-vineyard wines, mainly in large or medium-sized oak barrels.

Among the many admirable wines here, I have always had a weakness for the dry Muskatellers, with their understated floral notes. Real depth, however, comes with the deep, mineral elegance of Sauvignon Blanc Nussberg and the precision of the Morillon from the same vineyard. With the Sauvignon Blanc Privat, made only in exceptional years, and with his personal favourite, Pinot Blanc, Gross achieves a rare level of profundity, balance, and artistry. The sweet wines, too, can be outstanding.

HARKAMP

Flamberg 46, 8505 St. Nikolai. Tel: 03185 30630. Fax: 03185 306304. Website: www.harkamp.at. Vineyards: 10 ha. White grapes: Sauvignon Blanc, Chardonnay, Pinot Gris, Gelber Muskateller, Pinot Blanc, Roter

Traminer, Welschriesling, Riesling.

The Harkamp empire is run by two brothers: Hannes, the winemaker, and Heinz, a chef who runs a nearby restaurant, a showcase for the wines. Most of Harkamp's wines are characterized by their clear and fine fruit, while his single-vineyard wines, aged in barriques, can be very baroque, with international wooded notes and caramel aromas that may or may not have their place in Styria. Recently, he has made some unoaked single-vineyard wines, and their profound fruit seems to me to be much more successful. Apart from the classic, dry wines, Harkamp's sweeties, an outstanding Grauburgunder TBA among them, can be very exciting.

LACKNER-TINNACHER

Steinbach 12, 8462 Gamlitz. Tel: 03453 2142. Fax: 03453 4841. Website: www.tinnacher.at. Vineyards: 16 ha. White grapes: Sauvignon Blanc, Chardonnay, Pinot Gris, Gelber Muskateller, Pinot Blanc, Roter Traminer, Welschriesling, Riesling. Red grapes: Zweigelt, St Laurent.

Franz Tinnacher's estate is set among hills, and he has to work on some frighteningly steep vineyards, but the result is wines with delicate fruit and acidity. Among the offerings is a memorable Pinot Gris, all smoky fruit and marzipan, and a fine Roter Traminer, as well as Sauvignon Blanc from the Welles vineyard, with finely tuned, elegant minerality.

Tinnacher is also famous for his fruit schnapps.

MAITZ

Ratsch an der Weinstrasse, 8461 Ehrenhausen. Website: www.maitz.co.at. Tel: 03453 2153. Fax: 03453 21537. Vineyards: 8 ha. White grapes: Sauvignon Blanc, Chardonnay, Pinot Gris, Gelber Muskateller, Pinot Blanc, Roter Traminer, Scheurebe, Welschriesling, Riesling. Red grapes: Zweigelt.

Wolfgang Maitz Junior. is one of the few ambitious younger producers in the area. His wines may still lack the ultimate refinement of the great Styrians, but he produces a fine Muskateller and a lean, stylish Morillon, both from the Schusterberg vineyard, which make this an estate to watch.

DOMÄNE MÜLLER

Grazerstrasse 71, 8522 Gross St. Florian. Tel: 03464 2155. Fax: 03464 211625. Website: www.domaene-mueller.at. Vineyards: 33 ha. White grapes: Chardonnay, Welschriesling, Sauvignon Blanc, Pinot Blanc, Pinot

Gris. Red grapes: Zweigelt, Cabernet Sauvignon, Blauer Wildbacher.

Some of the world's best wines are lying in Günter Müller's cellars – Müller is also the main Austrian importer of some of France's finest. Before he took over the estate and also bought the nearby Prinz Liechtensteinsche Weingut, he worked as a wine merchant in Paris and London and studied oenology in Bordeaux.

Müller is not a timid man. He has "corrected" an entire hillside in order to perfect its exposure to the sun. He makes impeccably crafted wines, often notably French in their inspiration. With its intense, fine, cassis and gooseberry aromas, Der Sauvignon Blanc is an aristocratic wine. Der Chardonnay is Müller's answer to Meursault, and with its richly exotic density and oak tones it always needs at least three years to come round. All the top wines of this domaine are made to age, and Müller is also ambitious about his reds, especially his Cabernet Sauvignon, which marries dense herbs and spices with berry tones and fine tannins. Müller's enthusiasm for the local rosé, Schilcher, is genuine, but it is his other wines that make him one of the region's best producers.

MUSTER

Schlossberg 38, 8463 Leutschach. Tel & Fax: 03454 70053. Vineyards: 10 ha. White grapes: Sauvignon Blanc, Chardonnay, Welschriesling, Gelber Muskateller. Red grapes: Zweigelt.

They still exist, the true individualists. Sepp Muster doesn't do anything the way his famous colleagues do; not from a desire to be contrary, but because he believes their way is not the best way. The son of a wine producer, Muster spent some years travelling (part of the time in India), before returning and taking over his father's vineyards, which are now tended according to Biodynamic principles. His vines are trained according to a reverse system, with the stems grown relatively high and the shoots left to hang down to give a greater leaf surface and thus, he finds, better ripening. Once in the cellar, everything is (or will soon be) fermented in wood using only ambient yeasts. In extreme years like 2003, his wines can have well over fifteen degrees of alcohol, and I must record that to my astonishment their mineral structure nevertheless made them seem balanced and elegant. "If a wine is alive it can take that sort of thing," he comments. More typical vintages, however, tend to have alcohol levels well below the Styrian norm.

The Morillon shows finesse, depth, and elasticity, while the Sauvignon Blanc Graf is a wine of understated noblesse with aromas of elderberry and summer leaves around a firm, mineral core. The top wine is Sgaminegg, a single-vineyard blend of Morillon and Sauvignon Blanc, rich and powerful, deep and with a complex play of exotic and varietal aromas, a wine with many dimensions whose length hints at its potential.

POLZ

Grassnitzberg 54a, 8471 Spielfeld. Tel: 03453 23010. Fax: 03453 23016. Website: www.polz.co.at. Vineyards: 45 ha. White grapes: Chardonnay, Pinot Blanc, Sauvignon Blanc, Riesling, Pinot Gris, Traminer, Welschriesling. Red grapes: Cabernet Sauvignon, St Laurent, Zweigelt.

The energy, charm, and enthusiasm of the Polzes, a team of three brothers and a sister, can sweep you off your feet. They have transformed a mid-sized family estate and made it into a winery of almost Californian dimensions; it is also a very successful export business. They also oversee a second winery, the Rebenhof, which has twenty-three hectares of vineyards, as well as owning the nearby Tscheppe estate and part-owning the Vino Miro estate in nearby Slovenia.

The Polz winery produces a whole range of wines, both traditional and internationally oriented. At the top end they may occasionally err in the direction of power, but mostly their great Morillons, Sauvignon Blancs, and Muskatellers are models of elegance, structure, and attention to individual terroirs. Between the vineyards Theresienhöhe, Obegg, Grassnitzberg, and Hochgrassnitzberg the estate commands some of the finest plots in the area, and their painstakingly careful vineyard work produces, for example, the excellent Sauvignon Blanc Therese, vinified in large oak barrels; Morillon Obegg, aged in new barriques; and Sauvignon Blanc Hochgrassnitzberg, aged in steel tanks for six months.

Walter and Erich, the driving forces behind the wines, are forever experimenting and pushing the boundaries, and it is this, combined with an almost mystical respect for their landscape, that makes Polz one of the best producers of the region.

SABATHI

Pössnitz 48, 8463 Leutschach. Tel: 03454 265. Fax: 03454 266. Website: www.sabathi.com. Vineyards: 12ha plus 23 ha under contract. White grapes:

Sauvignon Blanc, Chardonnay, Welschriesling, Gelber Muskateller, Pinot Blanc, Pinot Gris.

Erwin Sabathi is still a young man, but he has already made his mark with his initiative, his entrepreneurial sense, and his excellent wines. Born into a family of small-scale growers, he persuaded his father to give him control over the family estate and he transformed it into a large, modern, export-oriented enterprise.

Sabathi does not compromise on quality. With his marvellously complex and long Sauvignon Blanc Merveilleux he proves that he can compete with the best in Styria, while his other wines hold a consistently high level.

SATTLERHOF

Sernau 2, 8462 Gamlitz. Tel: 03453 2556. Fax: 03453 5732. Website: www.sattlerhof.at. Vineyards: 25 ha. White grapes: Chardonnay, Pinot Blanc, Pinot Gris, Riesling, Sauvignon Blanc, Welschriesling. Red grapes: Pinot Noir, St Laurent, Zweigelt.

Two generations of wine pioneers have made the Sattlerhof into one of Austria's great estates. Today, Willi Sattler is anything but settled in his ways and is constantly searching for new vineyards to plant, as well as enlarging his already labyrinthine cellars. The steep hills determine every aspect of the winemaking here: like many local growers, Sattler has to battle with vertiginous slopes, but the depth and mineral purity in the wines make it worth the fight.

The Sauvignon Blanc Privat, barrique-aged and produced only in top vintages, shows great depth and definition, elegant acidity, and enormous ageing potential. Other wines, notably the Morillon Pfarrweingarten and Sauvignon Blanc Sernauberg, are matured in steel or large wood and show breeding, minerality, focus, complexity, and length.

SKOFF

Eckberg 16 and 99, 8462 Gamlitz. Tel: 03453 4243. Fax: 03453 424317. Website: www.weingut-skoff.com. Vineyards: 36 ha plus 20 ha under contract. White grapes: Sauvignon Blanc, Chardonnay, Pinot Gris, Gelber Muskateller, Pinot Blanc, Roter Traminer, Welschriesling, Riesling. Red grapes: Zweigelt.

Walter Skoff is one of the most consistent Styrian producers of wines with character and clear varietal fruit. With their emphasis on alcoholic punch and purity of tone these wines can be on the rustic side, but when the balance is right these can be wonderfully satisfying wines with good ageing potential – all at a very attractive price.

TEMENT

Zieregg 13, 8461 Berghausen. Tel: 03453 4101. Fax: 03453 410130. Website: www.tement.at. Vineyards: 45 ha. White grapes: Chardonnay, Pinot Blanc, Sauvignon Blanc, Traminer, Welschriesling. Red grapes: Blaufränkisch, Cabernet Sauvignon, Zweigelt.

This estate owes its existence to two misfortunes in one man's life. Initially, Tement *père* had wanted to become a priest, but a lack of money forced him into making wine for the Carmelites. Then a stretch as a prisoner-of-war in France broadened his wine horizons. His son Manfred has built an entirely new winery overlooking some of his finest vineyards and has overseen the rise of the House of Tement.

Tement's wines combine power and elegance, fruit and structure in a way that is very close to ideal; they clearly take their bearings from international rather than local styles. The Sauvignon Blanc Zieregg is one-third aged in 300-litre barriques, blended with steel-aged wine and then put into either steel or large wood. This is one of Tement's flagship wines: with concentrated, elegant, and complex fruit, it is a commanding performance with enormous potential for the future. The second lead is played by the Morillon Zieregg, a powerful and dense giant, aged for at least fourteen months in new oak, with enormous promise for those few patient enough to lay it down. Among his other wines are always one or two excellent BAs or TBAs. To me, however, the most remarkable newcomer is a fine and delicately layered Pinot Noir, not only an exception in this region, but also one of the finest Pinots of central Europe.

Manfred Tement is also one of the three people (with F.X. Pichler and the late Tibor Szemes) behind Austria's most publicized red wine, Arachon (*q.v.*)

TSCHERMONEGG

Glanz an der Weinstrasse 50, 8463 Leutschach. Tel: 03454 326. Fax: 03454 32650. Website: www.tschermonegg.at. Vineyards: 17 ha. White grapes: Sauvignon Blanc, Chardonnay, Pinot Gris, Gelber Muskateller, Roter Traminer, Gewürztraminer, Müller-Thurgau, Pinot Blanc, Welschriesling, Riesling. Red grapes: Zweigelt, Cabernet Sauvignon.

Erwin Tschermonegg is determined to build on his good reputation and to make wines that can contend with the region's greatest. His new, gravity-driven cellar puts all the technical means at his disposal. So far, his wines have always appeared to me to be competent (as well as very reasonably priced) rather than extraordinary, with good, clear fruit, plenty of punch, and skilfully used wood.

WOHLMUTH

Freising 24, 8441 Kitzeck. Tel: 03456 2303. Fax: 03456 2121. Website: www.wohlmuth.at. Vineyards: 35 ha. White grapes: Sauvignon Blanc, Chardonnay, Pinot Gris, Gelber Muskateller, Gewürztraminer, Pinot Blanc, Welschriesling, Riesling. Red grapes: Zweigelt, Cabernet Sauvignon, Merlot.

Always restless, always on a mission to make better wines and to make them better known abroad, Gerhard Wohlmuth is one of Styria's most dynamic producers. This spirit of innovation is reflected by his wines, notably in his Semillon, which is the only one in the region, and possibly in the country. In addition, Wohlmuth offers two Zweigelt-based red wines and a kosher wine.

Among the more orthodox Styrian varieties, the best come from the Steinriegl vineyard: a Sauvignon Blanc combining mineral depth with well-integrated oak, a delicately pale Muskateller, always among the region's best, and a honeyed Gewürztraminer.

SOUTHEAST STYRIA (SÜDOSTSTEIERMARK)

Vineyards: 1,115 hectares.
Soils: basalt, volcanic, sand, loam.
White grapes (eighty-two per cent): Welschriesling, Pinot Blanc, Traminer, Riesling, Chardonnay, Pinot Gris.
Red grapes (eighteen per cent): Zweigelt, Blauburger, St Laurent, Blauer Wildbacher.

Very much larger than South Styria, the Southeast has fewer distinguished wine-growers, although it is certainly possible to grow excellent wine in the area.

The soil here is very different from anything found nearby: basalt and other volcanic stones, partly overlaid by fossil chalk. Like all of southern Styria, it lies between the Pannonian and Mediterranean climatic zones. It has an annual mean temperature of almost 10°C

(50°F) and a little under 1,000 millimetres (39.4 inches) annual rainfall. The eighty hectares around Straden in the west have a particularly warm climate, and can produce wines with beautiful fruit.

In contrast to Southern Styria, this area has traditionally cultivated Traminer, which takes well to the basalt soils. As this variety has gone out of fashion in recent years, it has often been replaced by red varieties, mainly Zweigelt. The best *Rieden* are Morafeitl, protected by forest and with deep loam soils, ideal for Sauvignon Blanc and Chardonnay; Saziani, with sandy, light humus soils on basalt; and Steintal. The vineyards around Schloss Kapfenstein (which partly dates back to the eleventh century, though the site has been settled since 3,000 BC) produce good Chardonnay, Pinot Blanc and Pinot Gris, and remarkable red wines. The Ried an der Kapelle with its gravelly and sandy soils on basalt, is planted mainly with Chardonnay and Pinot Gris, while Kirchleithen, with sand and sandy loam, has mainly Traminer, Sauvignon Blanc, Welschriesling, Pinot Blanc, and Pinot Gris. Rosenleithen, with sand and sandy loam again, has Pinot Blanc and Chardonnay. Winzerkogel has gravelly and loamy sand on which not only white but also red grapes ripen well.

The vineyards around Klöch are both relatively extensive and old – the Romans made wine here. Another castle, now a ruin, overlooks the area. The basalt, tuff, and sandy loam of the Klöchberg offer ideal growing conditions for Traminer, which ripens here better than anywhere else in the country.

Another part of Southeast Styria and another castle is the Riegersburg. Situated on a steep basalt rock (460 metres/1,500 feet), the Riegersburg is one of the largest strategic buildings of the Middle Ages in Europe and was extended several times during the Renaissance and the baroque periods. It is an impressive structure, and now belongs to the princes of Liechtenstein. Most of the vineyards here are within the large defensive wall systems and benefit from the mesoclimate they create. The Süd-Bastei and Burggraben are especially famous.

Top Growers

FÜRWIRTH
Deutsch-Haseldorf 46, 8493 Klöch. Tel: 03475 2338. Fax: 03475 2334.
Website: www.fruewirth.at. Vineyards: 11 ha. White grapes: Sauvignon
Blanc, Welschriesling, Scheurebe, Pinot Blanc, Gelber
Traminer/Gewürztraminer, Chardonnay, Müller-Thurgau. Red grapes:
Zweigelt.
As well as Morillon and Pinot Blanc Fritz Fürwirth produces particu-
larly fine Gewürztraminer, which is especially remarkable as a Spätlese.

GIESSAUF-NELL
8493 Klöch-Hochwart 63. Tel & Fax: 03475 7265. Website: www.giessauf-
nell.at. Vineyards: 6 ha. White grapes: Welschriesling, Riesling,
Gewürztraminer, Sauvignon Blanc, Gelber Muskateller.
Josef Nell is a Gewürztraminer specialist. His Gewürztraminer Selection
is a wine with good ageing potential, while the punning
Gewürztraminer SensatioNell is opulently charming.

NEUMEISTER
8345 Straden 42. Tel: 03473 88308. Fax: 03473 83084. Website:
www.neumeister.cc. Vineyards: 23 ha. White grapes: Chardonnay, Pinot
Blanc, Pinot Gris, Welschriesling, Sauvignon Blanc, Traminer, Muskateller.
Red grapes: Zweigelt, Pinot Noir, Merlot, Cabernet Sauvignon.
Set into a steep hillside, the gravity-driven, avant-garde Neumeister
winery combines function and design. During the past decade,
Neumeister has continually refined his style and has emerged as one of
the finest local producers, making highly individual wines.

Sauvignon Blanc produces the greatest wines from this estate, among
them Zieregg, a monumental wine with wonderfully expressive
minerality and deep fruit, and Morafeitl, elegant, exotic, with perfectly
judged ripeness and acidity. With its power and focus, the Morillon
Morafeitl shows Neumeister's mastery of Chardonnay, too. Other
excellent wines are his complex Pinot Gris Sazani, and a surprisingly
fine Pinot Noir.

PLATZER
Pichla 25, 8355 Tieschen. Tel: 03475 2331. Fax: 03475 23314. Website:
www.weinof-platzer.at. Vineyards: 25 ha. White grapes: Sauvignon Blanc,
Chardonnay, Pinot Gris, Pinot Blanc, Gewürztraminer, Roter Traminer,

Welschriesling, Riesling. Red grapes: St Laurent, Zweigelt.

Still one of the lesser-known Styrian producers, Manfred Platzer makes reliable and individual wines vintage after vintage, including an opulent Chardonnay Aunberg and a similarly generous, exotic Pinot Gris.

RIEGERSBURG

Andreas Tscheppe, Glanz 75, 8463 Leutschach. Tel: 03454 391. Website: www.at-weine.at. Vineyards: 13 ha. White grapes: Sauvignon Blanc, Chardonnay, Pinot Gris, Welschriesling, Pinot Blanc, Roter Traminer, Welschriesling. Red grapes: Cabernet Sauvignon, Zweigelt.

The Riegersburg is a magnificent old pile, perched on an almost unassailable hill, and accessible only on foot. The vineyards within its walls, which possess a unique mesoclimate, are tended by Andreas Tscheppe, who also has vineyards outside the castle confines. His Sauvignon Blanc AT has good complexity, while the Morillon Langegg shows pleasing fruit.

WINKLER-HERMADEN

Schloss Kapfenstein, 8353 Kapfenstein 105. Tel: 03157 2322. Fax: 03157 2324. Website: www.winkler-hermaden.at. Vineyards: 26 ha. White varieties: Chardonnay, Pinot Blanc, Pinot Gris, Riesling, Sauvignon Blanc, Traminer, Welschriesling. Red varieties: Pinot Noir, Zweigelt, Cabernet Sauvignon.

Situated underneath his old family home, the magnificent, medieval Schloss Kapfenstein, Georg Winkler-Hermaden's winery suffers from only one problem: the wines are sold out so fast that he has to turn away many a hopeful customer. The soils are of volcanic origin and, unusually for Styria, Winkler-Hermaden concentrates on red wines. The most notable are Olivin, named after the olive-green volcanic minerals found here, and a very classy Zweigelt (with just a little Cabernet?) with finely structured tannins and dense body, good extract, smoky, plum aromas and wonderfully intriguing length. The Pinot Noir is increasingly good. Among his white wines, the finely chiselled Traminer Kirchleiten shows great elegance, while the Morillons Kirchleiten and Rosenleiten have an emphasis on stylishness, length, and purity. The Morillons especially show elegance and lean, intense aromas of apple underlaid with fine caramel tones, and good persistence on the palate. There are also outstanding sweet wines, such as the fine Kirchleiten TBA (Chardonnay/Pinot Blanc). All wood-aged wines are vinified in oak barrels originating from local forests, and their balance and structure give them an excellent ageing potential.

WEST STYRIA (WESTSTEIERMARK)

Vineyards: 433 hectares.
Soils: gneiss, slate.
White grapes (fourteen per cent): Welschriesling, Pinot Blanc.
Red grapes (eighty-six per cent): Blauer Wildbacher, Zweigelt.

West Styria, though beautiful, does not on the whole produce wine that is remarkable either for quality or quantity, though wine was produced here by the Celts and Romans, and there is evidence of winemaking as early as 400 BC.

The most important and traditional grape of West Styria is the Blauer Wildbacher, which is vinified as a rosé and made into a light, acidic, and fruity summer wine called Schilcher. It is produced by all growers in the region, though I know of no full-time producer who grows this grape exclusively. There is also tank-fermented Schilcher sparkling wine and, when nature allows it (about once in three years) nobly-rotten sweet wine. Made for immediate drinkability, Schilcher nevertheless has the ability to age remarkably well.

The soil of West Styria is dominated by crystalline gneiss and slate, often covered by sedimentary soils. Many vineyards are on steep hills and are higher than those in other parts of Styria, usually between 420 and 600 metres (1,380 and 1,970 feet), in order to escape night frosts in the valleys. Wind is less of a problem here than in eastern Styria, as the area is protected by the foothills of the Alps.

The best *Rieden* are Hochgrail and Engelweingarten near Stainz, both planted entirely with Schilcher, and Burgegg below Landsberg castle, a *Ried* which in the 1920s was one of the first to be planted with the newly bred Zweigelt.

Top Growers

JÖBSTL

Am Schilcherberg 1, 8551 Wernersdorf/Wies. Tel: 03466 423791. Fax: 03466 423753. Website: www.joebstl.at. Vineyards: 8 ha. White grapes: Sauvignon Blanc. Red grapes: Blauer Wildbacher.

Johannes Jöbstl makes not only Schilcher and Blauer Wildbacher, but also a well-judged Sauvignon Blanc.

OSWALD VULGO TRAPL

Lestein 40, 8511 St. Stefan. Tel & Fax: 0363 81082. Website: www.trapl-schilcher.at. Vineyards: 2.5 ha. White grapes: Klevner (Pinot Blanc). Red grapes: Blauer Wildbacher.

Good, creamy Schilcher from this traditional producer who still works with a tree press built in 1867.

REITERER

Lamberg 11, 8551 Wies. Tel: 03465 3950. Fax: 03465 3956. Website: www.weingut-reiterer.com. Vineyards: 45 ha. White grapes: Sauvignon Blanc. Red grapes: Blauer Wildbacher.

Christian Reiterer is by far the biggest producer in the area. His Schilcher Frizzante skillfully uses the grape's acidity to produce a stylish sparkler, while the Engelweingarten Alte Reben is a delicately acidic rosé.

8

Above and beyond:
Bergland Österreich

Though the overwhelming majority of Austrian wine is produced in the eastern part of the country, there are some wine-growers in other areas. Most of them work on one hectare or less. For the sake of completeness, here are a few general remarks.

The term Bergland Österreich comprises all regions not discussed earlier in the book and has a total surface area of twenty-one hectares under vine, with thirty-four producers scattered around the country.

VORARLBERG

Vorarlberg, on the Swiss border at the very western tip of Austria, boasts a long winemaking history, but has only twelve hectares of vineyards today. The Romans brought vines to this province, and in the fourteenth century two-thirds of all farmers here made wine. The greatest expansion of vineyards was reached in the seventeenth century, when the area had 700 hectares under vines. From there, however, wine production went downhill and the phylloxera blight spelled the beginning of the end of Vorarlberg winemaking. Today, Grüner Veltliner, Burgundian varieties, Müller-Thurgau, Bouvier, Riesling, Traminer, Blauer Portugieser, Zweigelt, Cabernet Sauvignon, and Merlot are being cultivated here.

Because of the low average temperatures, Vorarlberg vineyards are situated on southeast- or southwest-facing hills, on the upper slopes and therefore away from the cold air that accumulates in the valleys. The warm Föhn wind in late summer and autumn helps the ripening of the grapes.

Only Franz Nachbaur makes wine on more than two hectares here, and among his offerings are a good, powerful Chardonnay and a turbo-charged Pinot Noir. (Franz Nachbaur, Zehentstrasse 4, 6832 Röthis. Tel: 05522 43251.) With just 1.5 ha, Peter Summer is also very respectable. (Fober 26, 6820 Frastanz Tel: 0552253671.)

UPPER AUSTRIA, TYROL, CARINTHIA, SALZBURG

Wine-growing in Upper Austria is negligible. Some wine is made in Carinthia and in Tyrol, but here the largest producer, Karl Reinhart, has one hectare under vines. (Karl Reinhart, 6170 Zirl. Tel: 05238 2600.)

Part 3

Appendices

I
The legal framework

Austrian wine legislation is among the strictest in Europe, a development partly triggered by the 1985 scandal. With Austria's entry into the European Union in 1995, Austrian wine laws were brought into line with EU legislation. In some respects, however, they remain even stricter than that of other countries within the Union.

THE REGIONS
(1999 figures)

Austria (Weinland Österreich): 48,558 ha, 32,044 producers

Lower Austria (Niederösterreich): 30,004 ha, 18,038 producers, comprising
Carnuntum: 892 ha, 745 producers
Donauland: 2,732 ha, 1,710 producers
Kamptal: 3,869 ha, 1,491 producers
Kremstal: 2,176 ha, 1,397 producers
Thermenregion: 2,332 ha, 1,282 producers
Traisental: 683 ha, 706 producers
Wachau: 1,390 ha, 867 producers
Weinviertel: 15,892 ha, 9,774 producers
Outside these regions: 38 ha, 66 producers

Burgenland: 14,564 ha, 9,654 producers, comprising
Middle Burgenland (Mittelburgenland): 1,877 ha, 1,098 producers
Neusiedlersee: 8,326 ha, 3,268 producers
Neusiedlersee-Hügelland: 3,912 ha, 3,652 producers
South Burgenland (Südburgenland): 449 ha, 1,636 producers
Styria (Steiermark): 3,291 ha, 3,821 producers, comprising

Southeast Styria (Südoststeiermark): 1,116 ha, 2,254 producers
South Styria (Südsteiermark): 1,741 ha, 1,066 producers
West Styria (Weststeiermark): 433 ha, 491 producers
Outside these regions: 2 ha, 10 producers.

Vienna (Wien): 678 ha, 497 producers

Bergland Österreich: 21 ha, 34 producers
The rest of the country, comprising Carinthia, Upper Austria, Salzburg,
Tyrol, Vorarlberg.
(*sources: wein-plus and AWM*)

MEASURING RIPENESS
The legal framework is drawn essentially from the German system of
classification, a fact regarded by many commentators as unfortunate.
German wine law classifies wine largely according to the sugar content of
the grapes when harvested, even if individual regions are now establishing
their own, geographically based systems of First or Great Growths. The major
disadvantage of the German system is its underlying assumption that higher
sugar content and alcohol are equivalent to higher quality. This is clearly not
necessarily the case, and in any case says little about the character of the
wine. German-style classification also means that labels can be difficult to
understand for non-specialists and for those who do not read German.

To make things even more difficult, the sugar content of the grape must
is not measured in Beaumé or Öchsle, but in KMW (Klosterneuburger
Mostwaage), a system measuring the must weight of the grape juice, which
in itself is coherent and practical, but does nothing to make for easier
understanding by foreigners. The following small conversion table may be
of some help in this respect.

OECHSLE	BAUMÉ	KMW
73	9.8	15
84	11.2	17.1
94	12.4	19
105	21	21
127	25	25

QUALITY CATEGORIES

Tafelwein: the simplest wines, with a minimum 10.6 degrees KMW.

Landwein: minimum 14 degrees KMW. Treated as Tafelwein, but must originate from a specific wine-growing area and must be made from legally sanctioned grape varieties. Maximum yield per hectare: 9,000 kilograms.

Qualitätswein: minimum 15 degrees KMW. The must may be chapitalized by up to 4.25 kilograms of sugar per 100 litres, up to a maximum 19 degrees KMW for white wines, 20 degrees KMW for reds. Alcohol content must be a minimum of 9 degrees for whites and 8.5 degrees for reds.

Kabinett: minimum 17 degrees KMW. Regarded as a Qualitätswein, but must not be chaptalized. Maximum alcohol content is 12.7 degrees. Residual sugar must not be higher than 9 grams/litre.

Prädikatswein: must not be chapitalized, and residual sugar must be the result of either interruption of fermentation or natural ending of fermentation. No concentrated grape juice may be added. Grapes must come from a designated wine-growing area. Export is only in bottles, not in tanks. May not be sold before May 1, with the exception of Spätlese, which may be sold after March 1.

Spätlese: minimum 19 degrees KMW. Grapes must be fully ripe. May not be sold before March 1.

Auslese: minimum 21 degrees KMW. All faulty or unripe grapes must be excluded.

Beerenauslese (BA): minimum 25 degrees KMW. Produced from overripe grapes or grapes affected by noble rot.

Ausbruch: produced only in the Neusiedlersee region, minimum 27 degrees KMW. Produced from nobly rotten, overripe grapes or naturally shrivelled grapes. Fresh grape must, Auslese or Beerenauslese from the same *Ried* may be added for harmony.

Trockenbeerenauslese (TBA): minimum 30 degrees KMW. Produced from overripe grapes, naturally shrivelled grapes, and those affected by noble rot.

Eiswein: minimum 25 degrees KMW. Grapes must be frozen when harvested and pressed.

Strohwein: minimum 25 degrees KMW. Produced from overripe grapes that have been stored and air-dried on straw or reeds for at least three months.

Bergwein: wine made from grapes grown on slopes or terraces with a steepness of over 26 per cent.

Wachau Classification

There is a special regulation for Wachau wines, containing three quality steps:

Steinfeder: maximum alcohol content 10.7 degrees.

Federspiel: minimum of 17 degrees KMW, maximum alcohol content 11.9 degrees.

Smaragd: minimum 18 degrees KMW. Minimum alcohol content 12 degrees. (No maximum.)

The members of the Wachau association Vinea Wachau Nobilis Districtus follow a strict policy of not chaptalizing their wines and of allowing ripeness and natural fermentation to dictate sugar and alcohol contents.

Sugar Levels

Trocken (dry): up to 9g residual sugar, if the total acidity is less than the residual sugar by a maximum of 2g per litre.

Halbtrocken (semi-dry): up to 12g per litre residual sugar.

Lieblich (semi-sweet): up to 45g per litre residual sugar.

Süss (sweet): over 45g per litre residual sugar.

Other Points

Wines harvested before 1995, apart from Landwein, must have a paper banderole or cap in the Austrian national colours, red-white-red. After 1995, this banderole was supplanted by a conventional plastic or paper bottle-cap with the national colours on top of it.

Wines of a higher category than Landwein and Tafelwein must have a *Staatliche Prüfnummer* (official analysis number), which is allocated after chemical and tasting analysis of the wine.

Labels must list the *Abfüller*, the estate or firm filling the wine into bottles or other containers. *"Erzeugerabfüllung"* is a designation indicating the wine has been filled into bottles by the producer.

II
Useful addresses

WINES OF AUSTRIA MARKETING BOARD

For all information about wines and producers, professional and marketing materials, and so on, the very active and professional Wines of Austria Marketing Board is a good place to start. Its website also offers a plethora of press releases, statistical information, and names and contact details of (most) wine producers. The Marketing Board is financed from public funds and contributions from all producers and cannot therefore promote individual growers.

Österreichische Weinmarketing Service GmbH
Prinz-Eugen-Strasse 34/7
A-1040 Vienna
Tel: +43 (0)1 503 9267
Fax: +43 (0)1 503 9268
Email: info@weinausoesterreich.at
www.weinausoesterreich.at; www.winesfromaustria.com

WEIN PLUS GLOSSAR

Another good source on the internet (in German) is the Wein Plus Glossar, an informative site devoted to German and Austrian wines with good information about regions, associations, terms, and, of course, growers.

www.wein-plus.de

THE AUSTRIAN WINE ACADEMY

The Austrian Wine Academy offers very well-respected courses and diplomas, and has also established a branch of the prestigious Master of Wine programme in Austria.

Weinakademie Österreich

Dr. Josef Schuller, Director

Hauptstrasse 31

A-7071 Rust

Tel: +43 2685 6853

Fax: +43 2685 64 31

Email: info@weinakademie.at

www.weinakademie.at

III

Austrian wine associations

The Austrians are very fond of clubs and associations, especially if they come with titles for their distinguished members. The names most likely to pop up on wine labels are the following – a small selection from the almost thirty different associations currently in existence, each of which comes with its own standards of quality and vinification. It would be very much in the interest of exporting producers to clear up this tangle of names.

CERCLE RUSTER AUSBRUCH
Fifteen members, dedicated to reviving the classical Ruster Ausbruch. These wines must mature in barrels for at least one year and in bottle for another six months before being sold.

KAMPTAL KLASSIK
Seventy-four members. Marketing association of growers around Langenlois, aimed at promoting both the wines and an Austrian style of vinification, as well as "natural" methods of cultivation.

PANNOBILE
Small and outstanding association in Burgenland with nine members, dedicated to developing wines of high quality with a character typical of the area, using indigenous grape varieties. White wines are assembled from Neuburger, Pinot Blanc, and Chardonnay, red blends from Zweigelt, Blaufränkisch, and St Laurent. In 2005 the members were: Achs, Beck, Gsellmann-Gsellmann, Gernot Heinrich, Matthias Leitner, John Nittnaus, Pittnauer, Helmut Renner, and Claus Preisinger. (www.pannoblile.at)

RENOMMIERTE WEINGÜTER DES BURGENLANDES (RWB)

Sixteeen leading Burgenland wine producers make up this association, which has an influential voice in Burgenland wine. The members are: Achs, Feiler-Artinger, Gesellmann, Hans Igler, Juris, Paul Kerschbaum, Kollwentz, Alois Kracher, Krutzler, Leberl, Pöckl, Rosi Schuster, Ernst Triebaumer, Umathum, and Velich. (www.rwb.at)

DIE THERMENWINZER

Ten member-association hoping to raise quality and typicity of their wines through regular tastings. Karl Alphart, Aumann, Biegler, Cristian Fischer, Reinisch, Schafler, Schellmann, Spaetrot Gebeshuber, and Stadlmann.

TRADITIONSWEINGÜTER ÖSTERREICH

Twenty-two members: Bründlmayer, Dolle, Ludwig Ehn, Hiedler, Hirsch, Jurtschitsch, Schloss Gobelsburg, Schloss Grafenegg, Johann Topf (all Kamptal); Geyerhof, Malat, Mantlerhof, Hermann Moser, Sepp Moser, Salomon Undhof, Unger, Weingut Stadt Krems (all Kremstal); Ludwig Neumayer (Traisental), Martin Nigl (Kremstal), Bernhard Ott (Donauland).

VIENNA CLASSIC

Not an inspired name, but a laudable goal: improving the quality and image of Viennese wines. Members: Bernreiter, Cobenzl, Fuhrgassl-Huber, Helm, Hengl-Haselbrunner, Leopold Klager, Mayer am Pfarrplatz, Petritsch, Reinprecht, and Schilling.

"VINEA WACHAU" NOBILIS DISTRICTUS

Founded by Wilhelm Schwengler (of Freie Weingärtner Wachau), Franz Hirtzberger, Franz Prager, and Josef Jamek, this is the Wachau association whose member vineyards account for about eighty-five per cent of the region and which effectively functions as an *appellation d'origine contrôlée*. It oversees classification into three levels: Steinfeder (up to 11 degrees of alcohol), Federspiel (up to 12.5 degrees), and Smaragd (above 12.5 degrees). It is an effective organization and has helped markedly to create a strong image for Wachau wines. All wines must be produced according to strict quality criteria and sample bottles are deposited in the association's cellars. The association is in 2006 deciding whether the requirement that Smaragd wines be closed with natural cork is to be changed, as cork taint is a persistent problem for some of these wines. There are also some voices wondering aloud about whether the tie between high quality and high alcohol really is the best way of assuring quality, but this is unlikely to change any time soon.

The Latin phrase that is the name of the association, incidentally, is not a modern marketing ploy but the designation given to this region by one of its former rulers, Leuthold I von Kuenring (1243-1312), whose silhouette is shown on the association label. (www.vinea-wachau.at)

WAGRAMER SELEKTION
Association of fifteen growers seeking to improve the quality of the wines of Wagram/Donauland. (www.wagramerselektion.at)

Glossary

Alter: In *Heurigen*, last year's wine, as opposed to *Heurige* wine, which is this year's.

Ausbau: The process of ageing a wine in the winery. Ageing in large wooden casks or, more recently, steel tanks is called *"klassischer Ausbau"*. The alternative is ageing in barriques.

Ausbruch: Sweet wine produced in Rust by adding healthy ripe grapes to others affected by botrytis.

Auslese: Pradikatswein classification for wine made from overripe grapes.

Barrique: See Cask ageing.

Beerenauslese: Pradikätswein classification for a wine made from selected overripe and botrytis-affected grapes.

Beisl: A city inn similar to a *Heurige*, in which local wine can usually be bought by the glass.

Bergwein: Wine from a slope of more than twenty-six per cent.

Botrytis (*Botrytis cinerea*): Noble rot: a fungus which, when it affects ripe grapes shrivels them and concentrates the sugar and acidity, while adding a distinctive aroma of its own. Grapes affected by noble rot are used to make sweet wines such as Auslesen, Beerenauslesen, and Trockenbeerenauslesen.

Buschenschank: see *Heurige*.

Chaptalization: The addition of sugar or concentrated grape juice in order to increase the alcohol content. In Austrian wine law chaptalization is forbidden for wines from Qualitätswein up.

Eigenbauwein: Estate-produced wine.

Eiswein: Icewine, made from grapes that are harvested and pressed when frozen (usually in November or December), so that the water in the juice is left behind and a sweet, rich juice is extracted. In years with little botrytis this is a popular second choice for growers around Lake Neusiedl.

Erzeugerabfüllung: Eestate-bottled.

Federspiel: Middle denomination of Wachau wine.

Gemischter Satz: The growing of different grape varieties together in the same vineyard, to be harvested together and made into one wine.

G'spritzter: Summer drink, (usually) white wine mixed with soda water.

Hang-time: The length of time the grapes spend on the vine. Longer hang-times are fashionable, and mean increased alcohol levels, but can also mean less freshness on the nose and palate if carried to excess.

Heurige: Both this year's wine, and the place where it is usually drunk, a country inn in which a farmer is allowed to sell wines made by himself.

Hochkultur: High training of vines, a system of trellising developed by Professor Lenz Moser. It was widely adopted in Austria as it facilitates better yields and makes work on the vines easier, but is thought not to produce the best quality. With a few exceptions, the more ambitious Austrian growers have abandoned this system.

Kabinett: Qualitätswein that may not be chaptalized, has to have a high natural sugar content (17 degrees KMW), and may not have more than 9 g residual sugar and 13 degrees of alcohol.

KMW (Klosterneuburger Mostwaage): a system for measuring the sugar content of the must that was developed in Austria. For a conversion table to Oechsle or Beaumé, see Appendix I.

Lenz Moser: Austrian viticulturist and developer of the eponymous training system for vines. Also one of the largest wine producers in Austria, though no longer controlled by the Moser family.

Lieblich: Semi-sweet. According to Austrian wine law, all wines with twelve to forty-five grams of alcohol can carry this names, though most growers have stopped writing it on their bottles, because of its connotations with German wine.

Lyre training: A double-canopy vine-training system developed in Burgundy and used in Austria by several growers, most notably Willi Bründlmayer.

Malolactic fermentation: A second, bacterial, fermentation during which malic acid is transformed into the riper-tasting lactic acid, thereby giving the wine a more mellow, buttery character. In Austria, malolactic fermentation used to be unknown and is now used for wines made in a more international style.

Mischkultur: See *Gemischter Satz*.

Novemberlese: Wine harvested in November, a form of late harvest practised particularly in the Kamptal.

Phylloxera: Pest that devastated European vineyards in the second half of the nineteenth century. In Austria the plague was at its worst during the 1880s and 1890s.

Prädikat: Late-harvested wine. Prädikat wines include Spätlese, as well as sweet wines such as Auslese, Beerenauslese, Trockenbeerenauslese, Eiswein, Strohwein, and Ausbruch. Chaptalization is not allowed. Few Austrian wines are today labelled in this way.

Ried, Riede: A single named vineyard, usually of higher quality.

Salon: An annual competition at which the wines submitted by Austrian growers are tasted blind and awarded prizes. The winners are entitled to call themselves Salon wines.

Schilfwein: A Neusiedlersee novelty. Similar to Strohwein, but dried on reeds, not straw.

Smaragd: Highest classification of Wachau wines.

Spätlese: Pradikätswein classification for wine made from fully ripe grapes (no less than 19 degrees KMW), harvested after other wines.

Steinfeder: Lightest classification of Wachau wines.

Strohwein: Wine made from grapes that have been dried on straw mats for several months, causing them to shrivel while retaining their sugar content.

Sturm: Still-fermenting grape juice, often made from Bouvier, drunk throughout Austria during the harvest season.

Süss: Sweet.

TBA: See Trockenbeerenauslese.

Trocken: Dry. Trocken wines must have less than 9 g residual sugar.

Trockenbeerenauslese (TBA): Pradikätswein classification for wine made exclusively from grapes affected by noble rot; TBAs are sweet wines of great concentration. The process of selection is very labour-intensive and the wines (usually sold in half bottles) are correspondingly expensive.

Vinothek: Wine cellar or wine archive. Most Austrian growers have a vinotheque of their own wines. There are also regional vinotheques in which the wines of the area can be tasted and bought.

Weinbau, Weingut: Estate.

Weingarten: Vineyard.

Bibliography

Bednarz, Klaus, *Spitzenweingüter Österreichs,* Neuer Umschau Verlag, Wiener Neustadt, 2005.

Dähnhard, Wolfgang, *Atlas der Österreichischen Weine,* Gräfe & Unzer, Bern, Stuttgart, 1995.

Fally, J. & A., *Gebert Blaufränkischland,* Fally-Eigenverlag, Deutschkrutz, 1997.

Hallgarten, S. F. and F. L., *The Wines and Wine Gardens of Austria,* Argus Books, Watford, Herts., 1979.

Heintl, Franz Ritter von, *Der Weinbau des Österreichischen Kaiserthums,* self published, Vienna, 1821.

Lantschbauer, Rudolf, *Die Weine des Burgenlandes,* Hugendubel, Graz, 1993.

Moser, Peter, *Falstaff Wineguide,* Falstaff, Vienna (updated annually).

Sandhofer, Hubert, and Tobias Hierl, eds., *Österreichs Salon-Weine,* Österreichischer Agrarverlag, Klosterneuburg (updated annually).

Schams, Franz, *Vollständige Beschreibung sämmtlicher berühmter Weingebirge in Österreich, Mähren und Böhmen in statistisch, topographisch-naturhistorischer und ökonomischer Hinsicht,* Vol. 1-3. Pesth: Wigand (3: Kilian) 1832-1835.

Schreiber, Georg, *Deutsche Weingeschichte,* Rheinland Verlag, Cologne, 1980.

Siegl, Viktor, Rudolf Steurer, *Die besten Weine Österreichs 2004/2005,* Ueberreuter, Stuttgart, 2004.

Index